ROUTLEDGE LIBRARY EDITIONS: EDUCATION IN ASIA

Volume 11

PROBLEMS OF CHINESE EDUCATION

PROBLEMS OF CHINESE EDUCATION

VICTOR PURCELL

LONDON AND NEW YORK

First published in 1936 by Kegan Paul, Trench, Trubner & Co. Ltd.

This edition first published in 2018
by Routledge
2 Park Square, Milton Park, Abingdon, Oxon OX14 4RN

and by Routledge
711 Third Avenue, New York, NY 10017

Routledge is an imprint of the Taylor & Francis Group, an informa business

© 1936 Kegan Paul, Trench, Trubner & Co. Ltd.

All rights reserved. No part of this book may be reprinted or reproduced or utilised in any form or by any electronic, mechanical, or other means, now known or hereafter invented, including photocopying and recording, or in any information storage or retrieval system, without permission in writing from the publishers.

Trademark notice: Product or corporate names may be trademarks or registered trademarks, and are used only for identification and explanation without intent to infringe.

British Library Cataloguing in Publication Data
A catalogue record for this book is available from the British Library

ISBN: 978-1-138-30826-8 (Set)
ISBN: 978-1-315-14674-4 (Set) (ebk)
ISBN: 978-1-138-31012-4 (Volume 11) (hbk)
ISBN: 978-1-138-31021-6 (Volume 11) (pbk)
ISBN: 978-1-315-14363-7 (Volume 11) (ebk)

Publisher's Note
The publisher has gone to great lengths to ensure the quality of this reprint but points out that some imperfections in the original copies may be apparent.

Disclaimer
The publisher has made every effort to trace copyright holders and would welcome correspondence from those they have been unable to trace.

PROBLEMS OF CHINESE EDUCATION

By

VICTOR PURCELL

LONDON
KEGAN PAUL, TRENCH, TRUBNER & CO. LTD.
BROADWAY HOUSE: 68–74 CARTER LANE, E.C.
1936

PRINTED IN GREAT BRITAIN
BY STEPHEN AUSTIN AND SONS, LTD., HERTFORD.

CONTENTS

		PAGE
	Preface	vii
CHAP.		
I.	The Old System	1
II.	Contact with the West	44
III.	The Aim of Education	76
IV.	The Language Problem	87
V.	San Min Chu I	161
VI.	The Present Period	207
	Appendix	235
	Index	251

PREFACE

The first two chapters of this study are introductory, but the information has not been collected elsewhere in the form considered necessary to illuminate the questions later discussed. The bulk of the fourth chapter, on language, is an examination of Chinese neologisms on a new system. In the fifth chapter a summary of *San Min Chu I* is given with the Chinese original of the key words and phrases in brackets. This is to enable the summary to be read in conjunction with the language chapter. The final chapter describes the situation at the present day and concludes with some tentative suggestions.

The Chinese characters rather than the romanized equivalent are nearly always given because romanization often conveys very little to the expert (especially to one who reads Chinese in some dialect other than Mandarin), whereas the characters convey everything. The reader who does not know Chinese will be made no wiser by romanization than he is by the characters. But an even weightier reason for inserting characters in the text is that they are necessary to give the proper " feel " to the subject matter. Romanized Chinese is insipid and grudgingly informative at the best ; Chinese characters are living things which reveal instantly their identity to the eye at the same time that they please it with their beauty.

The original intention was to provide a complete conspectus of Chinese education, but it was found that the mass of laboriously collected statistics, translations of extracts from books by teachers, and descriptions of educational organizations, clogged the narrative and obscured the essential issues. In looking over the material discarded at this juncture, I find that the only omission I now regret is an account of the Mass Education Movement associated with the name of Mr. Y. C. James Yen.

One thing this study has revealed and that is the warming

truth that a student has only to decide which of the savants of the world can best guide his special course and they with the generosity of learning will at once agree to do it. To daily conversations with Dr. Van Stein Callenfels I owe an increased sense of the modest scale of my enquiries compared with the astronomic stretches of pre-history. To Sir Arthur Keith I owe an enhanced belief that cultural differences must not too readily be interpreted in terms of anthropology. To Professor Rupert Emerson, of Harvard, I owe the discovery that humanism, especially American humanism, can be an intellectual as well as emotional creed. To Professor Moule who directed my studies at Cambridge I owe the beginnings of a Chinese literary education and a sense of perspective lacking from my severely practical studies as a civil servant.

At this point an uneasy feeling comes over me that a catalogue of indebtedness is in the nature of a promise of repayment of some sort in the present study (a promise, I fear, without hope of fulfilment), but nevertheless I must continue it. I am grateful to Professor Duyvendak, of Leiden, for the close scrutiny he have to my fourth chapter, and to Professor Ernest Barker for the equally minute way in which he commented upon Chapter V. The suggestions of Professor Duyvendak I have, I trust, followed in every point; those of Professor Barker I have endeavoured to follow similarly, but my deficient knowledge of political science has, I know, prevented me from doing this with uniform success. I thank Mr. Li Chi Wa, Inspector of Schools, Mr. Chan Ping Kee, Mr. Cheng Hui Ming, and Mr. Lin Chong Hsin for the assistance they gave me, and not least of all Professor Dyer and my wife who have read over the complete manuscript.

VICTOR PURCELL.

PROBLEMS OF CHINESE EDUCATION

CHAPTER I

THE OLD SYSTEM

Innovation is more acceptable to a people if it is offered to them as a reversion to a former age in their own history rather than as a novelty invented at home or imported from without: in Rome the new *jus gentium* was ultimately hailed as the natural law; Rousseau in France harked back to a time when man was still uncorrupted. The Chinese within the last few decades have been induced by the force of events to abandon almost entirely an age-old system of literary education in favour of one derived from the West, and the native sponsors of the change, whilst constrained to admit that the models offered are Western in their immediate origin, are yet able to point to their prototypes in ancient China. It is a game that the Chinese have been playing from at least the sixth century B.C., when Confucius and Mo Tzŭ, under traditional appearances, and perhaps with the authentic desire to revert to the principles of antiquity, yet turned upside down the existing state of things without reproducing anything that had been known before.[1] In 1865 Prince Kung relied upon historical argument to advocate the introduction of mathematics as a subject into the hitherto purely literary civil service examinations—" We find," he said, " that Western sciences borrowed their roots from ancient Chinese mathematics. Westerners still regard their mathematics as coming from the East," [2]—and the many persons who memorialized the

[1] Maspero, *La Chine Antique*, Paris, 1927, p. 372.
[2] 近 代 中 國 敎 育 史 料, Chung Hua Book Co., Shanghai, 1928, vol. i, p. 8. Quoted from another source in *Nationalism and Education in Modern China*, by Cyrus H. Peake, New York, 1932, p. 4.

Throne during the latter reigns of the Chʻing Dynasty in favour of Western innovations, always resorted to historical argument and searched through China's past in quest of precedents.[1] Contemporary writers on education still find themselves able to indicate a period in Chinese history when utility and not literature was the basis of public instruction. Their contention is that before the Han Dynasty, education did not end with a mastery of the classics but economic needs were given a first place in the curriculum.[2] Thus is a leaf of native and often plausible gilt found for an alien pill.

What sort of things was a Chinese taught in this pre-Han period, and how was he taught them? The information given by the classics themselves is not always in the round; it fades so often into feudal remoteness. The Book of Rites, *Li Chi* (禮記), which purports to describe the ancient ritual, tells us that, " for the purpose of education among the ancients, each village of twenty-five families had its school (塾), each district of five hundred families its academy (庠), and each department of two thousand five hundred families its college (學),"[3] but in default of a description of what these institutions were like and what their curriculum was, the terms I have used rather arbitrarily in translation

[1] When a few years ago a phonetic alphabet was adopted to simplify the language, the symbols for it were not borrowed from the Roman alphabet or the international phonetic script, but from the *Shuo Wên* (說文), a dictionary of the first century A.D. (e.g. ㄅ, ㄆ, ㄇ, ㄈ), 古書今讀法 by 胡懷琛, Shanghai, 1932, p. 15. " Ku Yen-wu, who founded the scientific branch of Chinese phonology, actually hoped that his studies might help to bring about a restoration of Chinese speech to the classical pronunciation of the ancients." Hu Shih, *The Chinese Renaissance*, Chicago, 1934, p. 77.

[2] e.g. 中國教育史大綱 by 王鳳喈, Commercial Press, Shanghai, 1926.

[3] Legge (*Sacred Books of the East*, vol xxvii, p. 346) says that the names of these different schools are very perplexing, and his quotation from a commentator of the eleventh century does not clarify the matter to any extent. Mr. 王鳳喈, in his 中國教育史大綱 (before cited), p. 34, gives a somewhat different list of schools in the Chou Dynasty, i.e. 塾, 商校, 夏序, and 虞庠.

THE OLD SYSTEM

may lead us far astray. At the beginning of the Chou Dynasty (1122 B.C. ?) all candidates for official employment were required to give proof of their acquaintance with the Five Arts—music, archery, horsemanship, writing, and arithmetic—and to be thoroughly versed in the rites and ceremonies of public and social life, an accomplishment that ranked as a sixth art.[1] The Book of Rites records that the Minister of Music devoted himself to honouring the arts of poetry, writing, ceremonial, and music in the tradition of the ancient kings. In spring and autumn he taught ceremonial and music; in winter and summer he taught poetry and the histories.[2] Ritualism, we see, had already established a hold on the Chinese mind, a hold that it was to extend in ages to come until, long before the Han Dynasty, a set form was prescribed for every action of the day. But as Dr. Kuo Ping-wên remarks, " the word ' ceremony ', often regarded as the equivalent of the work *li* (禮), does not at all convey the true import of the word, for *li* includes not only the external conduct, but also involves the right principles from which all true etiquette and politeness spring."[3] The Minister of Ceremonies and Public Instruction on one occasion assembled the old men of the capital at the Imperial College. He then went through archery practice in their presence in order to do honour to those who shot well, and he drank their health in order to do respect to their age. Chosen pupils of the college were present to profit by the Minister's example. The Imperial College admitted the most promising pupils of the realm,

---

[1] Martin, *Hanlin Papers*, London, 1880, p. 56.
[2] *Li Chi*, book iii, sec. iv.
[3] *The Chinese System of Public Education*, New York, 1915, p. 11. In his *Outlines of the History of Chinese Philosophy* (中國哲學史大綱), Commercial Press, Shanghai, 1925, p. 134, Dr. Hu Shih (胡適) says, " *Li* in a broader sense means all proper action and behaviour recognized by the Government. It was first applied to religious ceremony and then to correct behaviour. It is intended to regulate men's passions, to cultivate their character, and to form good habits."

and once they were entered no further reference was allowed to the elevation or baseness of their birth.

The education of the Chou Dynasty (1122 B.C. ?–255 B.C.) has at all times been the object of admiration of the Chinese themselves. The curriculum is described in the Book of Rites. It consisted in the Six Virtues—wisdom, benevolence, goodness, righteousness, loyalty, harmony—the Six Praiseworthy Actions—honouring one's parents, being friendly with one's brothers, being neighbourly, maintaining cordial relationships with relatives by marriage, being trustful, and being sympathetic—and the Six Arts—ritual, music, archery, charioteering, writing, and mathematics. A liberal education included five kinds of ritual, five kinds of archery, five ways of directing a chariot, six kinds of writing, and nine operations of mathematics. Music was stressed as having an influence in modelling the character. The musical instruments were the drum, the bell, the lute, and the Pandean pipes; dancing was with the shield, lance, plume, and flute.

The Book of Rites gives in detail the model careers of a boy and a girl [1]:—

"At six years, they were taught the numbers and the names of the cardinal points; at the age of seven, boys and girls did not occupy the same mat nor eat together; at eight, when going out or coming in at a gate or door, and going to their mats to eat and drink, they were required to follow their elders—the teaching of yielding to others was now begun; at nine, they were taught how to number the days.

"At ten, (the boy) went to a master outside, and stayed with him (even) over the night. He learned the (different classes of) characters and calculation; he did not wear his jacket or trousers of silk; in his manners he followed his early lessons; morning and even he learned the behaviour of a youth; he would ask to be exercised in (reading) the tablets, and in the forms of polite conversation.

[1] Legge, *Sacred Books of the East*, 1885, vol. xxvii, p. 478.

THE OLD SYSTEM

"At thirteen, he learned music, and to repeat the odes, and to dance the *ko* [*shao* 勺] (of the Duke of Kao). When a full-grown lad, he danced the *hsiang* [象] (of the Duke of Wu). He learned archery and chariot-driving. At twenty, he was capped [冠], and first learned the (different classes of) ceremonies, and might wear fur and silk. He danced the *ta hsiâ* [大夏] (of Yü), and attended sedulously to filial and fraternal duties. He might become very learned, but he did not teach others;—(his object being still) to receive and not to give out.

"At thirty he had a wife, and began to attend to the business proper to a man. He extended his learning without confining it to particular subjects. He was deferential to his friends, having regard to the aims (which they displayed). At forty, he was first appointed to office; and according to the business of it brought out his plans and communicated his thoughts. If the ways (which he proposed) were suitable, he followed them out; if they were not, he abandoned them.[1] At fifty, he was appointed a Great Officer, and laboured in the administration of his department. At seventy,[2] he retired from his duties . . .

"A girl at the age of ten ceased to go out (from the women's apartments). Her governess taught her (the arts of) pleasing speech and manners, to be docile and obedient, to handle the hempen fibres, to deal with the cocoons, to weave silks and form fillets, to learn (all) woman's work, how to furnish garments, to watch the sacrifices, to supply the liquors and

---

[1] This sentence is translated quite differently by Dr. Kuo Ping-wên in his version of the passage (p. 20, op. cit.). He renders it as: "If the orders of his superior are conformable to good rules then he obeys them, if not he withdraws from public life." The Chinese words are 道合則服從, 不可則去. M. Callery, in his translation of part of the Book of Rites (I say *part* because he had lit on one of those expurgated editions once common), gives, ". . . on marche d'accord dans la même voie (avec son souverain), de manière à occuper toujours l'emploi qu'on a; car, si on ne peut pas marcher d'accord (avec lui), il faut se retirer . . ." The commentary by 鄭玄 (second century) renders the passage: "If the way is fitting, then he obeys and follows (it); if he cannot do so then he goes." Whether *Tao* (道) is proposed *to* him or *by* him cannot be determined by the text, though the probabilities are in favour of the latter.

[2] Dr. Kuo (op. cit.) gives "sixty" as the age for retiring, but "seventy" is given in all the Chinese texts I have been able to consult.

sauces, to fill the various stands and dishes with pickles and brine, and to assist in setting forth the appurtenances for the ceremonies.

"At fifteen, she assumed the hairpin; at twenty she was married, or, if there were occasion (for the delay), at twenty-three. If there were the betrothal rites she became a wife; and if she went without these, a concubine."

In China, as elsewhere, teaching was originally not a specialist function. Social customs were preserved by imitation and parental precept. Teachers, when they appeared, had the double function of teachers and ministers of state. In China schools were an early development, though what the people at large were taught does not clearly emerge from the classical writings. Dr. Kuo Ping-wên claims that in early times popular education was given at public expense, but states that in later times the discovery of talent and not universal education was the aim. It seems clear that the curricula described in the Book of Rites, the Ceremonial Rites of Chou, and the Decorum Ritual, were intended for the class of feudal nobles and for selected candidates from the common people. No doubt more could be ascertained in a field as yet virgin to foreign research, though Dr. Kuo Ping-wên has done something towards mapping out the ground. But I need not delay at this point. The age of purely literary education extends back nearly two millenniums from the modern period I have set out to examine, and if I am able to describe the development and perfection of this literary system I shall have given my inquiry more than enough mould to cover its roots.

Education is the perpetuation of a culture, and all culture, especially intellectual, is built upon language[1]: this

---

[1] "Language is one of the great forces for the development of a race," says Sun Yat-sen in *San Min Chu I*, the official Bible of modern China (Nationalism, Lecture i).

THE OLD SYSTEM

statement is perhaps truer of China than of any other country, and here language means rather the ideographic written medium than the spoken dialects. I must endeavour then to sketch a philological back-scene. This back-scene will be indispensable later when I come to discuss the adaptability of the language to the cultural revolution of the twentieth century.[1]

The written languages of other countries have changed with the change of speech, whilst in China the characters, and their meanings, have remained as they were two thousand years ago. In the British Museum there is exhibited an actual manuscript of the second century A.D. of the Aurel Stein collection. Each and every character in this is written exactly as it would be by a Chinese to-day, and yet in the second century the form of the characters had already been fixed for centuries.

> "The literary language has been an artificial thing for a thousand years or more, and for all its stylistic variations it has been essentially the same throughout the ages. Once a Chinese has succeeded in mastering it, it is the same for him, from the point of view of language, whether the poem he is reading was written at the time of Christ, a thousand years later, or yesterday; it is just as comprehensible and enjoyable in either case."[2]

Yet the Englishman cannot without special study understand anything in English literature more than three or

---

[1] The Chinese have always taken the greatest interest in etymology. The *Shuo Wên* (說文) is a dictionary of the language as it appeared at the close of the first century A.D., comprising 10,600 characters in the lesser seal script (小篆) with meanings and etymological notes. The etymology, however, is based on the apparent form of the lesser seal script and is not always correct. Mr. L. C. Hopkins has probably done more for Chinese etymology than anyone else in the West in recent years. In the above skeleton account of the Chinese written language, Dr. Karlgren's excellent *Sound and Symbol* has been largely followed, though corrections from Mr. Hopkins's work in the *Journal* of the Royal Asiatic Society have been accepted.

[2] Karlgren, *Sound and Symbol in Chinese*, London, p. 37.

four hundred years old. And just as a Chinese is in touch with the ages through the medium of his script, so is he with a coeval Chinese at the other end of the empire, for although he would be unable to understand a word the other said, the written language they use is one and the same. The political union of China through the centuries can be attributed to the unifying force of the written language more than to any other factor.

Somewhere about four thousand years ago Chinese writing originated in crude pictures of objects.[1] Six hundred and eight of these pictures, or "pictographs", are enumerated by Chinese scholars amongst the 23,265 characters of the present language, and a few of them are still something like the objects they stand for, such as 木, a tree.[2] They first varied with the perception or caprice of the artist-writer, but were detailed enough to convey their meaning without the help of a previous knowledge of what they were meant to be. Later on they were standardized with an impressionist economy of line. Up to the introduction of the brush as an instrument for writing, the pictographs still resembled their subjects fairly closely, but the limitation of the brush as compared with the stylus destroyed the direct representation value of most of them. A brush will spurt if worked against the hairs, and for this reason twists and curved lines tend to be eliminated. Characters at this epoch, two thousand years ago, took the square form of the "normal script" (楷) which they still retain.[3]

[1] The history of the origin and development of Chinese characters is fully dealt with in 中國文字之起源及變遷 by 吳貫因, Commercial Press, Shanghai, 1931.

[2] Dr. Karlgren gives 人 as an example of this and says it suggests Shakespeare's "bifurcated radish", but 人 is from a profile 𠂉, as Mr. Hopkins has shown from the Honan finds.

[3] Dr. Lionel Giles points also to a change about the fifth century A.D., when the characters became smoother and less blobby than before. Was this due to a change in writing instruments?

THE OLD SYSTEM

A selection of characters shown in their primitive form and in the normal script will illustrate the adaptation of pictographs to the brush: ⊖, 日, "sun"; ☾, 月, "moon"; 火, 火, "fire" (rising flames); ⌒ (or ⛰), 山, "a mountain"; 鳥, 鳥, "long-tailed bird"; 隹, 隹, "short-tailed bird"; ♡, 心, "heart"; 木, 木, "a tree"; 谷, 谷, "valley" (an image of a dell widening towards its mouth); 酉, 酉, "wine", "spirits" (the vessel containing them); ㅂ, 口, "mouth"; and 雨, 雨, "rain" (drops of rain falling from heaven).

Abstract ideas could also, to a certain extent, be rendered by drawings of the idea. Thus — "one"; ⚌ "two"; ☰ "three"; 上 (now 上) "above"; 丅 (now 下) "below"; 八 "to divide"; and 中 "middle". One hundred and seven of these "symbols indicating thought", as the native philologists call them, are to be found in the language.

Another system of using or forming characters soon suggested itself. That was to use a pictograph to suggest an abstract idea closely associated with the object it represented, or by a certain condition of that object. By this method 交, 交, a man with crossed legs, stood for "to cross, entangle, connection"; 高, 高, "high," was the picture of a tower; 行, 行, 行, the picture of "crossways", meant "to walk".[1]

Still another method was to borrow a pictograph of the same sound as the word in the spoken language it was wished to convey, and to make it do duty in both its own and the borrowed sense (compare "date" in English standing both for a fruit and a day in the calendar. See also footnote on p. 12). This method, though, was likely to lead to ambiguity and could not be widely adopted.

[1] Dr. Karlgren says "footprints", basing his opinion on the first form given above, but Mr. Hopkins shows it to be from the second form, "crossways."

A more promising line of development for characters expressing abstract ideas was the manufacture of compounds from two or more pictographs. These " suggestive compounds " pointed to some property or relative circumstance. An excellent example is 日 " sun " and 月 " moon " in juxtaposition to form 明 " bright ". Chinese scholars identify 740 of these compounds in the language.

Other examples of suggestive compounds are 坐 " to sit " (two men 人, on the ground 土) ; 好 " good, happy " (女 " woman " plus 子 " child, man ") ; 友 " a friend " (two hands together) ; 東 " east " (日 " the sun " rising behind the " trees ", 木). 開 is " to open " (" two hands " removing 一 " the bar " of " a door " 門) ; 算 " to calculate " (" two hands " 廾 using 目 " an abacus " made of " bamboo " 竹) ; 焦 " to roast " is 隹 " a bird " over " a fire " 灬 (shortened form of 火). Three women together is 姦 " lewdness, falsehood " ; 看 " to look at " is 手 " hand " shading 目 " an eye " ; 田 " a field " and 力 " strength " together formed 男 " male ", i.e. the strength that tilled the fields.

The suggestive compound method did much to develop the written language, but to multiply characters to the number of thousands in this way was, Dr. Karlgren suggested, too great a tax on the invention. At any rate, the Chinese themselves seemed to consider that the method had its limitations, and they set their minds to invent a more practical one. The device that they hit upon cannot perhaps be classed with revolutionary inventions like the alphabet, the ploughshare, or the wheel, but as an evolutionary factor in China it very nearly ranks with them, for by this new method the Chinese were enabled to develop their written character endlessly.

It is quite likely that the new device was suggested by the method referred to above of borrowing a character

THE OLD SYSTEM

representing one word to represent another word of the same sound. There was, for instance, a spoken word *kung* meaning "work" that was represented by the character 工 in the written language. There were also several other words also pronounced *kung*, or something very near it, but meaning things as different as "red", "a bench", "merit", "dispute", and "a river". If the character for "work" were used in all these other senses as well, how could one decide which particular sense was intended? Someone hit on the idea of placing next the character for "work" another character that gave a hint of the meaning. Thus when "red" was intended, the character for "silk" was added (紅); when "a bench" was meant, the character for "wood" was placed alongside it (杠); "merit" was indicated by 工 plus 力 "strength" (功); "dispute" by 工 plus 言 "words" (訌), and "river" by 工 plus 氵 "water" (江). By choosing a character to convey the sound and adding to it another character to give a hint of the meaning, the Chinese found that they could manufacture as many characters as they wanted. It was not necessarily a pictograph they chose, but sometimes a combination character, and later on a character that contained in itself both a meaning indicator and a sound indicator. The part giving a hint of the meaning has become known to Western students of Chinese as the "radical" (Dr. Karlgren calls it the "signific" to distinguish it from the radicals used for the headings of a dictionary), and the sound indicator as the "phonetic". Of the 23,265 characters of the language, 21,810, or over nine-tenths, are built up in this way.[1]

---

[1] These figures are the estimate of Chinese philologists. K'ang Hsi's *Dictionary* contains very many more than 23,000 characters, but a vast number of these are alternative and obsolete forms.

As early as the Chou Dynasty, the written characters of China were subdivided into the Six Scripts : (1) *Hsiang Hsing* (象形) pictograms;

It is convenient to state here that the value of the radicals as logical categories was nil, and as mnemonic assistance in learning the characters very little more. The phonetic, too, which originally gave the exact sound, now often only gives a rough hint of it, and in some cases gives no hint at all.

What is given above is no more than the barest analysis of the primitive origins of Chinese characters. The danger risked is giving an effect of crudity. It is only an extensive study of the language that would convince us that Chinese writing deserves to be ranked very high amongst the achievements of human ingenuity. The merits of the language as a medium for the expression of ideas is reserved for discussion in a later chapter. There is, however, one fact that should be recorded at this point, and that is the divorce that has taken place between the written and the spoken languages.

The characters were first invented to represent words in the spoken language. The Chinese still attach sounds to their characters, and the sounds vary with the speaker's dialect. But the spoken language is very poor in separate sounds. The Peking dialect has only about four hundred of them. This number is eked out by pronouncing the sounds in various tones of voice, but even then there are dozens of meanings allotted to a single sound in a certain tone—homonyms, that is to say, as if with us the sound " reed " (or " read ") meant forty different things instead of two or three. This difficulty the spoken language overcomes by joining synonyms in pairs, by attaching to a verb its inherent object (read-book, etc.), by the use of classifiers

---

(2) *Chih Shih* (指事) indicators ; (3) *Hui I* (會意) ideograms ; (4) *Hsieh Shêng* (諧聲) phonograms; (5) *Chuan Chu* (轉注) deflections, and (6) *Chia Chieh* (假借) borrowed characters. See C. A. S. Williams, *Outline of Chinese Symbolism and Art Motives*, Shanghai, 1932. Dr. Karlgren's classification is founded on the traditional one.

of nouns, and other devices. The written language has no need of such expedients. Though a passage in a book will be impossible to understand if read out, owing to the hearer not being able to decide which of a dozen characters with the same sound is intended, no such difficulty is presented to the reader himself. The identity of a character is established at once by its unique shape. Since the written character had such facility for multiplying its words and ran no risk of ambiguity through homonyms, it refused to be held back by the infirmities of the spoken language. Thus the two parted company. The written language soared in its full career, though reaching soon the limit of altitude and gliding rather than flying, whilst the spoken language stayed on earth and underwent all the changes which speech is unable to escape.

With the written language grew the literature of China. The simplicity of the Odes [1] gave place to the precise aphorisms of the Confucian classics, and the language reached its perfection in the hands of the Horatio-Wordsworthian poets of the T'ang Dynasty. But in the end it became the preserve of the professional stylists and the scholars. It was they who in conformity with their own esoteric ideals, multiplied its subtleties, linked it in an associative literary tradition, and brought it to the limits of the refined-obscure.

There were four rebirths of culture during this period, but they did not dissolve the accumulated crystals of traditional thought—the T'ang poets, the invention of Zen Buddhism, the secular neo-Confucianism of the Sung Dynasty, and the Drama of the thirteenth century.

It is perhaps not doing an injustice to Chinese literature to say that it is, like Théophile Gautier, less interested in the subject than in the form in which it is presented. Indeed,

---

[1] Some are exceedingly simple; others are exceedingly obscure.

the highly artificial style of Gautier is the best of the far-fetched analogies available to convey what Chinese became in the hands of the stylists. It is ultra-chryselephantine in the ornament of allusion, yet at the same time (and unlike Gautier or any other Western writer) exercises a verbal parsimony amounting to baldness. But in European languages lucid expression is reckoned an indispensable quality of style, while in Chinese the stylist was often one who led his reader groping through labyrinthine corridors in search of the tenuous allusion whose capture alone could give meaning to the text. For ordinary official purposes, indeed, the language was straightforward enough, and books on practical subjects and official dispatches were written in workaday language intended to be understood.[1]

Some foreign scholars have referred to Chinese literature as containing "untold treasures"; others with equal right to speak have referred to it as "a barren wilderness". The fact is that different Europeans have applied entirely different criteria, and even a single European is disposed to apply different criteria in different moods. If the Western reader expects to find anything in Chinese corresponding to the Western imagination, he will be disappointed. Chinese literature is of an entirely different inspiration, of a different tempo of existence, and he who would live in it in the real sense must be willing to die and be born anew. But without doing this we can see that although the Chinese have set themselves narrow limits, they have within these limits displayed prodigious activity, and the interplay of brain

[1] In his work on the *Tao Tê Ching*, "The Way and its Power," London, George Allen and Unwin, 1934, p. 59, Mr. Waley says: "During the fourth century B.C. it began to occur to the Chinese that words move in a world of their own, a region connected only in the most casual way with the world of reality." The rift, because of the nature of Chinese, was more pronounced than in other languages. But the attempt to bridge the discrepancy between language and reality came to nothing, and the rift became wider.

The whole of this section of Mr. Waley's book on the "language crisis" merits study.

THE OLD SYSTEM

cells alone must at times overawe our minds and still our criticism.

" Employ the able and promote the worthy "—this had long been a maxim of Chinese policy. To begin with, ability had been measured by practical, if approximate, methods. In the Han Dynasty the officials were appointed by selection pure and simple, based on reputation for ability or virtue. Confucianism was now established as the state philosophy, and remained so in spite of the occasional setbacks at the hands of Buddhists, Taoists, and eunuchs, and in spite of the invasions and dynastic upheavals which took place every few centuries. Gradually a system of education was adopted in which the classics became the sole test.[1] The road to advancement in the public service was through a command of letters, and every Chinese family aimed at giving its sons a chance to tread the path of ambition. With the exception of some changes in the Sung Dynasty the literary system of education I am about to describe was the same in China from about A.D. 600 until the beginning of the twentieth century.[2]

The boy (the education of women was comparatively neglected, though there were scores of " blue-stockings ")

---

[1] Even though it be only in a footnote, mention must be made of Wang An-Shih (王 安 石) (1021–1086). " He attempted to reform the examination system, requiring from the candidate not so much grace of style as a wide acquaintance with practical subjects. ' Accordingly,' says one Chinese writer, ' even the pupils at village schools threw away their text-books of rhetoric, and began to study primers of history, geography, and political economy.' He was the author of a work on the written characters, with special reference to those which are formed by the combination of two or more, the meanings of which, taken together, determine the meaning of the compound character." H. A. Giles, *Chinese Literature*, London, 1915, p. 221. He is the subject of a work by H. R. Williamson, of which the first volume was published in 1935.

[2] Kuo Ping-wên, op. cit., 書院制度考 by 周傳儒 (privately printed), and 王鳳喈's work 中國教育史大綱 which says, 自漢至清之前半期,中國的社會與教育無多大的變動. In the Sung Dynasty, however, Mencius was for the first time considered as a classic proper. But see footnote on p. 43.

vegetated at home till he was seven or eight.¹ Even if a father was a literary man he seldom instructed his sons, and maternal training was supposed to be limited to giving right direction to the morals. Complete directions for the bringing up of children are given in the *Hsiao Hsüeh* (小 學), or *Juvenile Instructor*, a manual for teachers by Chu Hsi (朱 熹, known as 朱 子), written in A.D. 1150, which attained a classical standing. A great deal of the work is, as the author acknowledges, taken from the classics. For example, the model careers for a boy and a girl, quoted earlier in this chapter, are copied from the " Book of Rites ".² Fathers are to choose from among their concubines those who are fit for nurses, seeking such as are mild, indulgent, affectionate, benevolent, cheerful, kind, dignified, respectful, and careful in their conversation, whom they will make governesses of their children. In the matter of indulgence, be it noted, the Chinese child, in spite of the demands of filial piety, was allowed a license, in his earlier years at any rate, which would scandalize most European parents, though it might be approved by certain modern educationalists. " When able to talk, lads must be instructed to answer in a quick, bold tone, and girls in a slow and gentle one."

The *Hsiao Hsüeh* was reprinted hundreds of times with commentaries several times its own length. In examining it one finds that it was written in a lucid style. It gives compendious instructions for the behaviour of youth, quoting the authority of the sages whenever possible. It is continually appealing to authority and antiquity, the phrase " men of old " (古 之 人) appearing on nearly every

[1] 敎 育 思 想 發 展 史 (A History of the Development of Educational Thought), Commercial Press, Shanghai, 1934, p. 4, says, " in ancient times boys went to school when they were six or seven."

[2] S. W. Williams quotes this passage at length as the original remarks of the *Hsiao Hsüeh*; whereas that work specifically states that it is taken from the Book of Rites—a work belonging to a period much more than a thousand years earlier. See *Middle Kingdom*, London, 1883, vol. i, p. 522.

other page. "Let children always be taught to speak the truth, to stand erect in their proper places, and listen with respectful attention." "The way to become a student is with gentleness and self-abasement to receive implicitly every word the master utters." "Persons of the first grade are good without being taught; those of the middle grade acquire goodness with instruction; those of the lower grade even if they are instructed never achieve goodness." The pupil, it seems, is tacitly allotted to the second grade. The child owes an obligation to his parents even for his body, and must treat it as property held on trust. Hence to break a leg is not merely painful—worse, it is unfilial. The Confucian code is faithfully interpreted. The pupil must keep away from contamination—Milton "cannot praise a fugitive and cloistered virtue"; Confucius and Chu Hsi definitely can.[1]

In practice, certainly in the later periods, the programme of the Book of Rites was not adhered to with much accuracy. The more active pursuits were all but dropped. A boy went to school at about seven years old. He was led to the teacher by his father. The teacher then knelt down before the name tablet of some one or other of the ancient sages and supplicated their blessing on his pupil, after which, seated himself, he received the homage and petition of the lad to guide him in his lessons. Thereupon the pupil received his *shu ming*, or "book name".

Originally teachers were peripatetic; later they kept schools in a fixed place.[2] They were usually failed candidates for office and received a poor salary supplemented by eatables, but as an offset they were objects of almost idolatrous homage. The influence of the teacher was paramount; the pupil was expected to receive implicitly every

[1] Good fortune consisted in "not seeing improper sights, not hearing improper sounds (words), in not using improper words".
[2] Martin, *Hanlin Papers*.

word his master uttered. The aim of education was not so much to fill the head with knowledge as to discipline the mind and purify the affections.[1]

The schoolroom (and these remarks hold good up to the present day) was rarely specially built for the purpose. It was usually in a temple or matting shed, often ill-ventilated and ill-lighted. In one corner were the tablets to Confucius, the " Teacher and Pattern for all Ages ", and to the God of Letters. Incense sticks burnt in front of both. On entering the room the boy bowed to the tablet of Confucius, saluted his teacher, and took his seat. School hours were from sunrise till 10 a.m., then came breakfast, and after breakfast a further session till 5 p.m. In summer there were no lessons after dinner, though evening school was held in winter. Holidays were few, and consisted of a few days at the Chinese New Year and of the twelve festivals.[2]

The school course consisted in committing to memory the canonical books and writing an infinity of diversely formed characters as a mental exercise in the first stage. This writing exercise provided a training for the hands strangely neglected in the West. The pupil gained a dexterity in contrast with the Western boy who is usually clumsy at drawing and similar accomplishments.[3] In the second stage the pupil translated books into colloquial language (i.e. reading) and lessons in composition. In the third stage there were belles-lettres and the composition of essays. Pupils learnt their lessons by heart and aloud (a lesson in concentration when all the other pupils were doing the same thing with another book or a different part of the same book), and recited them when learnt with their backs

[1] Martin, ibid.
[2] Williams, *Middle Kingdom*, London, 1883, vol. i, p. 526.
[3] ". . . as a physiologist I note that I need as large an area of my brain to control my hands as my vocal organs . . . And as a scientific worker I note that some of my colleagues appear to do most of their thinking with their hands . . ." J. B. S. Haldane.

THE OLD SYSTEM

to the teacher. There were no graduated classes; in fact, there were as many classes as there were pupils.

The first manual of the syllabus was the *San Tzŭ Ching* (三字經), or Trimetrical Classic, a work by Wang Po-hou (A.D. 1050).[1] It contained 1,068 words, of which 534 were different characters. This standard hornbook, because it was the first book learnt, was known to the great majority of Chinese. It started off with a statement as to the perfect nature of man in the beginning of things, and then proceeded to a survey of learning in general. It exhibited the Chinese fondness for numerical categories. The classic enumerates the Three Great Powers, the Three Lights, the Three Bonds, the Four Seasons, the Four Cardinal Points, the Five Elements, the Five Cardinal Virtues, the Six Kinds of Grain, the Six Domestic Animals, the Seven Passions, the Eight Materials for Music, the Nine Kinds of Kindred, the Ten Social Duties. It then gives a list of books, sets out the motives for learning, and recounts anecdotes of Hsing T'o and Confucius and of devotion to learning. The pupil hears of the youth who studied his books by glow worm's light or the reflection of snow, or who tied his books to the cow's horn when ploughing. He hears, too, of infant prodigies, of Yung who at eight could recite the Odes, and Pi who at seven could explain the game of chess in verse.

The *San Tzŭ Ching* has been described as a "syllabus of studies" rather than a textbook. Its influence was very great among the Chinese, not only because it was the first book studied, but also because so many thousands were forced by circumstances to discontinue their education after having read it, and it thus became the sum total of their literary knowledge. "Its influence," says Wells Williams, "has perhaps been as great as the classics during the last four dynasties."

[1] Translated by H. A. Giles, Shanghai, 1873. In the same volume is also a translation of the Millenary Classic.

The student next studied the *Pai Chia Hsing*, or " Century of Surnames ", a work of obvious use later to him in social intercourse.[1]

After this came the study of the *Ch'ien Tzŭ Wên* (千字文) or " Millenary Classic ", a work of a thousand characters in which no two characters are the same. It was written about A.D. 550 by Chou Hsing-ssŭ. It was a *tour de force* in verse, and rhyme and rhythm were carefully observed, though it was quite devoid of poetic inspiration. Julien, who translated it into French, said, " Since it is arranged in methodical order which embraces the knowledge most essential to children, whoever has read it, copied it, and learnt it by heart, retaining in his memory the little notes which accompany the classic editions, already possesses exact notions on a number of facts of history, geography, literature, morality, the duties and the domestic virtues." He goes on, however, to lament, " rien n'est plus vrai que l'obscurité de ce livre." It started off with the universe (" the heavens are sombre ; the earth is yellow "), mentioning the constellations, and went on to the calendar, meteorology (" the clouds ascend and bring rain "), geology (" gold is born in the River Li ", " Jade is found on the summits of Mount K'un-lun "), horticulture, fruits, the ocean, and many miscellaneous branches of knowledge.

The Millenary Classic was followed by the *Yu Hsüeh Shih-t'ieh* (幼學詩帖), or " Odes for Children ". This work was in rhymed pentameters, praised the literary life, and alluded to the changes of the seasons and the beauties of nature. It gave instances of intelligent youth rising to the highest offices of the state.

---

[1] The *Pai Chia Hsing* (百家姓) contains, not a hundred but 408 surnames. It dates from the tenth century. Giles gives about 2,500 surnames in his dictionary, and the *T'u Shu Chi Ch'êng* (圖書集成) contains about 5,000.

THE OLD SYSTEM

The course was supplemented by the *Hsiao Ching* (孝經), or " Canons of Filial Piety " (" ever think of your ancestors, reproducing their virtue "), and some of the hundreds of toy books such as the " Twenty Four Filials ", containing anecdotes such as that of Wu Wang whose parents were too poor to buy mosquito curtains and who attracted the mosquitos away from his parents to feed on his own naked person. In due course the pupil passed on to the Classics proper, in particular the Four Books which comprised, from the Sung Dynasty, the *Ta Hsüeh* (大 學), the *Chung Yung* (中 庸), the *Lun Yü* (論 語), and *Mêng Tzŭ* (孟 子).

By dint of learning by heart and by writing compositions the pupil gradually acquired the " feel " of the language. He learnt, in Dr. Martin's words—

> " that the characters are endowed with a sort of mysterious polarity which controls their collocation and renders them incapable of companionship except with certain characters, the choice of which seem to be altogether arbitrary. In this, as in other things among the Chinese, usage has become law. Combinations which were accidental or optional to the writers of antiquity, and even the errors, to their imitative posterity, became the *jus et norma loquendi*." [1]

The first thing a pupil had to learn in composition was to yoke together double characters ; the second was how to reduplicate their binary compounds and to construct parallels. For instance, the teacher writes " wind blows ", the pupil adds " rain falls "; the teacher writes " rivers are long ", the pupil adds " seas are deep " or " mountains are high ". The construction of the " antithetical sentence " (對) was only a step further. For example, the model given is, " the emperor's grace is as vast as heaven and earth," and the antithetical compliment supplied is, " the sovereign's favour is profound as lake and sea." " In heaven there

[1] Martin, *Hanlin Papers*, p. 90.

is everlasting happiness: on earth there is no enduring peace" (天有永樂, 地無長安) is an example of an antithesis constructed by a Christian scholar. These couplets often contain two propositions in each member, accompanied by all the usual modifying terms; and so exact is the symmetry required by the rules of the art "that not only must noun, verb, adjective, and particle correspond to each other with scrupulous exactness, but the very tones are adjusted to each other with the precision of music".[1]

The last peculiarity which extends to Chinese composition generally is excellently illustrated by the remarks of Sir E. Backhouse [2]:—

"The tones are, for literary purposes, divided into sharps and evens, and no decree, no advertisement written to catch the literary man's eye, ever ignores the essential antithetical balance between the tones in consecutive sentences. Take, for instance, the fine imperial decree of abdication: its last sentence runs:—

ch'ang^l shou^o kuo^o min^l chih^l yu^l li^o
ch'in^l kuan^l chih^o chih^o chih^l kao^o ch'êng^l

[長　受　國　民　之　優　禮
　親　觀　邦　治　之　告　成]

where the words marked *l* are evens and those marked *o* are sharps. It is essential that the second, penultimate, and ultimate characters in antithetical phrases shall alternate sharp and even sounds. In a seven-lined couplet the fourth character would also preferably differ in tone. It is immaterial whether sharps or evens reverse their order, so the second line quoted above could with perfect propriety change place with the first. Foreign proclamations, as for instance,

---

[1] Martin, op. cit.
[2] Article on the Chinese language in *China Year Book*, 1933. The Chinese characters for the quotation from the abdication decree are not given in the article, and I am indebted to Sir Reginald Johnston, K.C.M.G., Professor of Chinese in the University of London, for telling me where they could be found.

THE OLD SYSTEM

in the Boxer Year, were sadly to seek in their neglect of this elementary rule of composition. It was possible to notice the literati's perusal of some of these well-meaning amateur effusions and the smile of good-humoured tolerance with which the outlandish character of the phrasing would be greeted."

The next stage after the antithetical sentence in the boy's curriculum was the *shuo t'ieh* (說帖), in which a single thought is expanded in simple language, and the *lun* (論), a formal discussion of a subject more or less extended, and letters addressed to imaginary persons and adapted to all conceivable circumstances. The Rev. A. H. Smith mentions a case which illustrates the nature of this exercise. A teacher, wishing to send a letter to his mother and having no time to write it himself, delegated the duty to a pupil who did not know the mother. When questioned by a foreigner as to this singular proceeding, the teacher replied, "Doesn't he know quite well what to say? For more than a year he has been studying literary composition, and he is acquainted with a number of elegant formulas. Do you think he does not know perfectly well how a son ought to write to his mother?"

These exercises are but preliminary steps leading towards the full-dress formal essay, the "eight-legs" (八股文章) of the public examinations.

It will be seen that the idea of progressive knowledge was foreign to the nature of Chinese composition. All knowledge resided in the classical writings; the well-informed man was the one who could point his finger at the place in the classics where a particular gem of knowledge was hid. The pleasure experienced by the essayist or the reader was that of responding to a situation in exactly the correct literary key. The sensation can be compared, more or less, to that of the person imbued with English literature who finds a building not merely large and enduring but " pyramidally extant ", or who on hearing the words " ancient valour " relives through volumes of resonant history. The feeling for logical inevitability is small; the warm feeling of authoritative literary support is great. It is the satisfaction we all derive from conservatism and the sanction of antiquity, when we are not troubled by the necessity of weighing and justifying. At its best, it is the splendour of tradition; at its worst, it is snobbery unabashed.

Schools were divided into primary where recitation and imitative chirography were learnt; middle in which the canonical books were expounded; and classical in which composition was the leading exercise. Often the divisions were all in one school.

The maintenance of the schools was left to private enterprise, and, to a small extent, to charity. The clans usually had their own schools.[1] The state took no part in organizing primary or secondary education, nor was there any provision for it from the national revenues.[2]

In the Sung Dynasty there came into being certain institutions which have been made much of by modern Chinese who wish to discover the progressive idea alive in the traditional China. These were the *Shu-yüan* (書院), or Provincial Colleges.

> " A Shu-yüan consisted usually of an endowment of land, a library, a well-known scholar as director, and a number of students, who were given a small allowance to cover at least part of their expenses... No lectures were given in the academy: the function of the professor was only to advise the students as to their reading and to criticise the results of their researches. Occasionally the professor or an outside

[1] Doolittle, *Social Life of the Chinese*, 1865, p. 376, says, "·There is no village tax or any aid from government. There are no free schools." But the last remark is certainly a misstatement.

[2] Parker, in his *China*, London, 1901, p. 198, written at the end of the Ching Dynasty, says that out of an expenditure of 31,000,000 taels only one two-hundredth part went in any way directly to the public. The 140,000 taels for " educational establishments " refers to Peking official colleges, or Manchu schools.

scholar would lecture on some selected topic, but, on the whole, the Shu-yüan was a place of self-study and a centre of research under expert guidance ... The spirit of scientific research which prevailed at these academies may best be illustrated by a maxim which the famous scholar, Huang Yi-chou, wrote on the walls of the Nanching Shu-yüan at Kiang-yin : ' Faithfully seek the truth, and make no compromises.' " [1]

Mr. T'ang Leang-li claims that the researches published by some of these academies, for example the " Series " published by the Nanching Shu-yüan, compare favourably with the best doctoral dissertations of European and American universities.

Attempts have been made to estimate the percentage of literacy in China at different times, but not with great success, for, to begin with, " literacy " is harder to determine in China, where so many can read in the sense of recognizing the characters but cannot understand what they read, than elsewhere. It is probable that literacy, in the real sense, at no time extended to more than 10 per cent of the population.[2]

---

[1] T'ang Leang-li, *China in Revolt*, London, 1927, p. 33. Mr. Chore's (周 傳 儒) monograph 書 院 制 度 考, before referred to, deals with the subject at length. The students were all of *chü-jên*, or higher standing, and their object was to prepare for higher examinations. See also 王 鳳 喈, op. cit., p. 153, which dates the beginning of these institutions in the T'ang Dynasty.

[2] The impression of a famous traveller is worth recording, though it must be remembered that it is only a traveller's impression and not the result of an exact inquiry. The time is the 'forties of last century.

" Of all countries in the world China is assuredly the one in which primary instruction is most widely diffused. There is no little village, not even a group of farms, in which a teacher is not to be found ... The schools are rather less numerous in the northern provinces ; it almost seems as if the intellects of the people were rendered duller and heavier by the rigours of the climate ... With some few exceptions, every Chinese knows how to read and write, at least sufficiently for the ordinary occasions of life. Thus the workmen, the peasants even, are capable of taking notes concerning their daily affairs, of carrying on their own correspondence, of reading the proclamations of the mandarins, and often also the productions of the current literature." *The Chinese Empire*, by M. Huc, London, 1855, vol. i, p. 111.

Dr. Martin estimated the proportion of Chinese who could read and understand what they read as one in twenty.

Those pupils who had the advantage of a full schooling were entitled to entertain hopes of entering for the public examinations. These examinations were, as I have stated, the main object of Chinese ambition, and every family aimed at supplying at least one candidate for academic honours.

Civil service examinations were originally confined to the Six Arts—music, archery, horsemanship, writing, arithmetic, and ceremonies. Under the Han Dynasty (206 B.C.–A.D. 220) the Confucian ethics had become current, and candidates were selected who had acquired a reputation for filial piety, but they were now subjected to intellectual tests as well. Subjects of examination were the Six Arts, civil law, military affairs, agriculture, the administration of the revenue, and the geography of the empire with special reference to the state of water communications. T'ang and Sung graduates were arranged in three classes, and officials in nine—a classification they retained till the end of the old system (1905).

But now that the written word was gaining its ascendancy, action was becoming depreciated.[1] Formerly candidates had been required to ride a race, to shoot at a target, and to sing songs of their own composition and to the accompaniment of their own guitars. In place of this examiners began to be satisfied with odes in praise of music and essays on the archery and horsemanship of the ancients.

The public examinations reached what was practically their final form in the T'ang and Sung dynasties (618–1126). The system, at the height of its development, was one of the most comprehensive and imposing the world has known. Towards the end of the nineteenth century two million candidates were examined annually, only one or two per

---

[1] A section of modern Chinese scholars regards the classics as inventions of the literati of the Han Dynasty (see T'ang Leang-li, *Foundations of Modern China*), but the researches of foreigners such as Karlgren by philological methods tend, in great measure, to re-establish their age and authenticity.

THE OLD SYSTEM

cent of whom were passed. The system has disappeared for ever, but there is plenty of evidence to show what ground the examinations covered and how they were conducted. Their position as keystone of the educational arch calls for an extended summary of their features.[1]

The first examination, in front of the Sub-Prefect, had two themes. The first theme was divided into two parts, the first for those over twenty who had received the cap of manhood (已冠文題), the second for those under twenty (未冠文題). Both were called *Shou T'i* (首題) or *T'ou T'i* (頭題). The themes were both taken from the Four Books. The same morning the second theme was set (次題). Since cheating and substitution of candidates were rife, Kien Long in 1788 established this second theme to make communication with those outside the examination hall more difficult. The second theme, or set of themes, was the same for both candidates (通塲次題). To this was added a theme in verse (通塲詩題). Once the themes and verse were finished they were transcribed in standard characters (謄眞繕寫) and also in cursive script. If these transcriptions differed in the least degree the composition might be rejected. Candidates had to avoid employing characters occurring in the personal and after-death names of emperors of the reigning dynasty.[2] There were eleven emperors of the Ch'ing Dynasty and each had a reign name (年號), an after-death name (尊諡), a name consecrated for the temple of his ancestors (宗廟), his own personal name (御名), and his personal name on decease (廟諱). The candidate had either to avoid the employment of the characters composing the personal and after-death names (M. Vissière shows that this meant avoiding only about eighteen characters in 1900),

---

[1] For this purpose the *Variétés Sinologiques*, No. 5, *Pratique des Examens Littéraires*, by Père Etienne Zi, has been freely drawn upon, though liberal supplement has been made from other sources.

[2] See Vissière, " Traité des Caractères Chinois que l'on évite par respect," *Journal Asiatique*, 1901.

or replace them by others (恭代). These rules were subject to certain modifications. It was permitted to make use of 福 and 臨 forming the personal name of the first emperor 福臨, whilst that of the second emperor 玄燁 had to be replaced by 元煜. Thus, in 1894, to describe the colour black (玄色) 元色 was written. Also certain locutions were prohibited, for instance simple homophones of imperial names such as 在田, a homophone of the personal name of the Emperor Kuang Sü. Taboos did not stop with imperial styles; Confucius' name 丘 was never to be employed, but by a decree of the Emperor Yung Chêng was to be replaced by 邱, and other characters were avoided for superstitious reasons. Candidates who ignored the prohibitions were expelled from the examinations.

If the Sub-Prefect had no literary degree and had bought his title, a literary outsider marked the papers.

The successful candidates were announced in a circular shaped notice with names radiating from the centre, and these could now present themselves for the repetition examination for the definitive classification (長案). The themes were now the same for the juniors as for the seniors, namely, extracts from the Four Books and the Five Canons with a piece of verse composition on a given theme. A second circular shaped list was now published with the number of names diminished. Usually there was a third " repetition " examination with a subject for amplification (commentary) and one for dissertation (論). The fourth " repetition " examination (四覆 or 終覆) was the last and by it the number of candidates was reduced to fifty or sixty. For this examination they brought two exercise books. In one they had to write out from memory a passage from the " Imperial Instructions " (in practice candidates brought a copy with them), in the other they made further commentaries, for example four exordia (走講).

The Second Examination took place before the Prefect (府考). It consisted of first and second repetitions. The results were published in a rectangular list. The Third Examination was before the Provincial Examiner. In this the subject for the first amplification was taken from the Four Books. The second theme, also from the Four Books, was given out after four hours. On this section of the examination the first classing was made, and it was followed by a second repetition and a second classing. Those candidates whose names appeared in the second classing had the certainty of the Bachelor's degree.

But the examination nevertheless continued with third and fourth repetitions. Nor even when he got his degree was the Bachelor allowed to rest permanently on his laurels. Unless he presented himself at the triennial examination he would be degraded. He was examined again in the Four Books and had to compose a piece of verse. Ten different grades of Bachelor were instituted from these triennial examinations.

The next examination was for the Master's degree (*chü-jên* 舉人). On a paper printed with themes (題紙) were given some characters from which the candidates had to choose their rhymes for the piece of verse composition; the same leaf prescribed the capital figures for indicating the characters added in recopying the drafts.

The following were the themes taken from the Four Books and set for the first test for the Master's degree in 1889 :—

(1) " There are three things which the sage reveres; he reveres the dispositions of heaven; he reveres eminent men; he reveres the words of the saints." (2) " For him who would understand the Sacrifices of Heaven and Earth, and who would penetrate the sense of the oblations offered every five years and each autumn to the shades of his

ancestors..." (3) "The visit of the Son of Heaven to the feudatories was called 'inspection of fiefs'; to inspect fiefs is to take a personal account of the territories of his (the emperor's) vassals. The coming of the feudatories to the court of the Son of Heaven is called 'to render accounts of one's administration', and is to describe the manner in which he (the feudatory) has managed the business of the lands."

The subject for the verse composition was :—

"The waters of the river present the shadows that are the precursors of autumn; the wild geese begin to take flight." Take the word 秋 (autumn) as the type of rhyme for this piece. (Here follows the sixty characters of the same rhyme or assonance from which the candidates are to choose their eight rhymes.)

A curious phenomenon in Chinese is that rhymes used in poetry are always those sanctioned by classic usage. Many words that originally rhymed have ceased to do so by the change in the spoken language which has in turn changed the sounds allotted to characters, but the versifier uses them as if they did still so rhyme. To use words that rhyme now, but which are not shown as so doing in the official rhyming dictionaries, is to write jingling doggerel.[1]

The prose commentary was not to exceed seven hundred characters. The verse was always of the kind called "five words eight rhymes" (五言八韻) having eight rhymed verses, each composed of two hemistichs (聯) of five syllables.

Other themes at Nanking in 1889 were, "strength and weakness are the emblem of day and night," and "the Emperor Shun (舜) offered a sacrifice to the crowd of spirits".

Sometimes the prose theme called for an essay in criticism. For instance :—

---

[1] The Commercial Press *Tz'ŭ Yüan* (辭源) gives a list of rhyming dictionaries.

" Question. Although the books 連山 and 歸藏 [titles of two books on the Changes (易)] are not mentioned in the history of the Han Dynasty, nevertheless the scholar 桓君山 could affirm with certainty in what spot these two books were hidden and what number of characters they contained, from which it follows that the works were lost in the Han Dynasty. When were they compiled? Some think that the commentaries on this double book made by Yung (庸) and Chên (貞) are authentic; which is the surer of these two opinions ? . . ."

A question that recalls European examinations, though the reply expected does not involve scientific methods of criticism, but proof by appeal to authority. That this should be so shows how the literary had ousted the beginnings of a scientific method, for Western scholars pay tribute to the skill of early Chinese archæologists and epigraphists.[1]

The learned *Variétés Sinologiques* gives examples of the texts of themes set for the formidable " eight-legs " essay (八股文章), but does not offer an example of how the candidate treated the themes. Such an example, however, is available without searching through Chinese archives. The *China Review* for 1879–80 contains the full Chinese text of an " eight-legs " essay with translation and notes by Mr. F. S. A. Bourne. The essay was written by the candidate who obtained the first place at the examination for the degree of Provincial Graduate (*chü-jên* or M.A.) held in Peking in September, 1879. His name was Chang Cheng-yu, aged 18. Thirteen thousand candidates presented themselves for examination and about 330 passed. The examination was held in all the provincial capitals as well as in Peking. There were other sections in the examinations, but the fate of the candidate largely depended on the first essay of the first period. The following was the candidate's first essay :—

[1] e.g. Karlgren, *Sound and Symbol in Chinese*, p. 13.

The theme set was: " Tzŭ-kung said to Confucius: Suppose there was a man of such unbounded beneficence and power that he was able to extend help to every one of the people (who needed it) what would you say of him? Might he be called humane? Confucius answered: Is humane the right word? Must he not be a Holy Man?"[1]

The candidate treated it in this way:—

" Analysis of the Theme (破題)—The meaning of the above words is that a humane man, as such merely, would not be able to reach to the degree of unbounded beneficence and power supposed by Tzŭ-kung.

" Amplification of Theme (承題)—That is to say that such unbounded beneficence and power could be manifested by none but a Holy Man; and it is this that Confucius conveys in his answer to Tzŭ-kung's doubting question—' Might he be called humane?'

" Explanation (起講)—For the term humane is applied to a man who has reached the full standard of that which humanity requires; but if too high a meaning is given to that term, the true standard of humanity may perhaps be passed by the man to whom it is applied. But Tzŭ-kung's question was prompted by his fervent wish that, the full possibility of his nature reached, even the humane man might be able to bring down the blessings of peace and prosperity on his generation; while Confucius in his reply raised Tzŭ-kung's estimate of the nature of a man who should be capable of the unbounded beneficence stated, pointing out that for such great power and wide beneficence we must look to the few Holy Men of antiquity [Yao, Shun, etc.]. Tzŭ-kung would make the attainment of humanity impossible, thinking that if his sympathies should be broad enough to take in all

---

[1] 子貢曰,如有博施於民,而能濟衆,何如,可謂仁乎,子曰,何事於仁,必也聖乎[堯舜其猶病諸]. The last six characters were omitted in the Theme, though the candidate from his store of knowledge would readily supply them. A candidate was not allowed to introduce into his essay the words that immediately followed the Theme in the classical text, in order to give scope to his literary skill. In the present case the essayist proved his skill by covert references to Yao (堯) and Shun (舜) without once introducing them by name.

men and things, then and not till then would he reach the full development of humanity; but he forgot the achievements and virtues, the record of which has come down to us from early times, and the distance that separates ordinary men from those highly endowed natures [Yao, Shun, etc.].

"Post Explanation (講下)—His Sacred Majesty, the present Head of the State, is the protection of his people, and has the interest of all at heart. But it must be a golden age, such as that not a man suffers want, before the unbounded beneficence and power supposed by Tzŭ-kung can be predicated of the Ruler. Can a humane man reach this standard? Tzŭ-kung's question was indeed a strange one.

"Argument 1st Division (題股)—Every man and woman below the sky, to whom Heaven has given body and soul, should have my sympathy in his joy and sorrow. But if you can say that one individual must suffer because I have not been able to reach him with help before I reach the whole measure of humanity, I reply that humanity is not so distant as this.

"2. If in reality I am compassionate and at peace with my fellows, my sympathy will extend to all places and persons; but if you say that my bounty must reach every place on which the sun and moon shine, before I can attain the limit of which humanity is capable, I reply that humanity is not so difficult.

"Re-assertion of Theme (出題)—Suppose, then, there were a man of such unbounded beneficence and power that he was able to extend help to every one of the people (who needed it), what kind of man would he be? And what kind of work that on which he was engaged? When Tzŭ-kung was in doubt whether such a man reached the standard of humanity, how greatly did he over-estimate that standard, and under-estimate the qualities necessary to unbounded beneficence!

"Argument 2nd Division (中股)—1. Tzŭ-kung, when he put this question, no doubt knew that work of such extent and difficulty was certainly not to be lightly accomplished, and he therefore allowed his imagination to wander and represent to his mind's eye a man possessed of boundless beneficence and virtue—a man whose work might perhaps be able to satisfy his own sincere love for the whole human race.

"2. But, to Confucius' unerring judgment, a state of things in which all men under Heaven should be as one family, and the whole nation of one mind, was sincerely to be hoped for, and therefore he could not restrain himself from looking afar and aloft [to the days of Yao, Shun, etc.]—for such great virtue and spiritual power belonging to the first Emperors, whom Heaven specially endowed.

"Argument 3rd Division (後 股)—Thus it was that Confucius replied without hesitation—How can you expect this from humanity? Can humanity reach this standard? Is the world so full of virtuous men and so united in opinion? Nature loves and hides the spirit that will make a good and great man, and often many hundreds of years elapse between one manifestation and the next, so that when such a man is born, he may be at once recognized as of extraordinary capacity; and thus the birth of a holy or enlightened man certainly cannot be depended on. But why should we not, however unlikely the realization may be, indulge the thought that the appearance is possible? Work of unusual difficulty must await the birth of a man whose mind is *en rapport* with Heaven and Earth (or who is able to assist Nature in her processes and to form a co-equal Trinity with Heaven and Earth, see *Chung Yung*, ch. xxii). From the earliest times unusually arduous undertakings have had to wait the appearance of specially endowed rulers (lit. Emperors who by their rule brought about such a state of equilibrium and harmony that a happy order prevailed throughout Heaven and Earth, and all things were nourished, see *Chung Yung*, i, 5). And when a period of calamity is reached, unless such a man is forthcoming, the people cannot be saved. But the humane man may have the desire to perform this work, and if he succeed so far that men look upon him with hope, who can help going back in imagination [to the days of Yao and Shun]?

"2. Are the people always in the enjoyment of peace and plenty? And when a period of bad fortune does come round, the lives and the property of the multitude await the delivering arm of an able Ruler. But how can we be sure that a Holy Man will suddenly come forth to the rescue? Yet what harm can there be in forming a wish, however impossible in its realization, that such a Being may appear? A time when all men enjoy plenty and happiness can only come about when one of these periods, predestined to be adorned by all men and their illustrious deeds, has come round. A Ruler who proposes to himself as his object the happiness of his people must be a man of the highest principle and in sympathy with Nature. When the work of saving a starving or drowning people is in question, none but such a man can be equal to the task. But the humane man can greatly assist in this work. Good fortune cannot make a man equal to such great undertakings; and (when we think of the need of such a man) who does not go back in imagination [to the days of Yao and Shun]?

"Confucius answered: Is humane the right word? Must he not be a Holy Man?"

In this translation 仁, usually translated "benevolent", is rendered as "humane", and 聖, usually translated "sage", is here more correctly rendered as "Holy Man".

Mr. Bourne remarks: "In writing his essay the candidate is not allowed to express his own thoughts in his own way. He must make his sentences conform in great measure to one of two or three recognized models. The division into cut and dried sections modifies in many cases the meaning. When, for instance, in the essay the theme is restated in the middle of the argument, if no notice were taken of the division, and the translation ran straight on, the author might appear to be begging the question or arguing in a circle."

Read in English the effect of the essay is of a meagre idea, excessively laboured, and held together by a series of *non sequiturs*. The Chinese text, however, which Mr. Bourne annexes to the translation, reveals that whatever its value as a contribution to classical exegesis, it is a marvel of literary ingenuity. A dozen references to the *Chung Yung* (Doctrine of the Mean), the *Lun Yü* (Analects), and to Mencius are dovetailed into the argument, and great skill is shown in alluding to the fabulous Yao and Shun without once introducing their names.

But although a candidate had survived what seems to us almost superhuman tests, and had joined the tiny percentage of *chü-jên* or Masters of Arts, he had as yet no right to public employment in the higher grades. He had merely risen higher in public estimation, wore a higher grade of gilt button when in dress, and put a board over his door proclaiming that he was a *chü-jên* or " Promoted Man ".[1] He had to pass still another examination, that of *chin-shih*, or Doctor of Literature, before he could hope eventually to attain high office. This degree he sat for in Peking. If successful he took one of the vacant posts that were distributed by lot. One more degree completed the crown of acdemic laurels, and that was the one entitling him to entry to the Hanlin (翰林, " forest of pencils ") at Peking, whose members constituted " the poets and historians to the Celestial Court, or were deputed to act as chancellors and examiners in the several provinces ".

Such was the vista of honour that stretched out before the ambitious Chinese. No one was excluded from the public examinations except the immediate descendants of play actors, executioners, yamen-torturers, or yamen-runners, from whom the candidate must be separated by three clear generations, and the descendants of barbers, priests, nail-cutters, and scavengers, though in the latter cases the inquiry was not so strict.[2] But in spite of this outlet for ambition there was a reverse side of the medal. A tiny proportion, as we have seen, obtained degrees at all, whilst of these only a small number ever got employment. About 14,000 Bachelors were added to the list every year. There were probably close on 700,000 graduates living at the end of the nineteenth century.[3] Douglas says that in 1894 there were 21,168 unemployed provincial graduates

[1] Dyer Ball, *Things Chinese*, Shanghai, 1925, p. 228.
[2] Parker, *China*. The river dwellers of Canton were also excluded on the ground that they had no domicile. [3] Parker, ibid.

alone, too proud, because they were literary gentlemen, to work at a trade, but not too proud to live on their relations or on charity.[1] " To pluck the mystic cassia and tread the azure clouds " was a heartbreaking vocation. The system, too, was " honeycombed with corruption ".[2] One censor reported to the Throne that everywhere personation was rife.[3] Giles combats this allegation, but the facts appear to be against him.[4] Yet on the whole the able candidate (able that is at solving literary conundrums) had a fair chance of getting through. In England the examinations are fair, there is no fear or favour, but success, for instance, in the civil service examinations, depends upon a special kind of training not available to the mass. The aspirant in China had no such handicap; the subjects taught were one and the same in any school in the Empire.

To appraise the moral code inculcated with this elaborate system it would be necessary to separate the living principles of Confucius from the dead formalism in which they were embedded. It would be necessary, too, to decide how far the doctrines of the orthodox classics were alloyed with Buddhism or Taoism. It is not possible to do these things with any certainty, though we are, like Gibbon with Christianity, safe in allowing much for the " inevitable mixture of error and corruption that " Confucianism " had contracted in a long residence on earth ". During the centuries formalism had encroached more and more on moral conviction. To appreciate this one had only to observe the " promoted man " (*chü-jên*) of the late Ch'ing Dynasty who, to prepare his character for office, suddenly takes an interest in practical benevolence (仁).[5] He osten-

---

[1] *Society in China*, London, 1894, p. 116.
[2] Ibid., p. 170. [3] Ibid., p. 171.
[4] *Civilisation of China*, London, 1911, p. 113.
[5] The five virtues were benevolence (or humanity) 仁, the duty of a man towards his neighbours 義, 禮 politeness, behaviour, 智 sagacity, and 信 sincerity.

tatiously burns incense and gives alms. If he sees a fish in the markets floundering on the hooks, he pays its price and restores it to its native element ; he picks struggling ants out of a rivulet made by a recent shower, distributes moral tracts or, better still, rescues chance bits of paper from being trodden in the mire of the streets.[1] These actions set him in bold relief against a society whose general callousness and apathy are freely admitted by the Chinese themselves and by their most ardent admirers.[2] But just as the ascendancy of the Pharisees does not throw doubt upon the Decalogue, the mummery of the literati cannot discount the value of the Analects. Besides, even principles that are fossilized into ritual can play a great part in giving social solidarity. As in the West the motives underlying acts in the public welfare would not always bear examination, and the tribute that vice pays to virtue is often as effective as virtue itself. It suffices to say that the classical morality of the Chinese, above all the principle of filial piety, disseminated by the complex machinery of the educational system, has been a good second to the literary language in holding the people together.

It is by now clear to us that Western standards cannot resonably be used for valuing the Chinese system. It is only because the West can at the moment demand recognition for its standards as absolute ones by virtue of the superior force of its civilization, that their application to China is at all justified. Progress, for instance, a dominant if not an ancient idea in the West, could have no place in China. To the Chinese an " onward march " was a foreign

---

[1] Martin, *Love of Cathay*, London, 1901, p. 317. The written character was sacred and no one would willingly tread on it. In many cities furnaces were provided at street corners for burning printed papers to save them from being trodden on.

[2] e.g. Sun Yat-sen, *San Min Chu I*, and Bertrand Russell, *The Problem of China*.

THE OLD SYSTEM 39

conception. The European visualizes himself as moving *forward* through time, facing the direction he is going in. He has a conviction of continuous betterment, though he recognizes the possibility of retrograde steps. The Chinese regards perfection as residing in the past, and all he can hope for is to reach some degree of emulation. If he moves at all he does so facing backwards. This feeling is well illustrated in the " eight-legs " essay given earlier in this chapter.

But even by Western standards it would be a mistake to regard the thought of China as flowing into stagnancy in the first centuries of our era. The educational system nearly choked invention, but it was still alive. " The age of Confucius and downwards gave birth to a succession of writers distinguished for the boldness of their theories and the freedom of their utterance." [1] Chinese writers educated in the West as well as at home, even claim to have discovered in China the counterpart of the restless political theory of Europe. One of them [2] speaks of " anarchists such as Lao Tzŭ, humanitarian socialists such as Mo Ti, commonalists such as Hsün Tzŭ, political economists such as Khuan Chung, progressive absolutists such as Shang Yang, co-operatists such as Hsü Hsin, practical socialists such as Wang An-shih, and constitutional monarchists such as Tung Chung-shu ". But the use of these terms from political science is anachronistic and misleading, and suggests a type of mental adventuring not to be found in Chinese thought. We can say, though, that the poets of the T'ang Dynasty sought their models from nature direct, and that speculation of a special kind was rife under the Sung emperors. Wylie, writing in 1867, even finds some signs of literary renaissance at that advanced period of stagnation.

[1] A. Wylie, *Notes on Chinese Literature*, London, 1867. Introduction, p. iii.
[2] Leonard Shih-lien Hsü, *The Political Philosophy of Confucianism*, 1932.

"The views of bygone ages," he says, "are fully canvassed; scholars are less under the mental domination of antiquity; and expositions of the classics which have long been held infallible, are anew submitted to the tests of criticism."[1] But the renaissance, if such were in train, never took place.

The purely literary nature of study meant that in China "men occupy themselves with words rather than with things; and the processes of acquisition are more cultivated than those of invention".[2] The conviction that knowledge was a definite quantity like the contents of a great treasure house, and not the working theory of a moment, encouraged the scholar to an exaggerated pride in his acquisition. Those whose measure of pride is the Spanish hidalgo can have no conception of the Chinese literatus in the heyday of his influence. The fact that he had no shirt to his back would not (and quite logically) abate his feelings of condescension towards the unlettered. This fact is noted time and again by foreigners; Giles (usually so lenient to Chinese failings) devotes an article to it in the *China Review*, and Biot, writing in 1847, speaks of "l'orgueil excessif des lettrés Chinois".[3]

We must bear in mind that nearly all the works from which we gain our impression of China were written by foreign observers in the period of her decline. Hence the imposing effect which an account of the old system of education and its manifold intricacies is bound to produce is much impaired when we come to view the material concomitants of the system at the close of the Ch'ing Dynasty. Confucius says, "The best way to govern a people is to enrich them, and having enriched them, educate them." The precept was not fulfilled. The house of the scholar was

---

[1] Wylie, op. cit., intro., p. xi.   [2] Martin, *Hanlin Papers*.
[3] *Essai sur l'histoire de l'instruction publique en Chine*, Paris, 1847. Though Biot gained his impression from documents, for he never visited China.

too often a windowless hovel; he sat for his examinations in little cells which a Westerner would think of as slums; the great Hanlin itself (a symbol of a system though not in actual use) was in ruins and its courts grass-grown for centuries. Public works like the Grand Canal or the Great Wall touch the reader's imagination : one is not prepared to find that they are in no sort of repair, and that education has not succeeded in producing enough public spirit to maintain in good repair a highway of any length, the capacity to deal effectively with flood, famine, or afforestation, or enough official integrity to secure any appreciable portion of the revenue for national purposes. The standard of living has always been low, and the literary system did nothing to raise it. As a cultivation of the mind the literary system of China was impressive ; as a creator of tangible wealth (at the end of its days that is) it was scarcely so. To find the material achievement of the culture one would have to seek within the tent-like yamens and houses of the wealthy to be rewarded by the graceful porcelain, the T'ang sculpture, the Sung painting, the wood engraving, the embroidery, the lacquer of the Ming. These are the triumphs, if but the relics, of *chinoiserie*. And it must be conceded that the spirit that made these beautiful things was still alive enough to give grace and proportion to the few cups and earthenware pots by the hearths of the " Hundred Surnames ".

Those who respond to a civilization in ratio to its æsthetic product will find, like Gibbon viewing the Arch of Constantine, much food for melancholy in looking upon the paltry imitation and feeble fancy of the rebuilt Summer Palace near Peking. They will be disposed to think lightly of China's cultural fruits. But in the Fitzwilliam Museum at Cambridge (to take a casual example) is a certain porcelain horse of the T'ang Dynasty. Who looking upon it can fail to believe that the Chinese system at the height of its health and vigour, produced things of beauty to vie with those of any other civilization ? And beauty is never a solitary evidence of the good : the Chou, the Han, and the T'ang reveal more and more to scholarship a high level of living and thinking within selected co-ordinates of reality.

If in its decline this system did not teach the people to create wealth, its learning could at least dignify poverty in a way we cannot understand in the West. True literacy, too, may not have been widespread, but the least educated shared much of the literary heritage of the nation, though they could only recognize a few hundred of the commonest characters. Over the doors of the poorest houses were quotations from the classics, fragments of Sung poetry, pairs of elegant antitheses. By word of mouth and by the incidence of the beautiful written character upon the eye, the Chinese illiterate was in communion with the choicest minds. Who can think of a quotation from *Hamlet* in large red or gold letters over the door of an English navvy (or peer of the realm for that matter) without his risibility being aroused ?

The educational system of China was entirely autochthonous ; it was the creation of the Chinese people and owed nothing to outside help. If it had any deficiencies, the Chinese were unaware of them. It had worked for two millennia and, so far as we know, would have worked for another two if left alone. Up to the middle of the nineteenth century not a Chinese would have believed that strife with the " outer barbarian " would reveal its weakness and inadequacy. The foreigners who had come in driblets since the sixteenth century were known to have skill in numbers and had rectified the calendar, but no educated Chinese regarded their uncouth written signs as possessing a serious literature. It needed the cannon of the First China War (1839-1842) to make a breach that in the end would bring

THE OLD SYSTEM

down the great edifice built upon the classics, the elaborate examination system, "eight-legs" and all, into a ruin. The metaphor, even though it somewhat over dramatizes the facts and ignores the decay from within, is still a valid one, but we must examine more closely what happened in order to understand it aright.[1]

---

[1] Confession is good for the soul. If I had read *Le Traité des Examens, traduit de la Nouvelle Histoire des T'ang par Robert des Rotours*, Librairie Ernest Leroux, Paris, 1932, before this book went to press, it is likely that the introductory chapter would have been more complete than it is, and it is likely that the statement on page 15 that the educational system of China did not change from *c.* 600 to *c.* 1900 would have to be somewhat modified. What one imagines to be the small tooth-comb of investigation is often nothing but a hay rake.

But there is nothing in this valuable work of M. des Rotours which affects my main thesis, namely that the education in China for a period of well over a thousand years before the present cultural revolution was essentially the same. In M. des Rotours' work are given a selection of examination questions of the T'ang Dynasty and of the answers given by candidates. Comparing these with the "eight-legs" essay of the candidate of 1879, one finds that the principal difference is that the T'ang are less stereotyped and more vital. There is also a more practical air about the T'ang productions as if their authors were really concerned to arrive at the truth. But the essays are equally authoritarian, and the method of argument is the same as that of the *Ta Hsüeh*.

Chapter II

CONTACT WITH THE WEST

The few medieval contacts with Europe did not disturb or influence the Chinese scheme. Travellers such as Marco Polo or Friar Odoric found that there was much they could take away with them, but little they could leave behind. The Renaissance, stirring but still imprisoned in the womb, was powerless as yet to arm the envoys of Church or State with presents or accomplishments that would impress the most civilized people then existing. Even when navigation snapped the bonds of Ptolemy's map, the Portuguese adventurers who pounced on the Chinese coasts in search of trade or loot did not seem to the natives of the Middle Kingdom to be much in advance of the aboriginal Miao, except perhaps in their ferocity and their weapons of destruction; but a few decades later the Jesuit missionaries whom the Roman Church sent abroad were not only animated with the vital zeal of the Counter-Reformation; they were equipped with the best scientific knowledge that the reborn Western learning could provide.

Those early Jesuits capture the imagination. They had talent that would have brought them honour in their own country; yet they exiled themselves, and for life. They entrusted themselves to a people whose character was an unknown quantity, and they had no consuls or gunboats to answer for their safety. More remarkable still, several of them attained to a knowledge of the Chinese written language which even the jealous literati recognized as

CONTACT WITH THE WEST

approaching scholarship.[1] There was Michele de Ruggieri, Matteo Ricci, Diego Pantoja, Sabbatini de Ursis, Giacomo Rho, Adam Schall von Bell, and (later) Ferdinand Verbiest, and the greatest of all, Ricci, was practically the first to come. His arrival in the capital after a twenty years journey from Macao, where he had been with a Portuguese mission, is described in The Ming History.[2] His account of Europe and its cultural attainment was received with politeness, but was considered to be much exaggerated. The *Ming Shih* further on says :—

"Those who have come to the East from this land are, generally speaking, all clever men, scholars sent for the purpose of propagating their teaching without seeking rewards of wealth. The majority of the books which they have written are what the Chinese have not yet treated of. And so all those who are fond of curiosities continually honour them, and scholars and officials like Hsü Kuang-ch'i, Li Chih-tsao, and P'ei Shou, approved of their works and added polish to the style of their writing, so that their teaching prospered rapidly."

They were geographers, mathematicians, and astronomers, and their skill was employed in rectifying the calendar.[3] Of the gifts they brought, clocks and watches were the most appreciated. The Jesuit teaching prospered or declined with the temperament or caprice of succeeding emperors, and as the jealousy of officialdom was excited or its fears allayed. Adam Schall von Bell was called upon to cast

---

[1] This was certainly the case, though Thomas, *Histoire de la Mission de Pékin*, quoted by Latourette in *A History of Christian Missions in China*, says that in most, if not all, of his writings Ricci was aided by Chinese scholars.

[2] See portion of the Ming History (*Ming Shih*) translated by Professor Moule in "The First Arrival of the Jesuits at the Capital of China," *New China Review*, vol. iv.

[3] Ricci was the favourite pupil of Father Clavius, one of the chief authors of the Gregorian Calendar. Hu Shih, *The Chinese Renaissance*, Chicago, 1934, p. 28.

A great Jesuit scientific triumph was their exact prediction of the eclipse of 22nd February, 1636, which discredited the rival native schools of astronomy which had made false predictions of the event.

cannon for use against the invading Tartars, and he did so though it troubled his conscience. The final cause of missionary failure was the jealousy between the Jesuits and the Dominicans who had now arrived. The two parties could not agree as to whether ancestor worship or the worship of Confucius should be tolerated among converts, or again as to the translation into Chinese of the word "God". Two infallible but quite contradictory bulls of Innocent X and Alexander VII did not improve the situation or the credit of the Christians in China, whilst a third bull of Clement XI giving a decision on these points opposed to one already given by the Emperor, brought the missionaries under suspicion of being subversive agents. After more than a century, during which there were intervals of proscription, Christianity was denied toleration in 1724, though a few missionaries were retained for scientific purposes in Peking.[1] There had been at times a fair chance of Christianity being adopted throughout the country, but now the chance had gone. Christianity had been tolerated as a rival to Buddhism, but its effect on the educational system was negligible; Buddhism itself in the centuries had scarcely influenced the system more.[2] Western science, at this stage in its development, did not get beyond the status of a curiosity, even if at times a useful curiosity. The Chinese felt no doubt as to the complete sufficiency of their classical literature, nor was there any reason why they should.

Contact with Europeans during the eighteenth and early nineteenth centuries was almost entirely through traders, and these were by 1757 confined to the port of Canton. The Dutch and English came for a quick profit and a quick

---

[1] Since this chapter was written a good general history of the Jesuits in China has become available in *Jesuits at the Court of Peking*, by C. W. Allen, Kelly and Walsh, 1935.

[2] Influenced the educational system, that is, not the beliefs of the people. For an examination of Buddhism in China see H. A. Giles, *The Travels of Fa-hsien*, Cambridge, 1923.

departure, and they were seldom of the type, even if they had had the opportunity, to spread the intelligence of their own countries' scientific progress. Two expensive embassies from King George III and four from the Dutch did nothing effective to break down the isolation of the Dragon Throne. Again, the Chinese wanted none of the European gimcrackery in return for their rice and tea; Indian cotton, woollens, and silver were practically the only things they would take [1]—that is until the foreigner discovered that opium would relieve the drain on his silver. In Europe in 1839 the first stages of the Industrial Revolution had been accomplished; Lavoisier, Priestley, Watt, and Faraday had started science off on an astounding stage in its career, but the foreign barques and brigantines that sailed the Pearl River, the main available evidence of material advance, betrayed to the native observer no marked superiority in construction to the junks that passed by.[2]

A work on education is no place to describe the origins or the conduct of the First China War, though one is at liberty to remark that it was scarcely more an " Opium War " than the Indian Mutiny was a " Greased-cartridge Mutiny ". This war, however, was the signal for the break up of the old system. Not, be it understood, that for many decades had the Chinese as a people any suspicion that the Four Books and the Five Canons were not enough for the Middle Kingdom to stand on for ever. But the suspicion started from now that whatever the cultural merits of China she was inferior in one respect to Europe, and that was in material strength. They started at once to imitate—but only

---

[1] Morse, *International Relations of the Chinese Empire*, London, 1910, vol. i, p. 175.
[2] The foreign vessels in Chinese waters in the first decades of the century were mostly East Indiamen of about 600 tons, and later Baltimore clippers of beautiful lines but light displacement (500 tons about), with an occasional warship. *Encyc. Britt.*, 14th ed., art. *Ship*.

the barest superficies. Amongst the war junks captured at Wusung were several new wheel-boats, having two wooden paddle-wheels turned by a capstan—not by steam but by interlocking its cogs into those upon a shaft which was worked by man-power on the gun deck.¹ This was China's answer to the paddle-steamboats brought into action against them. And though China suffered complete and utter defeat, it needed years of time and another equal defeat before she condescended to go a step beyond this kind of half-hearted imitation. The official classes must have been aware of the danger and they sought with all the weapons of diplomacy to save their civilization by keeping it isolated, not by copying the barbarians' methods.² But forces were against them. Yet speaking as recently as 1924, Dr. Ts'ai Yüan-p'ei, one time Minister of Education and later Chancellor of the National University of Peking, was constrained to say, " Though in contact with the West from the thirteenth century, we have learnt very little about physical science except the evil effects of it." ³

The story of China's dynastic renewals can be compressed into a few sentences without much loss of accuracy. The country has ever been subject to the devastation of flood and famine, and its resources have never been well enough organized to ensure that a surplus from unaffected areas was available to relieve adequately those areas that were distressed. The result was that desperation was always creating centres of disorder. Under a strong government these centres were isolated and the inhabitants starved in

---

¹ Williams, *Middle Kingdom*, 1883, vol. ii, p. 534.

² It would seem that the famous Commissioner Lin did not share the views of his colleagues. Mr. Gideon Chen in his *Lin Tse-hsü : Pioneer Promoter of the Adoption of Western Means of Maritime Defence in China*, the French Bookstore, Peiping, 1935, attributes the *Hai Kuo T'u Chih* or *Illustrated Record of the Maritime Nations*, published in 1844, to Commissioner Lin, and in this work the adoption of Western ships, weapons, etc., is strongly advocated.

³ *The Development of Chinese Education*. A paper read before the China Society, 1924.

an orderly manner : under a weak government these centres of disorder spread (the more virile of the sufferers set out in bands to maraud the unaffected territory) and in extreme cases, when the reigning dynasty was effete, it was overthrown and a new and strong one took its place. Then the process started all over again. Sometimes the change-over was accompanied by foreign invasion, and in such cases the interbreeding of conqueror and conquered resulted in a vital impulse and a renewed culture. Such was China's normal process of self-renewal. Before the middle of the nineteenth century the Manchu Dynasty had reached an advanced stage of decay, the Banners were degenerate, and the bonds of government were loosened. Inevitably the forces of disorder gathered strength and started the great T'ai P'ing Rebellion. I say " started the rebellion ", for it was these conditions which made the ground fecund for Hung Siu-tsuen with his claims to blood relationship with Jesus Christ and later to the Imperial yellow. For fourteen years China suffered every imaginable misfortune—murder, rapine, pillage, and a loss of twenty million or more in population. The European powers, fearful that they would be robbed of the diplomatic recognition that they were wringing by slow degrees from the reluctant Manchu Emperor, and that they would have to start at the beginning again, lent their indirect aid to the Manchus, and it was enough to turn the tide.[1] The rebellion fell to pieces, and the Manchus lingered on through another fifty years of limp authority. Sustained not by their own will to govern (excepting always the redoubtable Empress Dowager) but by the absence of an effective opposition, the dynasty disintegrated at last rather like the subject of the experiment

[1] Morse and MacNair in *Far Eastern International Relations*, New York, 1931, p. 256, say, " The Ever-Victorious Army [Ward and Gordon] ... had helped stem the tide of rebellion, a task of which the imperial troops were, by themselves, apparently incapable." But a contrary view is taken by W. J. Hail in *Tsêng Kuo-fan and the T'ai P'ing Rebellion*.

of Poe's Dr. Valdemar when the hypnotic influence was removed.

It is not to be expected that during this long period of disorder and effete government the educational system remained in a robust condition. As we have seen in the first chapter, the dead wood of formalism choked the growth of healthy fibre, and corruption set in. If the impact of Western materialism had coincided with the latter half of the seventeenth century instead of the nineteenth, it is likely that there would be a different story to tell. Either the native system would have successfully resisted the Western cultural aggression, or else, more likely, the system would have modified itself by grafting with greater success. But it did not turn out in this way.

In preparation for the opening up of China Dr. Robert Morrison, the first Protestant missionary in the country, had been labouring secretly in a godown in Canton preparing a Chinese-English dictionary and a translation of the Bible. By the time the Treaty of Nanking was signed he was dead, but his successors were prepared with their plan of campaign. Writing of these missionaries Dr. Kuo Ping-wên says :—

> "They lost no time in establishing schools as an instrument for the dissemination of Christian knowledge and faith. The schools thus founded, though not strictly confined to the children of the Christians, remained chiefly as the place where the new converts were educated and preserved from too intimate contact with the unbelieving world. At all events the work of these pioneer missionaries did not have the scope and character which it has assumed in recent years. They had no well-established educational policy. Each school was opened as the exigency of the occasion demanded and the funds of the home board permitted. Their schools were, moreover, confined to the children of the humbler classes. The few who acquired a Western education therein had little prospect of employment in the government. In spite of these

and other shortcomings, it must be admitted that for some time the schools of the missionaries were practically the only institutions where some form of modern knowledge was taught and for this reason they must justly claim to have been the first modern educational institutions in China."[1]

But this account, fair as far as it goes, does not give adequate credit to Christian influence on Chinese education and a closer examination of missionary activity is called for.[2]

The edicts of toleration following on the Treaty of Nanking were taken advantage of at once by missionaries, both Catholic and Protestant. Amongst the Jesuits there were those who wished to renew the scientific mission to Peking which in the seventeenth and early eighteenth centuries had been of such assistance to the Church, but counsels were divided, and the anti-foreign reaction at Court which came with the accession of Hsien Fêng in 1850 made the project impracticable. Schools were established by the Catholics for the children of converts, but no attempt was made to introduce Western learning to the pupils. The main object was to maintain and strengthen the converts in their faith and to prepare candidates for the priesthood. Enough knowledge of the Chinese classics was inculcated to command the respect of the educated. The great work of the Jesuits was to be in the tradition of their early missionaries. At first the Catholics resumed scientific research in a small way only. Armand David, a Lazarist, studied natural history and made a collection of specimens, and in 1869 the Jesuits began to organize a museum of natural history as a means of approach to the Chinese. Then in 1872 was established at Zikawei near Shanghai, on land given centuries before by one of Ricci's converts, a centre for scientific research which has

[1] *The Chinese System of Public Education*, New York, 1915, p. 64.
[2] K. S. Latourette, *A History of Christian Missions in China*, has been followed in this account of missionary education.

grown ever since. Here is now an observatory from which emanate daily weather reports and forecasts, a large library, a printing establishment, and here originate the scholarly monographs on various aspects of Chinese life known as the "Variétés Sinologiques". Séraphin Couvreur, the lexicographer, was also a Jesuit and a member of the mission in south-eastern Chihli.

The Catholics did most for pure scholarship; the Protestants most for education. The Morrison Education Society, dating from 1835, maintained a school from 1839 to 1845, first of all in Macao and then in Hong Kong. At this school Yung Wing, who was to be China's first "returned student", and who is referred to later in this chapter, received his early education. Wong Fun, the first Chinese to take a Western medical degree, was also at this school. Other schools came into being from time to time. Among them were the Presbyterian boarding school for boys at Ningpo, and Miss Aldersey's school for girls in the same place. The Ningpo dialect was romanized and used as a medium for instruction. The American Presbyterian boarding school was established at Macao in 1845 but soon removed to Canton. In 1850 the Church Missionary Society began a school in Hong Kong which later became St. Paul's College, and which undertook the training of catechists and clergy. The American Methodists' girls' school was opened at Foochow in 1851, and in 1859 a boarding school for girls was started under the same mission. The Protestant Episcopalians, the American Board, the English Presbyterians, had all opened schools by the early 'fifties. The last body was the most ambitious and contemplated starting an education scheme on the lines of the one in India, but the time was not yet ripe.

The missionary schools and colleges soon became too many for separate enumeration. Among the institutions established between the Second China War and the native reform movement of 1898 may be mentioned the American Presbyterian Central Theological School in 1862, the school for preparation for the church begun by Mateer in 1864, the divinity college founded by the Church Missionary Society at Foochow in 1878, and St. John's College, later St. John's University, founded at Shanghai by the American Episcopalians in 1879. In 1889 the University of Nanking started life with rather an ambitious title and in 1890 the University of Peking was founded. The Canton Christian College began in 1893.

At the conference held in 1879 Mateer said that the purpose of Christian education was to provide a native ministry, to train teachers for Christian schools and "through them to introduce into China the superior education of the West", to prepare men "to take the lead in introducing to China the science and arts of Western civilization" as "the best means of giving access to the higher classes of China". This was in response to, and in exploitation of, the growing demand for Western knowledge. But Mateer's view was not accepted by all parties. For instance, Timothy Richard, of the Welsh Baptists, was principally concerned with adapting Christianity to the Chinese background.

In the early years the missions had great difficulty in getting pupils for their schools. Right to the end of the century and beyond, both Catholics and Protestants had to resort to something like bribery to keep their schools going, giving their pupils not only their tuition for nothing but their food, lodging, and clothing as well. It was only as China became awake to the advantages of Western knowledge that schools, especially those that taught English, were able to pay even part of their way from school fees.

Chinese classics were usually taught, since a grounding in the national literature was considered essential. English was taught in a large number of schools of the higher grade and was usually the medium of instruction in the higher subjects. The question of whether English was to be taught or not and, if so, how much, divided the opinion of the missionaries. The curriculum of the higher schools was " humanistic " rather than technical and professional, and consisted of Latin, Greek, philosophy, mathematics, and by 1879, sciences of various kinds, history, and English literature. But the first and candid object of the Protestant Missions was to further the study of the Bible, and the main *raison d'être* of the high schools was to bring forth native leaders in the work of spreading the Gospel.

It remained true till the end of the century and beyond that the Protestant schools were practically the only ones in which Western learning could be acquired, but, as we shall see, Western learning until the 'sixties and 'seventies was in no great demand, and as places of preparation for the all-important public examinations the missionary schools were inferior to the native ones.

The importance of mission schools in an account of Chinese education is that they were pioneers in the movement to come. Some of the principal leaders in the reform movement had received at least part of their education at mission schools—Kuo Ping-wên (P. W. Kuo), Chang Po-ling, C. T. Wang, Wang Ch'ung-hui, W. W. Yen, Chang Ying-hua, C. C. Wang, and last but not least, Sun Yat-sen. The founders of the great Commercial Press were trained in part at the mission presses. But numerically mission school pupils were not important in the nineteenth century. In 1876 5,917 pupils were reported in mission schools and in 1889 16,836. These schools were still looked down upon by the vast majority.

For all these activities the official classes displayed no interest whatever in Western education between the Treaty of Nanking of 1842 and the Treaty of Tientsin which concluded the Second China War in 1860. The T'ai P'ing

Rebellion and a second defeat at the hands of the Westerners had now, however, begun to persuade some of the more intelligent of the authorities that something must be done to improve the Chinese material efficiency. But the actual initiative was thrust upon them by foreigners.

Up to 1860 China had no Foreign Office. This deficiency was part of the policy of maintaining the isolation of the Middle Kingdom [1] by ignoring the existence of other political entities, and it was this state of affairs that the foreigners were intent on remedying. A clause in the Tientsin Treaty provided for the creation of the Tsungli Yamen—a Foreign Office, indeed, even if with limited powers and importance. A further clause provided that for the next three years all foreign dispatches would be accompanied by a Chinese translation, but after that they would not be so accompanied. It became necessary, therefore, for the government to make provision for the training of interpreters, and there was established at Peking a school known as the T'ung Wên Kuan.[2] The Maritime Customs under Sir Robert Hart financed and indirectly controlled the school. In 1866 it was raised to the rank of a college, and from 1869 onwards for many years it was presided over by Dr. Martin. About the time of Dr. Martin's appointment a scientific department was added to the school, which was an important step in the direction in which China was eventually to be led. Branches of the T'ung Wên Kuan were soon established in Shanghai and Canton.[3]

So far what had been done towards a modern system of

---

[1] I have seen it stated that *Chung* (中) in *Chung Kuo*, the " Middle Kingdom ", does not mean the geographical centre of the world, but is taken from *Chung Yung* (中 庸), the Doctrine of the Mean, but I do not know what authority there is for this view.

[2] Martin, *A Cycle of Cathay*, New York, 1900, p. 301.

[3] *Tsui Chin San Shih Wu Nien Chung Kuo Chiao Yü* (最近三十五年之中國教育), Education in China in the Last Thirty-five Years, Commercial Press, Shanghai, 1931, p. 55. Also Kuo Ping-wên, op. cit., p. 65.

education had been done as the direct result of foreign insistence, but the Chinese were now to start instigating changes on their own. The motive was, as it has remained ever since, to render China strong and able to stand up to her enemies. Arsenals had already been set up in China, but under the direction of foreign engineers and mechanics. In 1867 the Viceroy Tsêng Kuo-fan, renowned as the conqueror of the T'ai P'ings, through the persuasion of Yung Wing, China's first "returned student", set up a school attached to the Kiangnan Arsenal at Shanghai to train Chinese in the theory as well as the practice of mechanical engineering. In the same year two naval schools, one French and one English, were established in Foochow, and in 1879 the Northern Government Telegraph College was started in Tientsin.

In the meantime Tsêng Kuo-fan had himself sponsored a work of historical importance. In 1865 he caused to be published from his military headquarters in Nanking a translation of the fifteen books of Euclid's *Elements of Geometry*. This translation was a continuation and completion of one begun by Matteo Ricci, the Jesuit, 250 years earlier. It is probable that Tsêng was influenced in his decision to publish the complete work by Ricci's preface to the six books translated by him. Ricci explained that geometry had value in making the calendar, in medicine, geography, commerce, etc., but above all in military affairs. He said that in the past a smaller nation had often conquered a larger because its military leader had a knowledge of geometry.[1]

Plans for the establishment of a modern university at Tientsin were long considered. In 1887 they were formulated by the noted Li Hung-chang, but for some reason no steps were taken to carry out the plan until after the Sino-

[1] Cyrus H. Peake, *Nationalism and Education in Modern China*, New York, 1932, pp. 5–7.

CONTACT WITH THE WEST

Japanese war of 1894 when the question of education reform came once again to the forefront.

But the most significant move of all was that taken in 1887, after twenty years of discussion.[1] It was the new defeat by France in 1885 which finally brought matters to a head. For the first time in history, mathematics and science were introduced into the public examinations. They were optional subjects, it is true, but the thin end of the wedge had been inserted into the very pedestal of the literary column. This, moreover, when the European nations themselves had not yet reformed their own examinations in a similar way. Algebraic equations and problems of light and heat were queer companions for the eight-legged king of letters to have to endure!

Amongst the educational institutions on Western lines established during this time were the Polytechnic Institution in Shanghai in 1874, and the first modern military school at Tientsin in 1885, which latter was staffed by German officers. In 1890 the Chinese Imperial Naval College was founded at Nanking, two professors being provided by the British Navy. In 1895 a government mining college of the Hupeh Board of Mines was established at Wuchang, and in 1893 a medical college for the army at Tientsin. It was

---

[1] It is to be remarked, though, that in spite of this general dilatoriness the Chinese were in one remarkable instance actually in advance of their Western enemies. Witness the following extract from *Merchants of Death*, by H. C. Engelbrecht and F. C. Hanighen, London, 1934, p. 47 :—

"... One Remington agent put on Chinese clothes, made his way to Peking and gained the ear of Li Hung Chang, who ordered rifles for the Chinese army. Thereupon a catalogue was issued in the Chinese language and more orders were secured.

" In fact, the Chinese were more progressive than the French. When the Remington-Lee repeaters appeared on the market the Chinese were among the first to buy them. Shortly afterwards they met the French in battle, and Chinese progressiveness defeated French conservatism. At the battle of Lang Son in the 'eighties the French with their Kropatchek guns were three times repulsed by the Chinese armed with Remington-Lees. The American-made guns could be recharged in a few seconds, while those of the French took much longer. The latter were at the mercy of the foe when their magazines were empty."

at Wuchang, too, that the reforming Viceroy Chang Chih-tung, whose book will presently claim our attention, attempted to introduce Western education. He set up colleges of agriculture, languages, mechanics, mining and military science, and professors were engaged from America, Belgium, England, Germany, and Russia.

In 1877 thirty Chinese engineers went to England, Germany, and France to study, and returned in 1880. In 1881 an admiral, sixteen officers, and 200 marines went to London to study naval tactics.

The practice of sending Chinese youths abroad to be educated was begun on the advice of Dr. Yung Wing, himself a graduate of Yale and, as I have mentioned, the first " returned student ". The commission set up for the purpose was placed in his charge and that of Chin Lan-pin, a Hanlin, who would from this fact be expected to watch the interests of the literati. From 1872–5 thirty students were sent to America every year. During their absence, however, a reaction set in, and on the pretext that the students were being affected with republicanism, and advantage being taken of the strong anti-Chinese prejudice then existing in America, all the students were recalled in 1881. The returned students were refused public employment and got no opportunity to use what they had learnt till many years afterwards.[1]

Meanwhile a number of translations of foreign works were appearing in China from the arsenal schools translation departments, from the T'ung Wên Kuan, and from private sources. Most of them were technical works, but a few were on education and general subjects. Western missionaries assisted in the process and K'ang Yu-wei, the reformer, admitted that he owed his conversion to reform chiefly to the work of two foreign missionaries.

In spite of the reaction which led to the withdrawal of

[1] Kuo Ping-Wên, op. cit., p. 68.

CONTACT WITH THE WEST

the students in America, the Chinese government still maintained interest in Western methods. This is evidenced by the commission sent abroad under Dr. Martin to report on foreign educational systems which visited seven countries between 1880 and 1882. The public examinations contained more questions than ever on military affairs which showed how the official mind was tending.

Now on the eve of the Sino-Japanese war over fifty years had elapsed since the Treaty of Nanking and China's first severe blow from foreign arms. Measures had, as we have seen, been adopted to remedy China's educational deficiency which was responsible, it seemed, for weakness in war, but the measures, often half-hearted, were adopted slowly and reluctantly. Besides, it was no rebirth from within but a borrowing from without. Mr. C. S. Addis, writing in 1889 or 1890, says :—

> "even to the most sanguine in discerning the signs of a renaissance in China, there are moments when they must view with misgiving the direction which the new growth is taking. It is as true of the nation as it is of the individual that all growth must proceed from within outwards, from the centre to the circumference.... If there be a change, it is a change of veneer ; the essential characteristics of the people remain unaltered." [1]

The war with Japan in 1894-5 was a swift affair. A few months and China was again on knees worn to horn in supplicating her enemies. This defeat, more than any that had preceded it, brought home the necessity for real educational reform.

> "The conviction became so prevalent that many of the literary men, some of whom were quite advanced in age, sought Western learning by attending missionary schools and colleges, by employing private tutors, by forming reform clubs, and by reading such translations of Western books as were available.

[1] *China Review*, vol. xviii, p. 205.

The Emperor Kuang Hsü himself became so interested in Western science and learning that he ordered his eunuchs to search out and bring to him all the translations of books on Western learning that could be found."[1]

At last the University of Tientsin, so long contemplated, came into being, and in 1897 the Nanyang College was established in Shanghai.

A flood of memorials to the throne signalized the renewed and extended awareness of the official classes of the need of national rejuvenation. As yet there was no suggestion that the sap was not flowing amply and healthily in the aged trunk of the tree of classical learning; it was thought to be well able to sustain the slips of Western science, geography, mathematics, and languages that should, it was urged, be grafted upon it. As before, the aim of education was to cultivate men of talent: universal education was not yet favoured in official circles. The military officer, until lately not highly considered by society, was to be raised to an equality of status and opportunity with his civilian confrère and to be tutored by more officers engaged from Germany.

The outcome of the war with Japan had encouraged the reformers to come more into the open and their ranks received the addition of converts. The hand of one of the reformers, Liang Ch'i-ch'ao,[2] who with his master K'ang Yu-wei[2] was destined to share the title of Father of the

[1] P. W. Kuo (Kuo Ping-wên), op. cit., p. 69. The Emperor read K'ang Yu-wei's books on the reform of Russia by Peter the Great, and on the reform of Japan in recent years. "His mind was immature, though he was now approaching his thirtieth year, and his ideas were crude; but in the spring of 1898 he had reached the point of feeling the necessity for a change if the state was to be saved." *Far Eastern International Relations*, p. 446.

[2] These reformers were actual experimenters in writing. They were both prose writers and poets in a kind of modernized *Wênli*. For their influence, especially in connection with the "Poetic Revolution" (詩界革命), see 中國近代文學之變遷 (*The Transformation of Chinese Literature in the Present Generation*) by 陳子展, Chung Hua Book Co., Shanghai, 1929, p. 7 et seq.

CONTACT WITH THE WEST

Cultural Revolution, is identified in the memorial submitted in 1896 from the Vice-President Li Tuan-fên, outlining a system of modern education and suggesting the systematic examination of technical, agricultural, commercial, military, and mining schools abroad. The Four Books, the *T'ung Chien Kang Mu* (通鑑綱目, a condensation of the " Mirror of History ") and the *Hsiao Hsüeh* (小學) were to be the background of the system.

At the same time it was realized by the more intelligent of the mandarins that Western methods were valueless unless they were adopted on a sufficiently large scale and care was taken to keep up to date. Western technique was constantly improving and already the machinery of the arsenal at Foochow was becoming obsolete. The Chinese were doing nothing to advance applied science, and this was not remarkable since they lacked the apparatus needed for experiment.

Chang Chih-tung's work, *An Exhortation to Learning* (勸學), appeared in the early part of 1898.[1] It was published together with an Imperial rescript approving it, as Catholic works are accompanied by the *Nihil obstat* of the Censor Deputatus, and its effect was enormous. A million copies were sold.[2] The argument of the book was that China must adopt Western learning at once or be destroyed. But Chang did not advocate the abandonment of Chinese learning. " The old and the new must be taught ; by the old is meant the Four Books, the Five Canons, history, government, and geography of China ; by the new, Western government,

---

[1] Mr. Peake says (apparently on good authority) that Chang Chih-tung collected a number of the better essays written by pupils at modern schools already established at Shanghai and published them under his own name (op. cit., p. 24).
An excellent translation of *An Exhortation to Learning*, under the title of *China's Only Hope*, by S. Woodbridge, was published in 1901. The French translation by J. Tobar gives the Chinese text.
[2] Introduction to S. Woodbridge's translation.

science, and history." He was, as is invariably the case with sponsors of innovations in China, careful to reconcile his proposals with orthodoxy. For instance, he says, referring to the favoured departments of Western learning, "All this is not what is called 'dangerous knowledge' in the Book of Rites." His warnings, too, are taken from ancient Chinese history—" Formerly Yuen Poh of the Lu Kingdom perished because he was unwilling to learn, and Keo Chien of Yueh flourished by reasons of years of instruction." The principles of Western natural science are said to be stated in the Doctrine of the Mean by Confucius, and the principle of what is now known as scientific agriculture was to be found in the Ceremonial Rites of Chou.

Enthusiastic as Chang was for China to share in the benefits of Western learning, he scarcely over-estimated the difficulty of obtaining a knowledge of it. Speaking of what is vital in the curriculum he says :—

"From fifteen years upward the following should be taught— classics (complete), general literature, moral philosophy, Chinese government of the present Dynasty within the last hundred years, with special reference to the memorials and edicts of the last fifty years ; geography of the present time, embracing the physical condition of China, her water courses, products, provincial capitals, canals, roads, strategic points, coast and boundary defences, open ports, . . ., comparative study of foreign geography, especially that of Russia, France, Germany, England, Japan, and America ; cursory survey of the size, distance, capitals, principal ports, climate, defences, wealth and power of these (*the time required to complete this course ten days*), mathematics (sufficient for a working knowledge of other branches)."

The italics are mine.

Chang Chih-tung summarized his conclusions in this way :—

"To sum up : Chinese learning is moral, Western learning is practical. Chinese learning concerns itself with moral conduct ; Western learning, with the affairs of the world. What matters it, then, whether Western learning is mentioned in the classics or not, if it teaches nothing repugnant, or antagonistic, to the genius of our books ? "[1]

The reform party—and by this is meant, not the handful of revolutionaries who were beginning to gather round the exiled Sun Yat-sen, but those persons of influence who sought reform as the fountain of national strength—had by 1898 firmly entrenched themselves in the confidence of the reform-minded young Emperor Kuang Sü. From June to September of that year there followed in quick succession a most sensational series of Imperial decrees. A system of modern schools was called into being, the "eight-legs" essay was abolished by a stroke of the pen and replaced by short essays on practical subjects, and a scheme for the sending abroad of young teachers was proclaimed. The riding, archery, and sword-brandishing tests which form the subject of the quaint illustrations to Father Etienne Zi's chapter on military examinations in the *Pratique des Examens Littéraires*[2] were consigned to the lumber room of the past, and mental tests were instituted in their stead. Another decree foreshadowed a conscript army.

But the conservatives, scandalized and frightened though they were, were not long in marshalling their forces. The zeal of the reformers had carried them too far. A plot to seize the Empress Dowager Tz'ŭ-hsi was betrayed to her, and in a flash she had turned the tables by imprisoning the Emperor and executing most of his advisers. Those who escaped fled abroad where they formed a nucleus of intellectual revolutionaries. The edicts were annulled and the hoary "eight-legs" was revived from the dead to

---

[1] Extracts from S. Woodbridge's translation.
[2] *Variétés Sinologiques*, No. 5, 1894.

straddle the brain pan of the literary candidate for three more dismal years.[1]

Reaction, once set in, went even further than reform. Identifying itself with the anti-foreign feeling which came to a head with the foreign concession hunting and native desperation of the end of the century, the reactionary movement culminated in the Boxer outbreak of 1900. The inevitable military defeat and national humiliation followed. The articulate part of the people was converted to educational reform and the conservatives had to yield. This time it was not the Emperor who sponsored the measures but the intransigent Tz'ŭ-hsi herself.[2] Henceforward the adherents to the old scheme were fighting a rearguard action.

In China, an order obeyed to the extent of 10 per cent is considered to be fully carried out, and one must not be surprised at the scope of a government instruction or the short time allowed for compliance with it. In January, 1901, a decree ordered all government offices and all ministers in Western lands to survey Western methods of governing and to report their finding within *two months*. But then Chang Chih-tung allowed only six months for the complete mastery of Western learning!

The air was buzzing with reform. Even now care was taken by the instigators of the new-fangled proposals to spare the feelings of the literary classes and to rake out a plausible precedent from China's remote history. For the first time, commerce and industry, as the new foundation for the national strength, received favourable mention in official documents instead of being treated with silence or Hellenic contempt.

[1] H. Cordier, *Relations de la Chine avec les puissances occidentales*, 1902, vol. iii, pp. 407 et seq. The Emperor was confined to an islet in the Imperial park.

[2] 中國近百年史 by 陳懷 and 孟冲, Chung Hua Book Co., Shanghai, 1932, p. 228.

The upshot of the Russo-Japanese war of 1903–5 gave an unexpected impetus to the reform programme. What Japan had done with Western learning China could assuredly do. Students in thousands flocked to Japan to imbibe the elixir at the nearest fountain head. From 1902–7 it is said that more than 10,000 Chinese youths passed through the Japanese academies.[1] The elixir, as I have called it, turned out to be very heady wine, and the innumerable books, pamphlets, and essays the young men tossed off in praise of the new learning were distinguished by exuberance and sometimes by violence.

In 1901 a modern university in Peking was planned, and it was resolved to convert the provincial Shu Yüan, or colleges, into modern universities on the same model.[2] The military examinations were reformed in the same year, and the establishment of military schools throughout the country was ordained. The literary examinations still stubbornly resisted dissolution. In August, 1901, the " eight-legs " was finally buried by Imperial decree.[3] From the point of view of orthodoxy the examination was crippled, but it still had the Four Books as lungs to breathe with. Chinese political history and current affairs were added as subjects of examination. A further decree of the same eventful year made it possible for graduates of the modern schools to proceed eventually to the literary degrees. The beginnings of the Ministry of Education are to be seen in a new Central Educational Affairs Bureau which is ordered to be attached to the Board of Rites. The energy of the officials was on the whole considerable, but the results obtained varied with the capacity of the provincial governors. The old literary examinations were felt by the thorough-going

---

[1] 近代中國留學史 (*History of Chinese Students Abroad in Recent Years*), Shanghai, p. 46.
[2] See 新中華教育史 by 孟獻承, Shanghai, 1932, p. 320.
[3] 大清教育新法令, Commercial Press, Shanghai, p. 2.

reformers to be a great obstacle to their plans, since, while they remained the main avenue to advancement, students could not be attracted in great numbers to the modern schools. It needed repeated bombardments of the die-hard forts, and it was not till 1905, just after the Russo-Japanese War, that they capitulated to the big guns of Yüan Shih-k'ai and Chang Chih-tung. On 2nd September of that year a decree was promulgated abolishing the lower examinations at once and the higher from the beginning of 1906. The system had lasted in the same form for about thirteen hundred years, nearly as long as the Roman Empire.

In the few years preceding the collapse of the Empire in 1911 the mandarinate showed great energy in the work of educational reform. The *annus mirabilis* 1901, in which the *Shu Yüan* were ordered to be turned into provincial universities and in which the " eight-legs " was finally interred, saw also the order that middle schools should be established in every prefecture and department; that higher primary schools should be established in every district, and lower primary schools throughout the country. In 1903 a commission was appointed to draw up a plan for a national public school system. Chang Chih-tung and two others were to form the commission. The plan they proposed received Imperial sanction and was adopted as the programme for the whole of China. It was closely modelled on the Japanese system.[1]

The aim of the lower primary school was to give children above seven years of age the knowledge necessary for life, to establish in them the foundations of morality and patriotism, and to promote their physical welfare. The subjects to be taught were ethics, Chinese classics, Chinese language, mathematics, history, geography, nature study, and physical training. The course was to be five years, and twelve out of the thirty school hours a week were to be

[1] Kuo Ping-wên, op. cit., p. 78.

CONTACT WITH THE WEST

devoted to Chinese classics.[1] The higher primary school with a course of four years was to cultivate the moral nature of the young citizen, to enlarge his knowledge, and to strengthen his body. The curriculum consisted of ethics, Chinese classics, Chinese language, mathematics, history, geography, nature study, drawing, and physical training. Of the thirty-six hours a week, twelve were given to Chinese classics. The purpose and scope of the middle school were also defined, but only 5 per cent of pupils went through this stage, and the ground to be covered by the higher school and the university was also plotted. Since the commission was considered not to have stated its aims specifically enough, a decree of 1906 further stated that the aim of education in China was not merely to discover men of talent, but to educate the whole nation and to inculcate loyalty to the throne, respect for Confucius, the awakening of the people to a sense of their national responsibility, the promotion of a military spirit, and the creation of a practical and realistic sense.

This system was not changed in principle till after the Revolution. The changes in detail were in the direction of adapting the system to the needs of diverse communities, in endeavouring to spread education over a wider section of the people, and in cutting down an over ambitious curriculum. The number of school hours, after being increased, was reduced again in the Lower Primary to twenty-four in the first two years, and thirty for the last two years of a standard four-year course.

The education of women had always been neglected in China,[2] though blue-stockings managed from time to time to acquire learning. It was left for an Englishwoman,

---

[1] Ibid., p. 80; Peake, p. 63; *Tsui Chin San Shih Wu Nien Chung Kuo Chiao Yü*, p. 12.

[2] This account of female education is drawn from *Tsui Chin San Shih Wu Nien Chung Kuo Chiao Yü*, vide ante.

Miss Aldersey, to open, in 1844, the first Chinese girls' school at Ningpo.[1] Another was opened at Tientsin in 1864, and another at Shanghai in 1881. All were established by missionaries. The first girls' school established by a Chinese (named 吳懷疚) was in Shanghai in 1898.[1]

Regulations published by the government in 1902 referred to the education of women, but only to their domestic training. It was not till 8th March, 1907, that the Ch'ing Dynasty issued a set of thirty-six regulations regarding girls' normal schools, and twenty regulations regarding girls' primary schools. This was the first time that female education had been recognized in China as forming part of the system. The course of study in girls' schools was to be one year shorter than in the boys' schools. Boys and girls were to be separated from one another and were not to study in the same class.[2] No middle schools, colleges, or universities provided for girls at all, the normal school being the highest. In 1912, after the establishment of the Republic, the Ministry of Education issued a decree that education for boys and girls should be equal.

Primary schools for girls were first opened in 1907. The course of study was to be four years in the Lower Primary Schools and four years in the Higher Primary. The school ages were to be 7–10 and 11–14 respectively. The curriculum in the Lower Primary was ethics, literature, needlework, and drill, the optional subjects music and drawing. In the Upper Primary Chinese history and geography were added, whilst drawing became compulsory and music remained optional. By the end of the year (1907) there were 391 girls' schools in China, representing 11,936 girls.

The growth of girls' primary schools was rapid. In 1918–19 there were 190,882 girl pupils as compared with

[1] The first Chinese girls' school in the world was established in Singapore by missionaries in the 'twenties of last century.
[2] See 教育文存, Chung Hua Press, Shanghai, 1923, Sect. 4.

4,177,519 boys in the Lower Primary, and 24,744 girls as compared with 421,893 in the Upper Primary. In 1922 the figures were 368,560 to 5,505,816 and 35,182 to 546,308. In 1919 there were nine government girls' Middle Schools with 622 pupils and 132 teachers, but there is no record of the private ones. In 1923 there were 522 Middle Schools for males, and twenty-five for females, with 100,136 boy and 3,249 girl pupils. The province of Kiangsu was the most advanced in female education.

Before the Students' Movement of 4th May, 1919, there were only three universities for females in China, namely, the Union Girls' University at Peking, Ginling Girls' University at Nanking, and the Hua Nam Women's University at Foochow. Thereafter girls were permitted to enter men's universities. By 1923 there were 123 universities for men, and two for women exclusively, but the total number of girl students was only 887 as compared with 33,993 men. In 1928 the number of women had grown to 1,596.

We have seen that after the age of seven etiquette demanded that boys and girls should not mix or sit at the same mat: therefore co-education in China was non-existent. In recent years, however, the prohibition has practically broken down.

The creation of the *Hsüeh Pu* (學 部), or Ministry of Education, in 1905 as an independent ministry in lieu of the Department of Education under the age-old Board of Rites, was a big step in a new policy of centralization of education. This policy continued until the fall of Yüan Shih-k'ai in 1916, when it was lost for some years in the political break up of the country.[1]

A significant and, as it turned out for the country, ominous fact was the continued establishment of military

---

[1] An account of the administration of education in China is given on pp. 243 et seq. of *Tsui Chin San Shih Wu Nien Chung Kuo Chiao Yü*.

colleges and the increase in the number of professional soldiers.[1] By 1911 there were 240,000 troops under arms in China, 85,000 of whom were properly organized and officered, and by 1930 there were between one and two million soldiers. The China Year Book for 1934 shows a total of 1,999,630 troops, excluding Militia, Local Vigilantes, etc., or Manchukuo troops. It was the existence of these troops without any proper control or outlet for their ambition which was the main cause of the " war-lordism " which has sucked the blood of China since the Revolution. Nor has this militarization done anything to increase the strength of China in the family of nations.

When the Revolution took place the new Minister of Education, Ts'ai, proceeded at once to restate the educational aims of China as they must be modified to agree with the republican spirit. Ts'ai Yüan-p'ei, who, it may be remarked in parenthesis, was born in 1867, was a *Hanlin*, and had set many examinations under the old scheme. The most important order he promulgated was that the Chinese classics were no longer to be taught in normal, middle, and primary schools. Compared with this epoch-making decision the new formula for the national educational aims, the stressing of Liberty, Equality, and Fraternity, and the military spirit, were of minor importance. Not unimportant, however, was the natural consequence of the Republic, the removal of the Emperor from the position of respect. Yüan Shih-k'ai, the Provisional President, was a strong supporter of Confucius though he favoured the aims of modernization and militarization. He attempted to restore the monarchy in his own person and strove hard to maintain the Confucian worship to this end. A decree of 1913 proclaimed Confucius' birthday a national holiday. Yüan himself publicly worshipped Confucius, and restored the Hall of Classics and the Temple of Confucius.

[1] Peake, op. cit., p. 68.

But his schemes did not accord with Japanese policy, and the Japanese were in a position to make their influence felt. In 1916, his ambitions thwarted, he died a broken-hearted man.

The Japanese system, adopted in 1903, had been founded on the German system. The defeat of Germany in the Great War had the effect of discrediting German education as a foundation of strength, and the country, or rather the intelligentsia, reacted strongly to the military aims of the Education Minister, Ts'ai Yüan-p'ei's, 1912 instructions. It seemed for the time there was much more to be gained by absorbing the spirit of pacifism and idealism typified by the League of Nations than by relying on the methods that had brought Germany to grief. Besides, Japan, Germany's pupil and China's instructor, had engendered hatred for anything Japanese by her Twenty-one Demands in 1915. The First Conference for the Investigation of Education accordingly jettisoned the Japo-German system and adopted the American one.

Returned students from the U.S.A., including Kuo Ping-wên (P. W. Kuo, 郭秉文), born 1880, Chiang Monlin (Chiang Mêng-lin, 蔣夢麟), born 1884, and Hu Shih (胡適), born 1891, took a prominent part in restating educational aims. " The new aim sought the cultivation of a strong and developed personality, and the development of the spirit of republicanism." From this time dates the beginning of the students' self-governing societies (自治會). They were intended to develop the student's capacity for running his own affairs, but they later became the source of such indiscipline that the whole educational system was threatened with stoppage.

The American system, adapted on the advice of educationalists such as Professor Dewey,[1] was continued until

---

[1] Peake, op. cit., p. 85.

1925 when two incidents, the "30th May Affair" at Shanghai, and the "Shakee Incident" of 23rd June at Canton, in both of which Chinese demonstrators were killed, gave rise to such an outburst of anti-foreign feeling that there was an irresistible demand throughout the country for education that should be first and foremost militaristic and nationalistic. The eleventh conference of the Federated Provincial Educational Associations held at Changsha in October, 1925, decided that education should henceforth emphasize the racial peculiarities of China. The textbooks were to be rewritten to arouse racial self-consciousness; the nation, both through its schools and by other means, was to be reminded daily and hourly of the humiliations and indignities suffered by China at the hands of foreigners. Military and physical training were to be intensified. The most liberal influences in Chinese education before long succumbed to the fury of the nationalist and anti-foreign movement.

There is a danger in a compressed account of this sort, designed as an introduction, of giving the impression of a cohesive system applied uniformly to the whole territory of the late Chinese Empire. Actually China has suffered severe territorial losses since the Revolution, and separatist movements became rife, especially after the death of Yüan Shih-k'ai. In particular, Canton under Sun Yat-sen and others was separate from the North for many years, and even now in 1935 the union is only nominal. During the post-war years the country has been in almost constant upheaval and disorder with generals in independent command of different areas, and other parts have been delivered over to banditry. In the last few years, too, communism has exercised a fluctuating control over thousands of square miles of the hinterland. It was only to be expected that the application of any educational system would be far from uniform.

CONTACT WITH THE WEST

The wave of strident nationalism which arose in 1925 has continued to the present. The military advance of Chiang Kai-shek leading to the formal reunification of the country under the Kuomintang in 1928, even increased its confidence and its volume. The First National Educational Conference under the new régime was convened in May. There were sixty-seven delegates from all parts of China. Once more the educational aims were changed and the *San Min Chu I* (" Three Principles of the People ") of the late Dr. Sun Yat-sen were adopted as the basis of all Chinese education in the future.[1]

The considerable rivulet of missionary education flowed apart from the main stream, though it mingled its waters with it and coloured it out of proportion to its own size. In the renewed demand for Western knowledge at the beginning of the century the missionaries, especially the Protestants, saw an unexampled opportunity.[2] Their schools and colleges had been the pioneers in introducing Western subjects to China ; now that there was demand for them they should certainly be in the forefront in satisfying it. For the first quarter of the century missionary education progressed rapidly. There were, as has been stated, only 16,836 pupils in missionary schools in 1889 ; by 1911 there were 102,533, and by 1915, 169,707. After 1918 the Americans were increasingly active.

The question that exercised the missionary bodies from

---

[1] 教育法令彙編 (Educational Orders of the Ministry of Education) 1933, p. 64, state that Chinese Education is to be based on the *San Min Chu I*. Its aim is to enrich the life of the people, to develop their social existence, and to prolong the life of the nation. Its object is to make the nation independent, to make democracy universal, to develop the life of the people, and to promote the peace of the world.
The draft of the proposed new Constitution of the Republic of China, published in an official English translation on March 8th, 1934, has as Article 1 of its General Provisions : " The Republic of China is a *San Min Chu I* Republic." *China Year Book*, 1934, p. 471.

[2] K. S. Latourette is again the authority followed on missionary education.

1900 onwards was whether or not they should seek registration with the state. If they did not, would their diploma be recognized in making official appointments and in framing the conditions of admission to government higher schools ? The attitude of the government itself was not uniform, but in 1907 the Ministry of Education decided, for fear of encouraging further extra-territorial claims, that no school established by foreigners should be registered. This remained the situation for many years, but since, in the shortage of teachers, graduates of Christian schools were readily employed by the government, there was no serious friction. For some years prior to 1925 there had been a growing agitation amongst the nationalist Chinese for bringing missionary institutions under strict government supervision, but it was not until the anti-foreign movement was under way that any action was taken. Finally, in November, 1925, regulations for the registration of missionary schools were drawn up. These regulations required that at least half of the board of management of schools should be Chinese, that religious propaganda must not be its purpose, and that instruction in religion was not to be compulsory. There was delay in applying these regulations, but the ascendancy of the Kuomintang eventually compelled their enforcement. By 1927 anti-foreign propaganda had reached its height. There was an exodus of missionaries (the " running dogs " (走 狗) of the Imperialists) and many of their schools passed under Chinese control. By many foreign missionaries this last happening was welcomed as a natural stage in development. Many Christian schools, though, were closed because of the government requirements and the limited religious freedom, but most of the best schools became self-supporting. It was estimated that at the beginning of 1933 there were still well over 100,000 pupils studying in Protestant schools, and more than that number in Catholic primary and catechetical schools.

The avowed object of the Christian schools was to spread Christian teaching: the avowed object of government educational policy was to give China material strength. For this reason there was bound to be a conflict of policy. But the number of pupils in government controlled schools was overwhelmingly and increasingly greater than in Christian schools. In 1909-1910 there were 1,626,529 pupils in government primary schools and 8,882,077 in 1929. In a broadcast address delivered from Nanking on 23rd September, 1934, the Minister of Education, Dr. Wang Shih-chieh, stated that there were 11,667,888 pupils in government primary schools in 1931. Since 1927 subordination to nationalist policy has become the condition of the continuance of the Christian schools.

At this point this book concludes its introductory study and essays the task of examining the spirit animating the educational movement and the present cultural revolution in China.

Chapter III

THE AIM OF EDUCATION

For the study of Chinese education there is an abundance, even a plethora, of material. There is the mass of publications by the Ministry of Education (regulations, statistics, curricula, instructions to provincial authorities, rules for the registration of overseas schools), studies on the subject of textbooks, vocational training, and the education of the masses, specialist periodicals by the dozen, discussions by experts on pedagogics, the syllabuses of 111 universities and colleges, and the annual reports of societies for female, kindergarten, mass, vocational, and other training. An industrious foreign research worker working with this material and without direct experience of China and the Chinese, would assuredly produce a large, perfectly documented work, which, however, would give an impression far removed from the truth. He, or his reader, would not be in a position to make allowances for the Chinese tolerance of a very large discrepancy between programme and performance, and would not from the evidence available be able to ascertain how much of the spirit of the matter of the modernized textbooks arrived at the pupil's intelligence, and what form it arrived in. Yet an inquiry of this sort is the only one that has any value.

As we have seen, the Chinese only reluctantly and at long last decided to modify their native educational system at all, and when they did all they wanted to achieve was the material strength that Western science appeared to give.

THE AIM OF EDUCATION

A slogan at the end of the nineteenth century gave a recipe for a rejuvenated China. It was *chung hsüeh wei t'i, hsi hsüeh wei yung* (中學爲體, 西學爲用),[1] "let Chinese learning be the essence, and Western learning provide material efficiency." At best it was only a vague recipe, and Chinese educationalists have spent ever since trying to discover the proportions of the mixture and the method of the blend. In the meantime many students educated in China under completely Western systems, and practically all those who went abroad to learn, were cut off from their own culture and, homeless and restless, formed centres of discontent.

It was obvious that reformers like Chang Chih-tung, K'ang Yu-wei, and Liang Ch'i-ch'ao, would be unable to decide the right formula for the eirenicon of the new education. They had themselves been educated under the old system which was a monopolist of monopolists, and they only had a second-hand knowledge through scanty and inadequate translations of Western books (often obsolescent in their country of origin) to enable them to appraise and select from Western culture. The returned students were correspondingly handicapped by having insufficient acquaintance with their own literature. What was required was a selected committee of men, who, whilst thoroughly versed in the Four Books and the Five Canons, the Dynastic Histories, and the poets and essayists of China, were at the same time equally at home with Goethe, Molière, or Shakespeare, as with Li Po, Su Tung-p'o, or Ssŭ-ma Kuang, able to decide critically between Schopenhauer and Bergson, between Mo Tzŭ and Yang Chu, and with a

---

[1] 體 is used for "style" and 用 for "use" in discussing Chinese composition, but here the former word means essence more than mere style. See 中國新敎育槪況 by 舒新城, Chung Hua Book Co., Shanghai, 1928, p. 1.

knowledge of the fundamentals of chemistry, biology, and (say) municipal government. Such a man or men might conceivably effect an eclectic choice whereby the moral and social structure of China might be preserved by a framework of Western science and philosophical strength. But no man or men such as these has or have yet existed, nor with the exception of one or two brilliant intellectuals like Hu Shih or V. K. Ting, any person with a considerable knowledge of both cultures without an overloading in favour of one or other of them.

Mr. T'ang Leang-li has well analysed the misapprehensions and the dilemmas of the early reformers, though he claims that the secret of fusion was eventually discovered by the *intelligentsia* of the National University of Peking. Speaking of K'ang Yu-wei and Liang Ch'i-ch'ao he says :—

> " If they were aware of the superior utility of the mechanical sciences, they did not realize that the mechanical methods of the West had their own appropriate systems of thought. They were only conscious of the insufficiency of the old Chinese learning and that it was necessary to supplement it. In their view China's demoralization and decay were chiefly due to her defective political organization, so unlike that of Western countries, and to them political reform became China's most pressing need. What they effected was therefore merely a change in unessentials which not only brought the nation no nearer to salvation, but actually aggravated the situation." [1]

Educationalists since K'ang Yu-wei and Liang Ch'i-ch'ao, though armed with much extra information and having their predecessors' mistakes to profit by, have not been unanimous as to China's needs. The authors of the first modern school system of 1903 defined the aims of primary education to be to give children the knowledge necessary for life, to establish in them the foundation of morality and

[1] *Foundations of Modern China*, London, 1928, p. 85.

THE AIM OF EDUCATION

patriotism, and to promote their physical welfare. The "knowledge necessary for life" was to be the Confucian ethic and Western science, but as twelve hours of the weekly thirty were allotted to Chinese classics and ethics, with six to mathematics and only one hour to science proper, the Sage had more than the lion's share of the time-table. The syllabus was modified in 1909 and in later years, but the same difficulty remained. In a European or American school the subjects which a pupil is introduced to are all more or less of the same inspiration, the scientific facts and the practical facts of daily life are actual, not only during the specialistic lessons such as physics or geography, but also when he is reading from a general reader or a selection from the national literature. The unfortunate Chinese pupil, on the other hand, was the subject of a diarchy. He was at different times of the day enjoined to accept two different sets of facts and ideals. Because of his traditional respect for authority he found it all the more difficult (if he thought about it at all) to make a convenient compromise. Indeed, to some extent the European pupil is in the same dilemma.

> "For instance," as Bernard Shaw points out, "you cannot reasonably order that during the religious instruction how the children are to be informed that all forms of life were created within six days, including the manufacture of a fully grown woman out of a man's rib, and, when the clock strikes, begin explaining that epochs of millions of years were occupied in experiments for the production of various forms of life from prodigious monsters to invisibly small creatures, culminating in a very complicated and by no means finally satisfactory form called woman."[1]

The confusion, however, is not too great in this case, because the pupil is so imbued with the scientific spirit

---

[1] *Intelligent Woman's Guide to Socialism and Capitalism*, London, 1929, p. 361.

around him that he accepts the second as probable fact and the first as religious allegory. The difficulty of the Chinese pupil was not so much reconciling contradictions of fact as in imbibing at one and the same time a native set of moral and social precepts and a set of Western facts which depended upon and were inevitably mixed up with another set of moral and social institutions.

Since (to fix a time) Bacon the spirit of inquiry has been abroad in Europe, though it was only quiescent in the ages before. Just as the Romans had for universal application the quantitive and other tests indicated by the adjectives *qualis*, *talis*, etc., so had the modern European schoolboy his " What ? ", " Why ? ", " How ? " for every fact that was offered him. The Chinese schoolboy had an age of authoritarianism to forget before he could begin to apply this, to him, impertinent questioning.

An incident which fairly illustrates this point is recounted by Mr. E. A. Ross in his book *The Changing Chinese*, published in 1911.[1] A foreign professor of mathematics called the attention of his class to certain tables of logarithms, and the next day the students complained of the lesson as " very hard ". They had tried to memorize the tables ! The same book refers to another professor who complained that not over a quarter of his students could *think*. They remembered words, but not ideas or trains of reasoning, and he doubted whether 10 per cent could handle with success a new type of problem for which they had been given no rule. But Mr. Ross is careful to add that " this would be very flattering to our race pride but for the fact that nearly all the educators attribute it to defective training rather than to race deficiency ".

There should be nothing to occasion surprise that at this early stage in the reform movement Chinese pupils had not yet learnt to think in the way we understand that process.

[1] London, 1911, p. 333.

THE AIM OF EDUCATION

The pupil under the old system, we remember, had been given thousands of lines to learn by heart before he was even allowed to start puzzling out their meaning. Excogitation came later, if it came at all.

To return to the basic aims of the 1903 curriculum. Through the oil and water nature of the mixture of East and West, the pupil received a dangerous encouragement to think of morals and practical knowledge as being divorced from one another. Patriotism, too, was a branch of the moral code for which traditional China had inadequately prepared him. The Minister of Education, whose memorial to the Throne in 1906 finally fixed the aims of the first modern educational system, recognized this fact and remarked, " at present, the Chinese people are selfish and divided. The people of one province, district, village, or even family do not recognize or know the other." It has often been remarked that the Allied capture of Canton in 1857 would have been impossible without the aid of Cantonese carrying coolies. Sun Yat-sen, writing as recently as 1924, still notes the same phenomenon. He says, " The Chinese have no national spirit; they only know their family and clan groups. Thus China is only a loose sheet of sand." [1] In 1932 while T'ang Yu-lin was making a world-record démarche and losing sixty million square miles in eight days, two generals, an uncle and a nephew, were matching their strength in Sze-chwan. Following the traditional practice of invoking the past, patriotism has usually been presented by Chinese publicists as the " recapturing of a lost national spirit ", just as the nation has been enjoined to regain an imaginary spirit that it once possessed, but the fact is that " patriotism " in its modern nationalistic sense is newer to China than it is to Europe. It is a political device designed to knit the four hundred millions into a nation.

---

[1] *San Min Chu I*, translated by F. W. Price, Shanghai, 1929, p. 5.

It is quite a different thing from the age-old pride of the "black-haired race" in their common cultural heritage. But this question of inculcating patriotism was not such a burning issue as it became after 1925.

The crucial questions that the Chinese had to solve can be suggested in this way. Can one adopt the motor-car or the wireless without at the same time adopting representative government or trade unionism? Can one have a first-class navy without having a Faraday or a Bessemer somewhere in one's history? Japan seems to assume the answer to the first question to be in the negative, for she has adopted Western material appliances and large sections of Western social systems practically simultaneously. But she had a vigorous and flexible social system of her own which digested the foreign matter with successful metabolism. She had none of the handicaps of internal war, of a relaxing central authority, of recurrent financial crises, real and artificial, of external pressure, of a huge territory and diverse population. The second question has not received an adequate answer, even from Japan. For instance, she has a powerful navy, but the construction of her battleships still, in essentials, follows European practice. To maintain her navy in the future she will not be able to rely on purely mimetic action, she will have to breed her Bessemers, her Parsonses, and even her Thomsons and Rutherfords. Maybe she is doing so.[1] An important and fascinating task would be to search for evidences of original thought in pure or applied science in modern China.

The question reimposes itself and asks for a more detailed answer—how is it that Japan succeeded in Westernizing herself in the period of a few decades whereas China so far appears to have failed? The probable answers to this

---

[1] The revolutionary Japanese invention, the Toyoda loom, can be accepted as proof that the abilities of this nation are, in one direction at least, far from being purely mimetic.

THE AIM OF EDUCATION

question are those provided or assembled by Dr. Hu Shih.[1] Dr. Hu Shih first of all eliminates what he considers the double-edged arguments which can be used either to prove his case or its contrary, as for instance the relative size of the two countries, since it can be alleged that the greater size and resources of China might have assisted rather than retarded her, and the contention that China was too proud to receive an alien culture since China has in the past received the alien Buddhist culture, and both China and Japan have, to begin with, reacted hostilely to Western influences. The facts he relies on are these : In Japan existed and exists a powerful ruling class from which all the great leaders for reform and modernization have come. In China there was no such natural leadership, there was only a civilian bureaucracy and no powerful intelligentsia. Long centuries of despotic domination, enticements of official life, and a purely literary and useless education had made the literary class passive, innocuous, and ineffective. Secondly, a necessary phase of Western civilization is the military phase which is behind the scientific, technological, and industrial civilization, and the existence of the highly specialized and dominant military caste in Japan has enabled the country to reach this phase almost at once. China passed through the feudal age two thousand years ago, and the soldier's profession has become relegated to the illiterate and unruly section of the superfluous population, both as regards officers and men. Thirdly, the peculiar political development of Japan in the last thousand years has bequeathed her a suitable and stable basis for a new political framework. To this may be added

[1] *The Chinese Renaissance*, Chicago, 1934, p. 3 et seq. The book which sets out in minute detail the impressive facts of Japan's educational reform since 1868, but which does not assist much in explaining the underlying causes, is *Die Modernisierung des japanischen Erziehungswesens in den letzten 50 Jahren* by Riotaro Takemaye, Jena, 1929, translated for me by V. A. Purcell (not published).

that a decayed stem will not receive grafting : it is necessary to uproot it and to sow the soil with new seed. Also we must not forget that China only started in earnest on her reform forty years after Japan had undertaken hers.

Foreign observers, as well as native publicists, were early satisfied that China would follow Japan's lead with ease. For example, Mr. Paul Reinsch, writing in 1911, said :—

> "The present tendency of affairs in China seems to indicate that our generation is to witness a repetition of the marvel of the Japanese Restoration and that a movement will take place in China which in rapidity and thoroughness may even excel that remarkable transformation." [1]

The prophecy has not so far been realized. The Chinese in 1935 are a very long way from emulating the Japanese (though the Japanese themselves have still great problems to solve). But this is not to say that there has been no progress towards the distant aim. A very great deal has been done. If interest in education is anything, the Chinese must still go far, and the spokesmen of the country are still as vocally sanguine as ever they were. A broadcast talk by Mr. King-chau Mui, Consul for China in Hawaii, is typical of this frame of mind. He said :—

> "Those who know China know that the last two decades are the most significant in a great historical evolution of the Chinese nation. During the period, however brief, convincing evidence has been accumulating of the rise of a modern spirit. Although in these two decades China has suffered grievously from wars, both civil and foreign, we must bear in mind that China's territory is a vast one, and the fighting has not impaired the foundations of social, economic, and political order in the country. . . . Fundamentally the great revolution which is taking place in China is not the political one of which one hears so much. . . . It is significant to note that at the outbreak of the Revolution of 1911, over twelve volumes of decrees,

[1] *Intellectual and Political Currents in the Far East*, New York, 1911, p. 187.

THE AIM OF EDUCATION

edicts, and memorials for educational improvement reform have been drawn up. Indeed, education on a Western basis since 1905 has spread amongst all classes of Chinese."[1]

We note here the characteristic tendency to confuse deeds with intentions.

Of greater weight, though, than the periodic articles and speeches intended to consolidate the national morale is the unbiased opinion of the League of Nations' Mission of Educational Experts which visited China in 1931-2 :—

> "It is with the greatest satisfaction," the experts say in their report, "that we take this opportunity of recording our strong sense of the educational progress since the Revolution and our admiration for the energy shown in coping with the difficulties by which progress has been impeded . . ."

At the same time they subject the educational system to severe criticism.[2]

It is premature at this point for me to attempt to appraise China's achievement to date in education. What I am concerned to do is to decide the exact nature of the difficulties which have so far hindered the modernization of China's system.

The search has always been for the formula for cultural combination. Mr. T'ang Leang-li claims that the Chinese intelligentsia connected with the National University of Peking some years ago discovered

> "what will eventually be the basis of national regeneration. They began to realize that the reconstruction of China had to come through something more fundamental than a mere change of government. They aimed at the rebirth of the old Chinese civilization by discovering the foundation of Western strength and absorbing its essence into their own philosophy so as to effect a new synthesis on an intellectual and spiritual basis."[3]

---

[1] Published in the *Chinese Republic*, 2nd September, 1933.
[2] *The Reorganization of Education in China*, Paris, 1932, p. 16.
[3] *Foundations of Modern China*, p. 87.

That is what is called the " New Culture Movement ". But whatever its value as an encouragement to the intellectuals of Young China, the formula to students of Chinese movements seems vague and unsatisfactory. It seems to be nothing but *chung hsüeh wei t'i ; hsi hsüeh wei yung* in a more verbose form. Unless the apostles of the New Culture Movement decide what exactly the foundation of Western strength is, and what are the essentials of Chinese philosophy, and how the two are to be driven in double harness, they can reach no further in their quest than the alchemists towards the philosopher's stone.

At the beckoning of Young China Western ideas thronged to the East. What sort of form did they assume when they were received into the Chinese language ? How is Chinese able to adapt itself to foreign conceptions ? How far has the complication hindered the mass education on which the cultural revolution depends, and what attempts, if any, have been made to simplify the language ? How much of the old system is managing to withstand the onslaught of the West ? Finally, what sort of ideas have in particular been selected as conveyors of the foundation of Western strength, and how are they conveyed to the Chinese mind ? If we go any way towards answering these questions we shall have done much more than if we made the most exhaustive study of educational programmes, methods, curricula, and pedagogics. This last method of approach, indeed, has its complementary value and so, properly treated, have statistics, but the evidence produced will be entirely misleading if it is not preceded by an exposition of the more fundamental problems of the change-over.

CHAPTER IV

THE LANGUAGE PROBLEM

Phrases such as the "modernization of China" reveal a lack of appreciation in the user of what is going on in that country: even uncompromising terms like "revolution" do not fairly describe the change. Revolution suggests a rearrangement, however complete, of integral parts of the same original entity, whilst what China is trying to do is to repair a system built up on "Rhythm", "Wisdom", "the Yin and the Yang", and "Tao", with elements of one based on "Ideas", "Logic", and "Philosophy".

Much injury has been done to the understanding of China by the fabrication of analogies between her systems and our own. One of the unfortunate results of the sense of weakness and inferiority that oppresses the mind of Young China is the need that her apologists, native and foreign, seem to feel for discovering counterparts or anticipations in Chinese history of every phenomenon of the West. Much ingenuity has been expended in this connection with the effect of deceiving the Western reader and confusing the mind of the Chinese. Thus to deny "philosophy" to China is to alienate the nationalist, ever sensitive to new wrongs, and the impartial reader might be inclined to sympathize with him until he reflects that there is no special virtue in the word "philosophy" except as a description of the imaginative word-magic which has had such an influence on Europe both for good and bad. Philosophy has a definite linguistic basis, and because of the fundamental differences in the nature of languages can only be rightly used to include systems in the Indo-European tongues.[1] There is a mighty potency in symbols.

M. Marcel Granet in *La Pensée Chinoise* [2] seeks to isolate the fundamental concepts of Chinese civilization. In the governing dualism of the Yin and the Yang he can find nothing comparable to our abstract categories—number, time, space, cause, genus, species—these concrete, synthetic, effective notions which play with us the rôle of principles of organization and intelligibility [3] :—

> "Chinese thought, common or even technical, never separates the consideration of Time from that of Space.... The Chinese scarcely concern themselves to conceive of Time and Space as two homogeneous media suitable for housing abstract conceptions. They have decomposed them conjointly into five great rubrics or rituals, which they make use of to divide the emblems distinguishing occasions and places. This conception has furnished them with frames of a kind of totalistic art. Relying on a knowledge which to us appears to be entirely scholastic, this art tends to realize, by the simple use of effective emblems, an ordering of the world which is inspired by the ordering of society. On the other hand, the Chinese have avoided seeing in Space and Time two independent concepts or two autonomous entities. They perceive in them a complex of rubrics or rituals identified as active wholes, as concrete groupings. Far from appearing incoherent, the interplay of these rubrics appears to them governed by a principle of order. This principle is inseparable from the feeling of the efficacy of rhythm. Manifest in the social organization, this efficacy did not appear to them to have less value when it was a question of organizing thought. One will see that the same idea of the universal efficacy of rhythm is to be found at the bottom of the Yin and the Yang."

Whether or not M. Granet has lit on the *primum mobile* of Chinese thinking I am not competent to determine, but I do

---

[1] See *Bentham's Theory of Fictions*, by C. K. Ogden, London, 1932, pp. ix et seq.
[2] Extracts translated from the edition of 1934.
[3] M. Henri Berr in preface to M. Granet's work above.

THE LANGUAGE PROBLEM

feel that in the passage above quoted he has indicated something of the fundamental differences between the Chinese civilization and our own. I feel, too, the truth of his observation in another part of the book that the rhythm of Chinese prose has the same functions which are fulfilled elsewhere by syntax and that the favourite rhythms of this prose are those derived from choral poetry. The logic which he denies to the literature has a linguistic basis. Bentham points this out in his theory of fictions.

" In short," he concludes a passage on the subject, " it was by fancying that everything could be done by putting together a parcel of phrases, expressive of the various imports of certain *words*, mostly of certain *general* words, without any such trouble as applying *experiment* or *observation* to individual things, that, for little less than two thousand years, the followers of Aristotle kept *art* and *science* nearly at a stand." [1]

So in denying logic to the Chinese we are not denying them the *sine qua non* of cogency.

The Chinese picto- and ideo-graphic written language, of whose growth we have formed some idea in the preliminary chapter, derived its character from the fundamental concepts of the culture and from the Chinese method of thought, whilst, *en revanche*, the nature of the language decided the method of thought and how it would build up into systems.

" The Chinese way of thinking," says Professor Duyvendak,[2] " is along concrete, descriptive lines. As a type of language, Chinese shows remarkable likeness to certain so-called ' primitive languages '. It does not summarize,[3] it does not analyse, but it sees all things apart in never-ending variety.

---

[1] *Theory of Fictions*, p. lxvii.

[2] J. J. L. Duyvendak, " A Literary Renaissance in China," *Acta Orientalia*, 1922-4. Professor Duyvendak's admirable article analyses the nature of Chinese better than I have seen it done elsewhere.

[3] There are names for several kinds of nut in Chinese, but no word for " nut " ; words for several kinds of orange, but no word for " orange ".

" In the order of invention, proper names come before common names. Common names are the result of generalization ; every common name is the name of a general idea." Bentham.

It accumulates one concrete simple image after another in the order in which they occur to the mind. It does not easily form comprehensive perceptions. To express these it has to recur to compounds; e.g. to express the comprehensive idea ' to bring ' it is necessary to use an associative formation like ' to take-come ' ... Theoretically the Chinese ideographic script might be set down as the ideal way of expressing thought. For the characters express the idea, so to speak, unveiled, without any bounds of time or space, free from all qualifying limitations. As a matter of fact, however, each word is connected, by a thousand subtle threads, to a whole world of ideas. All its associations are defined by the trend of Chinese thought which we may trace in the classical scriptures ... The trend of thought is universalistic ... When I say ' East ' (東) I evoke the idea of spring, wood, the planet Jupiter, green, sour, the musical note *chüeh* (角), the spleen, and still more. When I say ' South ' (南) the association with summer, fire, Mars, red, bitter, the musical note *chih* (徵), and so on is aroused ... The Chinese mind has learnt to think by way of analogies, not along lines of causality. The development of an idea is effected by the juxtaposition of the parts of a sentence in which each describes a different aspect of an idea. It is like the unrolling of a series of images of a film; when the end has been reached, the film is rolled back the other way, and in reverse order all the evoked images pass once more before the mental eye. Only when back at the starting-point is the argument considered complete. What in the introduction to the *Chung Yung* is said of that book is truly typical of the Chinese mode of arguing in general. ' In the beginning the book speaks of one principle, in the middle it spreads it out so as to become all things, and in the end it returns and comprises them all again in one principle. Unrolled it fills the universe from Zenith to Nadir, from East to West, from South to North, rolled up it returns and lies hid in mysteriousness ' ... Almost the only means of developing an idea is the use of rhythmical antithetical phrases ... Rhythmical interplay by its very nature belongs to the old Chinese conception of a harmonious universe, in which microcosm and macrocosm, in fact all things, were interrelated in some intimate way, which is quite different from

THE LANGUAGE PROBLEM

the 'unity' which a modern logical mind will sometimes discover in the universe..."

Professor Duyvendak further says that while the descriptive power of the written language was wonderfully exploited, the means for developing an idea remained atrophied.

There is a quality of the language which does not appear to have attracted the attention of sinologues generally (though Mrs. Florence Ayscough has devoted some space to the subject),[1] and that is the associative power of the components of the characters. Chinese characters have their etymology written into them much more clearly than European words. In English it requires some thought, if not specialist knowledge, to discover the history of any word, but in Chinese it is often evident to the reader's glance. For instance, 男 "male" readily analyses itself into 田 "fields" and 力 "strength", and the present meaning of the parts together cannot fail to be influenced by this fact. That "language is a gallery of faded metaphors" is true of alphabetical languages: in Chinese, metaphors, when they occur, are not so often faded, and this is an additional reason for the concrete nature of the language.[2] Sometimes the characters have changed in form through the vagaries of stylus or brush, and the apparent etymology is a false one.[3] Nevertheless the meaning of a character is likely to be influenced by the apparent etymology, real or false. In 愁 "melancholy" the components are 秋 "autumn" (grain + fire) and 心 "heart". The reader cannot fail to be subconsciously affected by the idea of melancholy as the "autumn heart". It is a matter of indifference whether the etymology is true

---

[1] *A Chinese Mirror*, London, 1925, p. 17.

[2] In *The Spirit of Chinese Poetry*, Shanghai, 1929, I have discussed this quality at length.

[3] Many of the etymologies given by the 說文, based on the apparent meaning of the lesser seal script, are false.

or false, or whether 秋 is phonetic or signific.[1] In ascertaining the sum meaning of a character even a component that is merely a phonetic cannot be excluded, for it has a meaning that is bound to adhere to it. But it must be remembered that there is a selective sense that keeps the more incongruous senses in abeyance, and it is quite easy to exaggerate this peculiarity of the language.

Giles ridicules the attempt to invent a grammar for Chinese.[2] The Chinese, he says, did not produce a grammar of their own language in twenty to thirty centuries,[2] then foreigners undertook to supply a want that no one had felt. Marshman said that "the whole of Chinese grammar depends upon position", but Giles points out that no rules of position can be laid down. A Chinese character may act as any part of speech, "voice, mood, tense, person, case, number, etc., must be determined by the context, by usage, by probability, by inference, and by the general drift of the subject.[3] 入 means 'to go into', but 入木 means 'to put into a coffin'; 傷 means 'to wound' and 風 means 'the wind', but 傷風 (an ellipsis for 受傷於風) means 'to catch cold'; 傷弓之鳥驚曲木 means 'a bird that has been wounded by a bow is afraid of a crooked stick'; and 傷春 means 'to (be wounded) grieve for the loss of spring'." "The Chinese language," Giles continues, "supplies the fundamental and leaves accessories to the reader." Alphabetical language, too, we might say, is a definite woof: ideographic language is a fleet of pictorial ideas sailing in loose formation.

[1] Though, as Professor Moule points out, this fact has not prevented the use of 愁 in the phrase 春愁 "spring melancholy". I suggest, however, that the use of 愁 must give a sense of antithesis, however remote and subdued it may be.

[2] Preface to *Chinese-English Dictionary*, 1912. But there have been Chinese grammars: there is one as early as 1798.

[3] But it is to be observed that there are many characters which are never used except as nouns and many that are never used except as verbs.

THE LANGUAGE PROBLEM

Wênli, the literary style, is often so brachylogical that it makes the well-known pleasantry " ' Manx ? No, 5.15 Down ' " seem garrulous in comparison.[1] The rule is, if you can possibly omit, do so. The result may be that the meaning is quite hidden, but the reader is supposed not only to have an encyclopædic knowledge to assist him in his guess work, but to have unlimited time for filling in ellipses. This does not mean that the language has no words to fill in the ellipses, or that there are no words to convey tense, number, or mood. It mearly means that the spirit of the language is against their use. Modern *Wênli* is tending to abandon this spirit. The result, at present, is often clumsy or amorphous. I have seen a little book on Peking Man (*Sinanthropus*) written by a bilingual Chinese in semi-colloquial in which the syntax is as nearly as possible copied from English. The result is a plague of 的's that would give a Hanlin bad dreams.

When Giles scouts the idea of a grammar for Chinese he has in mind the attempts that have been made for drawing up a set of rules for speaking or writing the language instead of allowing people to gain a knowledge by the surer methods of experience and " feel ". Nevertheless, if the relationship to one another of words in a sentence is part of grammar then there is a grammar of Chinese.[2] The characters have a chameleon nature and a large degree of infinitiveness in their sense, so that there is a choice of meanings in certain constructions, but at the same time, at the moment of cognition in the reader or hearer's brain, the characters are joined by definite bonds. At a signal from the admiral (the writer) the fleet of pictorial ideas sails into a new formation : in the mind of the spectator (the reader) they are chained solid by the grappling irons of causation.

---

[1] The full text is : " ' Is that a Manx cat ? No, its tail was cut off by the 5.15 Down Train.' "
[2] Cf. C. W. Mateer, *Mandarin Lessons*, 1909, p. xxix.

Let us see how far the descriptions of comparative philology help us to understand what goes on in the mind of a Chinese reading, writing, speaking, or hearing his own language. We are told that Chinese is "monosyllabic" and "isolating". "The relation of these monosyllabic words to the whole sentence is not expressed by any marks in the words themselves but in the first place by a fixed word-order, and secondly in the spoken language (and in a less important degree) by the addition of words, the original concrete sense of which is so far faded that they can be used for formal purposes somewhat like our so-called auxiliaries."[1] Inflexions are therefore absent. Chinese, the philologists say, is not for this reason a primitive language which has not reached the inflexional stage, but one that has *passed through it* and in which vestiges of this prehistoric stage remain. English, considered by Jacob Grimm and Karlgren and many other foreign authorities to be the most efficient of European languages, is also the least inflected, and there are signs that in the end it will be quite without synthetic terminations. But at the same time it has developed methods of expression lacking in uninflected Chinese.

The consequence of the lack of inflections is that, generally speaking, Chinese has no formal parts of speech. Karlgren claims that the Chinese "of course, have the same psychological categories as we have, but they have no parts of speech corresponding to them".

If we experiment we are likely to find that most Chinese sentences seem to hold together eventually in much the same way as do our own. Though the lengthier compositions often appear to be immune from what we regard as the universal laws of causation, the units of thought usually adhere to these laws.

---

[1] F. N. Finck, *Die Hauptypen des Sprachbaus*, Leipzig, 1910, quoted in Karlgren's *Sound and Symbol in Chinese*.

THE LANGUAGE PROBLEM

Let us examine at random the classical proverb from the Four Books, 己所不欲勿施於人,[1] which is equivalent to our " do unto others as you would be done by ".

The root meanings of the words (ignoring any that would not apply in the context) are self, that-which, not, desire, do not, do, to people. Filling in the ellipsis the sentence would read 己所不欲人施於己(者)勿施於人, i.e. self that-which not desire *people do to self* do-not do to people. 不欲 " not wish ", a negative meiosis, must be replaced by an active word such as 惡 " hate ". The sentence now reads 己所惡人施於己(者)勿施於人. 所, the relative, which has force in both clauses, can conveniently be replaced by a symbol x, thus 己惡人施 x 於己；勿施 x 於人. We must now arrange it in a more causative form, thus 人施 x 於己, 己惡：勿施 x 於人. The historical sequence is now clear. People do x to self (you); you hate (i.e. experience an unpleasant sensation); (Therefore) don't do x to people (the inference being in Chinese as in English, both moral and prudential). But how does the idea build up in the Chinese mind? The sense is not complete until the whole proverb has been read. The idea then probably reasserts itself in the order I have suggested. 人, the simple pictograph (see p. 9 n.), here brings to mind the real, perceptible, generalized entity man, men and women, or people, and here, as it is in antithesis to 己, it means " others ". The image is given a space position in the field of the mind's vision ; the time position is indefinite, or rather continuing. 施 is expand, behave to, give, display. Here it is an operator (in the sense that Mr. Ogden uses the word).[2] x (representing 所 in the original sentence. 所 was first " a place " and was later used as a relative). 惡 is a fictitious entity derived from an aggregate of unpleasant sensations—" injury " shall

[1] *Lun-yü*, xv, 23.
[2] Introduction to Bentham's work cited *ante*. *Fictions* and *real* are used in the sense given to them in Bentham's work.

we call it. 於 is " to " (sometimes it takes the place of other English prepositions, in, at etc.). 己 is a second perceptible entity. Action originates from the image " people " operating (pushing, giving) *x* to (towards, against) the image " self ". This produces the consequence, unpleasant sensations in 己 represented by the fictitious entity 惡 " hate " (不 欲). Now follows another consequence, the moral of the proverb. 勿 (etymologically a signalling flag with three streamers) is " do not " or simply " not ". It is likely that in the Chinese sentence there is a third person introduced as the giver of the injunction " do not ", but 勿 may be merely a negative of refraining suggested by the preceding circumstances. To make the causation evident the last part of the sentence had better be arranged again thus, 施 *x* 於 人, 勿, wherein 己 giving *x* to 人 (the reverse process to that in the first part of the sentence) is visualized and then cancelled by the negative " not ", since an idea cannot be cancelled before it is conceived.

If we apply our simple cause and effect technique to Chinese sentences on a large scale we shall find that in many cases they build up, so far as sequence of idea goes, in a manner not unlike our own. The only essential difference is that of form, and while we may be willing to believe, say, that *ut sementem feceris, ita et metes* is the same as " As you have sown so also shall you reap ", we know that as units of language combining with other units they make very different thought-patterns. And in the case of our proverb above we have lit on a not very characteristic construction. It is only when we begin to explore the peculiar Chinese syntactical forms with 之 and 者, etc., that we begin to have doubts about Dr. Karlgren's dictum concerning the psychological categories.

The genitive or possessive case is found in Greek, Latin, French, German, etc. The word *chih* 之, in addition to its

THE LANGUAGE PROBLEM

meanings go to, arrive, hence, to, he, she, it, this, that, those (demonstrative pronouns),[1] an expletive,[2] a particle denoting that the action is finished, and zigzag, is used where we should use the genitive case; thus it is described in Chinese-English dictionaries as a mark of the genitive. Of course, genitive and possessive are mere words to suggest a relation, and neither word describes the relation in any exact way. The question is whether what is described by the genitive and possessive in English is the same relation as is represented by 之? The etymology of 之 is doubtful (Karlgren quotes the 說文 derivation, "a growing plant"); the root meaning is probably to go or arrive (Mencius uses the word in the latter meaning though in other meanings as well). Bullock says that careful analysis will show that through the latter meaning the most difficult combinations can be resolved. 心之所之 is translated by Giles as "what the heart desires". It is clear, then, that in this example "arrive" cannot be put for 之 in both cases. For the first 之 the genitive rendering is satisfactory, i.e. "heart's that which goes to". 有德之人 "a man of virtue" shows 之 in an alleged genitive use, "have virtue's man." If 之 is truly genitive or possessive, "have-virtue" must be taken as a fictitious noun-substantive and man as the possession or generation of the fiction. But does the Chinese language think this way?

The Commercial Press *Tz'ŭ Yüan* describes 之 in its sixth sense as a "join belong-to word" (連屬詞), and gives an

---

[1] 學者須知其所當之而之之也 (Giles) "learners should know the direction in which they ought to go, and go in it", shows the use of 之 as demonstrative pronoun (?), verb, and personal pronoun, and 不知之之之路 "he does not know the way there", in which Giles explains (1) 之 = to go; (2) 之 = there; and (3) 之 = sign of genitive.

[2] According to Giles, but Professor Duyvendak doubts it.

example 大學之道, 中庸之爲德, but it does not follow that generation or possession are implied. The Chinese often use 之 where we should use the genitive, but just as we mean something different by the possessive in Brown's nose, Brown's country, and Brown's enemies, I suggest that hidden under the imponderabilia of translation is a different set of methods for conceiving these particular kinds of relationships. 之 is here perhaps a conveyor of the quality of " have-virtue " to " man ". At any rate, it is likely that the prime sense arrive at, go to, of 之 (it is used often as meaning 適 and 往 in Mencius) gives the character a force other than that of our genitive and possessive.

The above was written before I came across in Karlgren's *Sound and Symbol* a much more likely explanation of the function of 之, but it may stand as disposing of the genitive rendering. Dr. Karlgren identifies 之 as one of the words of faded meaning referred to by F. N. Finck as acting as auxiliaries (see p. 94). " All sense of its status as an independent word has disappeared, and it has dwindled to the equivalent of an English inflexional affix. It is to be likened to the definite article in French which has no meaning by itself but stands for the demonstrative pronoun *ille*, long forgotten. It is placed after a word-group to mark it as an attribute of a following word." Karlgren says that by doing some violence to the English language the force of 的 (and hence of its exact literary equivalent 之) may be rendered by using the ending -*y* (German -*ig*), e.g. *Chang-san-ti-niang* " Chang-san-y mother " (Die Chang-san-ige Mutter)—Chang-san's Mother ; *shou-hua-ti yang-tzŭ* " speak-word-y manner—manner of speaking. 的 is connected with the older and literary 之. Modern 的 has no cognate pregnant meaning in the colloquial, whilst 之 has the meaning of " this, these ", etc. As the sign of the attribute

THE LANGUAGE PROBLEM

it is therefore only a weakening of a demonstrative; "the father's heart" was expressed by "father this heart". 有德之人 would now be "have-virtue-y man".

If the -*y* rendering is correct, then what precedes has the force of an adjective or adjectival clause. What is an adjective? Bentham says, "the *substantival name* of a quality presents the idea in the character of a complete idea, conceivable of itself; the *adjectival denomination* of that same quality presents the idea in the character of an incomplete idea, requiring for the completion of it the idea of some object in which it may be seen to *inhere*." Mr. Ogden describes an adjective (qualifier) as a word which expands the description given by a noun.[1] How does the adjective expand a substantive or inhere into it? In *maison rouge* the French postulate a neutral-tinted substantive and paint it red afterwards; in "red house" the qualifier "red" is created but has no body until it has "house" supplied to inhere into. According to Mr. Ogden's definition the substantive grows larger (expands) by the addition of red. The Chinese have their own special psychological processes for qualifying substantives. We should be nearer to understanding how a Chinese thinks if we could say what those processes were.

Even with the adjectival -*y* rendering 之 still remains as elusive as ever. 足見此事之必不能成 means "one sees fully the impossibility of accomplishing this", literally, "sufficiently see this thing-y certainly not can accomplish." If 之 is to be explained as "placed after a word-group to mark it as an attribute of the following

---

[1] i.e. from the standpoint of Basic English, in its deictic or directional aspects. If we ask where the adjectives "pleasing", "good", or "red" are pointing, the answer, for the Basic teacher, is "at ourselves, at some psychological reaction or feeling". Other adjectives, such as "political" or "electric", which may telescope in one word a descriptive sentence or even a page, behave formally in the same way as these essentially psychological epitomizers.

word ", such an explanation does not help.¹ If anything, "certainly not can accomplish" is an attribute of "thing". 之 as a demonstrative pronoun would make sense, so would 之 as a genitive, and also 之 " to arrive at ", but which of these, if any, is correct it is difficult to say.²

¹ " 之 here certainly marks a genitive or attribute. 必不能成 is the *object* of 見. The absolute idea is the 'impossibility of accomplishing'. 'This thing' 此事 is a further definition or attribute of that main idea." Professor Duyvendak.

² I record my adventures with 之 rather in the chronological order of their occurrence than in logical sequence. In commenting on the passage Professor Duyvendak states the position more consecutively. He says:—

" In the discussion of 之 three things should, I think, be distinguished:
(a) its original full meaning.
(b) its meaning as an auxiliary.
(c) how (b) could ever evolve from (a).

" The original meaning is certainly ' to go *to* ' (never ' to go ' alone—it indicates a tendency, a direction in which one moves). I believe that this is the whole clue to explain its further auxiliary uses. It indicates the tendency of the mind, the direction in which the thought moves, hence it has a demonstrative value, pointing towards something, either concrete or abstract. In the *Shih-ching* 之女 is ' (thought) direction—girl ' —' that girl '. In more complicated cases it joins one group of words to another group, making the first into an adjectival or genitive clause: 有德之人 ' having virtue (thought) direction—man,' i.e. indicates that the first idea refers to the second, it moves towards the second, as it were. In phrases like 惻隱之心人皆有之, Mencius, vi, the second 之, which is the object of 有, is really a demonstrative referring to the previous clause, establishing the connection, the thought-tendency.

" This psychological connection with 之 ' to go to ' is only found upon reflection, and I don't think that the Chinese themselves feel it any longer. The meaning is certainly faded into a grammatical auxiliary. Nevertheless it is important for understanding the fundamental structure of the language. Chinese seems to me a true type of what Finck calls ' centrifugal languages ': everything moves away from the speaker *towards* the main idea that is before the mind. Chinese is, so to speak, a language where everything is ' on the go '. Its type is ' red-house ' and not ' maison-rouge '. Relative clauses are also treated as adjectival and placed before the main idea. That is why we so often have to translate a Chinese sentence backward!

" I find an interesting parallel for the development of 之 in 的. Karlgren thinks they are phonetically related. Quite possible. But in any case the primary meaning of 的 is ' target ', i.e. the aim towards which one directs one's efforts. Here again is ' tendency ' (*tendance*). 的 as an auxiliary forms adjectival or genitive clauses, just as 之. It does not, however,

In examining units of language up to the length of a sentence and sometimes longer we are persuaded that the Chinese mind operates with a sense of causation. Yet we often get complete propositions that might be the major or minor premises of a syllogism, but we rarely get the conclusion. What intervenes is the rhythmic complement, the legacy perhaps of "rhythmic thinking" and of choral poetry.[1] In prose with a practical end this rhythm sense is more or less subdued, but it is there. For this reason in a passage from a modern Chinese encyclopædia in which a train of reason is translated from a European source, the prose seems unnatural; it scarcely seems Chinese at all.

Once we had decided the precise meanings of the elementary constructions we could attack sentences with greater confidence. Let us consider for a moment in what directions our further experiments would lead us. For instances, the validity of Descartes' "cogito : ergo sum" has been disputed by some later thinkers, but most of us still obtain from it a sense of the relation between consciousness and existence. We will see what the Chinese translators make of it. The *Hsin wên hua tz'ŭ shu* renders it as 我思考所以我存在. 思, to think, reflect, consider, has long been used in the combinations 思想, 思念, etc., but its use with 考 "examine" appears to be new in the sense of "think, cogitate". The Commercial Press *Tz'ŭ Yüan* explains 思 as meaning at different times 慮, be anxious, plan; 念, think, remember (Mencius); 慕, love; and 悲, grieve, showing that the kind of thought meant by 思 was primarily emotional. It will be seen that both 思

function as pure demonstrative or object, owing, I suppose, to the further development of the language which made sharper distinctions when 的 came into use."

[1] The effect of music on the written language is brought out in an article on Chinese music in the *China Review* by Choa Mei-pa. Music, in turn, is based on the cosmic rubrics.

and 想 contain the heart radical, and 心 is used in Chinese for mind. These facts are significant. Chinese literature is not concerned with pure thought but with human relationships. "Therefore" conveys an inevitable consequence: 所以 (以 to cause), which cause, has not the same force, though why this is so could only be explained by copious extracts from Chinese texts. 存 means to be in existence (as opposed to 沒) and 在 means to have or occupy a place, as distinct from 是, to exist as the subject of some predicate (Giles compares *ser* and *estar* in Spanish). For the rendering of such simple root European ideas as "think" Chinese seems to be forced to use near-synonyms yoked together in pairs.

We have now passed from the discussion of syntax and have started on vocabulary. The question is as important as and much easier to discuss than syntax and I propose to analyse a number of examples of the neologisms which have been coined to express European ideas. But before I do this it is convenient for me to describe a development of Chinese, namely the *Kuo Yü*, or National Language Movement. Mandarin, of which *Kuo Yü* is a modification, owns the new vocabulary in common with the literary language, or *Wênli*. In fact, as the late Rev. C. W. Mateer observes, "the line of demarcation between Mandarin and *Wênli* is but vaguely defined. They pass into one another by insensible gradations."[1]

A newly accepted principle of education was that the aim should be to educate the people as a whole, and not merely to discover men of talent for ruling the country. A prime obstacle to the attainment of this aim was the extreme difficulty of learning the written language. Before he was able to regard the language as a servant and not as a master the student was well advanced in life. He had to devote

[1] *Mandarin Lessons*, 1909, Introduction.

THE LANGUAGE PROBLEM

many of his best years to obtaining command over what, after all, was only a *medium* of expression.

Since form and content were more inextricably allied in Chinese literature than in any other in the world, there appeared to be no prospect of relinquishing the one without relinquishing the other. The classics were dropped from the curriculum of primary schools because they had hitherto been learnt there without being understood and because they took up time that was required for modern subjects. But the literary language was still used as the medium of instruction. It now lacked more and more its indispensable background of the classics. It still had its perplexing condensation, its ellipses, and its curious syntax, or absence of it, and it was still as difficult to write or understand. But what, if anything, was to be the alternative to it?

The spoken language, as I have said, was early divorced from the written, but they still influenced one another at a distance. Official business, for instance, demanded a greater lucidity than the ornamental written language was disposed to allow, and whilst due concession was made to the group mind by the frequent use of classical allusion, the intervening passages of official documents sometimes dangerously approached the vernacular. The Buddhist priests, who could take liberties of the sort without much social risk, often dropped the pretence of writing literary Chinese, and recorded their conversations with their disciples in characters representing the contemporary spoken word. Chu Hsi (1130-1200), the famous author of the *Hsiao Hsüeh* and of philosophical works, adopted the practice in his letters and written conversations and made it more respectable than it would otherwise have been.[1] This style was employed by his followers in certain branches of philosophical literature. The written vernacular, however,

[1] J. J. L. Duyvendak, op. cit.

became popularized by the playwrights and novelists, especially of the Mongol Dynasty. The famous novels *San Kuo Chih Yen I* (三 國 志 演 義) and the *Hung Lou Mêng* (紅 樓 夢) were written in this medium. But the vernacular style never obtained recognition from the literari and the large number of works in it were passed over in silence in the standard histories of literature. Thus the suggestion, when it came, that *pai hua* or vernacular should be used as the literary and educational medium of China was considered as threatening the very foundations of Chinese culture. But the foundations were rocking in any case.[1]

On 28th July, 1898, the Chancellor (軍 機 大 臣) presented a memorial to the Emperor pointing out the difficulties and disadvantages of the Chinese written language and recommending the adoption of the system of simplification described in books written by Lu Ch'uang-chang (盧 戇 章), Li Chieh-san (力 捷 三) and two others who had spent many years developing it. This system was based on K'ang Hsi's Dictionary. Before anything definite could be done the counter-revolution had taken place and the idea was forgotten in the general reaction. It is noteworthy that the promoters of this phonetic innovation were southerners (Cantonese and Fukienese), the northerners being then hostile to it. In 1900, Wang Chao (王 照), a native of Chihli, published a book called *A Mandarin Sound Alphabet* (官 話 合 聲 字 母), at Tientsin, and for a time it sold like hot cakes. It was no more than a list of abbreviations for beginners to enable them to master the language more easily. In 1907, another book appeared entitled *A Complete List of Abbreviations* (簡 字 全 譜) by Lao Nai-hsüan (勞 乃 宣) of Chekiang. It was an elaboration of Wang

[1] *Education in China in the Last Thirty-five Years*, Shanghai, 1931. Commercial Press. (最 近 三 十 五 年 中 國 敎 育).

THE LANGUAGE PROBLEM

Chao's system. In 1908, the author was summoned to appear before the Empress Dowager to explain the usefulness of his work. In consequence of this the Board of Education was instructed to report upon it, but the report was delayed and nothing came of it. Like many other inventors, Wang and Lao were before their time.

In 1912, when the Revolution had taken place, the Board of Education convened a conference at Peking to consider means for promoting the language and to fix for this purpose a phonetic alphabet (注音字母). After much discussion the "Forty Symbol System" was settled, but was not brought into use until November, 1918, and then by the Minister of Education, Fu Tsêng-hsiang (傅增湘).[1] So far, however, these attempts had been mainly directed towards simplifying the learning of the written language or *Wênli*.

The *pai hua* movement was started in the National University of Peking, though there had been increased composition in Mandarin from the beginning of the century. A periodical called *Hsin Ch'ing Nien* (新青年), or "New Youth" had been started by the young professors of the university in 1915.[2] It was written to begin with in the ordinary literary language. Early in 1917, a Chinese student in America, Hu Shih (Hu Suh) (胡適),[3] contributed an article in which he maintained that the written language should be abolished, and that *pai hua* should be elevated to the rank of a literary medium. The editor of the periodical, Ch'ên Tu-hsien, who was also dean of the literary faculty of the university, saw the possibilities of the idea, and gave

---

[1] By a proclamation of the National Government of 21st April, 1930, the term 注音字母 was changed to 注音符號, or "Phonetic Symbols".

[2] J. J. L. Duyvendak, op. cit.

[3] He at first called himself Hu Suh in English, but it is by the Wade romanization of his name Hu Shih which he later adopted that he is best known.

it his support. He wrote an article in which he enumerated these principles: (1) "Overthrow the old aristocratic literature and establish a literature of the people"; (2) "Overthrow the literature of classicism and establish a literature of realism"; (3) "Overthrow the literature that is secluded from the world and establish a social literature." Hu Shih now contributed a translation of a story by Maupassant in *pai hua*, and a number of other writers followed the lead he gave. From January, 1918, onwards, the paper was practically entirely in *pai hua*. More revolutionary still, it began to publish poetry written in the vernacular—crude, amorphous stuff for the most part, but some of it hinting at future achievement.[1]

The movement naturally incurred fierce opposition from the conservatives. Prominent amongst those who ridiculed the heretics was Lin Ch'in-nan (林琴南), the well-known translator of Dickens and Scott. The controversy soon became mixed up with politics. The students of the university had followed the lead of their professors in supporting the *pai hua* movement, and it happened that they also gained prominence by their agitation against the "Twenty One Demands" of Japan. The triumph of the political party favouring their action meant also the triumph of the *pai hua* movement. Literary men and long standing reformers such as Liang Ch'i-ch'ao allied themselves with the movement, and in January, 1920, the Minister of Education ordered that the spoken language should be used for the teaching of Chinese in the primary schools.[2] From that moment the *Kuo Yü* (國語) or National Language as *pai hua* was called, became of the first importance.

Pai hua had the advantage over the literary language, or

---

[1] There is a bitter attack on the *pai hua* school of poets in 中國詩學大綱 by 楊鴻烈, Commercial Press, Shanghai, 1928, p. 242.

[2] *Journal of the Ministry of Education* (教育公報), vol. vii, No. 2.

Wênli (文理) of being much more easily learnt, but it was far clumsier and more discursive. What could be said in four characters in *Wênli* might require ten or twelve in *pai hua*. It laboured under the difficulties of the spoken language. The poverty in separate sounds necessitated the coupling of synonyms and the attaching of its inherent object to a verb. But there were other difficulties weightier than this. The *pai hua* used by Hu Shih and his followers was the written form of the Mandarin dialect spoken in Peking. Now China, as is notorious, has a large number of distinct dialects. Those spoken in the northern provinces and over a wide area extending to Yunnan are closely related to Pekingese, but those spoken in the centre and southern maritime provinces such as Cantonese, Fukien, Foochow (Fuchou), Hainan, etc., have no recognizable resemblance to this dialect (though the differences are not, philologically speaking, fundamental).[1] These dialects have a *pai hua* of their own which in some cases has been reduced to writing. Cantonese, for instance, possesses a considerable popular literature (俗話). Thus, for the inhabitants of non-Mandarin speaking districts to use and understand a Peking *pai hua* meant that they first of all had to learn what was to them a foreign language.

The form of *pai hua* that was made standard for schools was called *Kuo Yü*, or the National Language (國語). It was an artificial language based on Pekingese, though effecting a compromise between northern and southern Mandarin, both in pronunciation and in vocabulary. Although it differed from Pekingese in many comparatively fine points, it did not sound different from Pekingese even so much as one type of Mandarin from another. This was

[1] For an account of the differences in the dialects, see *A Phonographic Course in the Chinese National Language*, by Yuen Ren Chao, Ph.D. (趙元任), Commercial Press, Shanghai, 1925. Also Mateer, *Mandarin Lessons*, 1909, which gives a comparative table of differences.

because the promoters of *Kuo Yü* agreed to use practically the same tones as those of Pekingese, and it is the tones, more than anything else, that characterize a dialect. It is doubtful whether it is anywhere spoken according to the rules laid down, each speaker of the Mandarin-speaking areas tending to revert to his own variety of the dialect.[1]

Kuo Yü, we see, was still, in writing, tied to the old ideograms,[2] though they were very often used in a different way than they were in the *Wênli*. There still remained, then, the necessity of learning several thousand characters before before one could read the literature that was coming into being with the new language, or the innumerable translations from foreign tongues. Williams, writing in the middle of the nineteenth century, gave it as his opinion that sooner or later, with the advance of what he called Christian civilization, it was inevitable that an alphabetic language would have to be substituted for " so laborious and unwieldy a vehicle of thought ". He was speaking, of course, of the literary language. But the invention of an alphabet or phonetic system that will effectively render Chinese, *Wênli* or even *Kuo Yü*, still seems out of the question. The reason is the great number of homophones.[3]

[1] A Society for the Unification of Pronunciation was formed in 1912, and later, a Society for the Unification of the National Language was organized under the auspices of the Ministry of Education to include wider aspects of the work. The result was a standard Dictionary of National Pronunciation with the pronunciation given in a new alphabet of 39, later 40 letters, called Chu Yin Tzŭ Mu (注音字母), or National Phonetic Alphabet. Yuen Ren Chao, op. cit.

[2] Attempts have been made to do away with the cumbersome radical system in using a dictionary, e.g. *System of Chinese Lexicography*, by Y. W. Wong, Shanghai, and *An Index to the Chinese Written Language on a New Non-Radical System*, by myself, Government Printing Office, Singapore, 1929.

Amongst the many attempts to simplify the writing of Chinese characters may be mentioned the *Shou T'ou Tzŭ* (手頭字) which is, however, merely a system of abbreviations.

[3] *Pai hua* borrowed characters from the written language with the same sound (in the *dialect* reading of the written language that is) as the spoken word it was wished to represent. For instance, " Where have you come

THE LANGUAGE PROBLEM

In the small Commercial Press Chinese-English Dictionary there are 113 characters all pronounced *li*, and even if these are divided up amongst the four tones with diacritical marks to distinguish them, there must still be room for about twenty-eight guesses each at the identity of li^1, li^2, li^3, or li^4. A Chinese, says Hillier, does not give public readings of his literary works, for the simple reason that he would not be understood if he did. The missionaries romanized several of the dialects for educational purposes. For certain dialects, notably the Amoy vernacular, which had no written *pai hua*, romanization was the only means of putting it down on paper. But romanization, apart from the constant dangers of ambiguity which arose (in spite of the spoken language's devices for avoiding it referred to above), destroyed at once the link with traditional China through the use of the ideographic character. The same objections applied to the Chinese invention of the *Chu Yin Tzŭ Mu* (or *Fu Hao*) with its forty phonetic characters (see footnote 1, p. 2), though this system proved useful in teaching the written

---

from ? " in Cantonese is *Nei hai pin shü lai ni ?* (你 喺 邊 處 嚟 呢). 你 " you " is the same in Mandarin. In the phrase 喺 邊 處, " Where ? " (lit. " in what place ? ") 喺 is the literary character 係, " to join ; be etc." with 口, " a mouth " added to show that the use is colloquial ; 邊 is a literary character meaning " a side " but here represents the colloquial word of the same sound meaning, " Which," " What " ; 處 " a place " is used in its literary sense, but pronounced *shü* instead of *chü* as it would be if read in a piece of *Wênli* ; 嚟 is borrowed from the literary character 黎, " the black-haired race ", plus 口, " a mouth " to show that the use is colloquial. 呢 is merely an interrogative particle. The speakers of the Amoy dialect had not troubled to build up a written *pai hua* ; hence the value of romanization to them.

In a letter to the *North China Daily News* of 12th December, 1935, M. Auxion de Ruffe contests the statement of Dr. Reifler that Chinese cannot be romanized and cites the Annamite language (a dialect of Chinese) which has been romanized since the French occupation of Annam, and points out that this romanization, *Quoc Gnu* has been for many years the official written language of Indo-China.

I have not studied *Quoc Gnu*, and there may be much in M. de Ruffe's claim, but to look at casually in the streets of Saigon it is terrifying with its plague of diacritical marks.

character and the sound in Mandarin. Besides, it was necessary for the speech of the whole country to be standardized before any phonetic would be intelligible to the country as a whole.

Kuo Yü is still on trial. M. Granet doubts whether the spoken language is fit to be used as a scientific language. He thinks that it will have the same defects as the written language so long as it is written in ideograms. " Tant qu'il s'écrira en caractères, le Chinois restera une langue morte." Professor Duyvendak, on the other hand, thinks that though in writing by means of ideographs the fact is recalled to mind that these words are really independent entities and not merely syllables, their constant use in combinations both in speaking and writing will tend to strengthen their unity and give their component parts the value of syllabic script. Professor Duyvendak has specially in mind the new double-word phrases which have been coined to translate foreign words.[1]

Opinion amongst European savants as to the capacity of the Chinese language, *Wênli* or *pai hua*, to express ideas is divided. Giles considers that criticism of Chinese on this score is due to insufficient acquaintance with the language.[2] Professor Heinrich Hackmann says :—

> " all culture, especially intellectual culture, is built upon language. But the nature of the Chinese language is such that it forbids the clear and accurate expression of philosophical ideas. The Chinese language is monosyllabic, tonic, and uninflected. As a result, there are only a small number of syllables, about 400, and only a small number of characters in common use, 2–4000. There are two inevitable results. 1. A paucity of words for expressing concepts with the result that it is impossible to express a highly developed world of ideas of objects and concepts, connections and relatives, such as is required for the development of an adequate philosophy, and (2) a paucity of means for expressing relationships—

[1] Op. cit.   [2] *Encyc. Britt.*, 11th edition.

THE LANGUAGE PROBLEM

something which is achieved in other languages by grammatical inflections with the result that it is impossible to attain scientific accuracy and exactness of expression in the absence of clear grammatical constructions."[1]

The first point appears to be due to a confusion of thought. The problem of homophones is one that affects the spoken language alone ; it has no influence on the number of words available for expressing concepts, and Chinese has many thousands of characters available to express infinite gradations of thought. Professor Hackmann's general conclusions are apparently supported by authorities like A. Forke and T. Suzuki, but opposed by Dr. Homer H. Dubs. Dr. Dubs thinks that " while the Chinese language may have to resort to clumsy means to express some of the concepts required for modern scientific and philosophical discussion, yet it is quite possible to express any conception in an exact manner by Chinese phrases ".[2]

Before I attempt to arrive at any opinion on these weighty questions I propose to try and contribute to the discussion by examining closely the neologisms which are being coined almost daily to translate Western ideas. Living as we do with ideas that are part and parcel of our culture and experience we rarely trouble to analyse them, and so in order to describe their metamorphosis in transit to China it is

---

[1] *Chinesische Philosophie.*

[2] It is amusing to recall the diatribe of Ernest Renan against the Chinese language :—

" Is not the Chinese language, with its inorganic and imperfect structure, the reflection of the aridity of genius and heart which characterizes the Chinese race ? Sufficing for the wants of life, for the technicalities of the manual arts, for a light literature of low standard, for a philosophy which is only the expression, often fine but never elevated, of common sense, the Chinese language excluded all philosophy, all science, all religion, in the sense in which we understand these words. God has no name in it, and metaphysical matters are expressed in it only by roundabout forms of speech." " Histoire de l'instruction publique en Chine " (*Mélange d'histoire et de voyages,* Paris, 1898).

Renan was a notable philologist, but he cast his net too wide to allow his opinion of Chinese to be of much authority.

necessary to decide as nearly as possible what they mean to us in Europe before they set out. I shall be bound to give a large number of examples and to analyse them with what may seem tedious minuteness, but things Chinese, unfortunately, cannot be delineated with the broad brush of the impressionist; the effect must be built up, like Richardson's "Pamela", with an endless series of tiny strokes.

Vocabulary

Long before the National Language Movement, *Wênli* had started the creation of new terms for new ideas, but *Kuo Yü* has now taken over the giant's share of the labour. The new words, though, may be used in both kinds of composition. Chinese lends itself to the coining of new characters, but as it has turned out, few new characters have been manufactured, but existing characters have been used to make phrases to express borrowed ideas. At the end of the small Commercial Press Chinese-English Dictionary is a list of twenty or more newly made characters which have as yet had no sound allotted to them. They are mostly equivalents of foreign weights and measures. Sometimes, too, old characters have been modified to suit China's emancipated point of view. For instance, 家 means a house, a family, and apparently represents a pig 豕 under a roof 宀.[1] For this 佂, i.e. three people under a roof, has been substituted. Similarly 婦 means a married woman, 女 a woman + 帚 a broom. This has been replaced by 娘 = 女 woman + 負 to rely on. Instead of the hausfrau with the broom she is now the person on whom the family relies. 國, a country, was frequently shortened by taking

[1] But Karlgren's *Analytic Dictionary* shows that this etymology is false, as 豕 is an abbreviation of 衆. We have, however, proof in this that the *apparent* form of a character does not escape the eye of a modern Chinese.

THE LANGUAGE PROBLEM

out the centre and substituting 王 a king, thus 囯. Nowadays the short form contains 民, the people, thus 圁. 他 meaning " he, she, it ", is now sometimes written 她 when it means " she ", and 牰 (牛 stands for 物) when it means " it ". But many of these forms are in the nature of curiosities and are little adopted. A playful, though widely used curiosity is 乒 乓 ping-pong. 兵 is a character pronounced *ping* and meaning a soldier. The new phrase, by leaving off the alternate legs of the character *ping*, gives a graphic idea of the ding-dong of the game. The addition to the language, however, has been almost exclusively in the shape of new phrases utilizing existing characters.

Evan Morgan's *New New Terms*, published in 1926 (2nd edition) contains 10,000 such newly born expressions, and several native collections have been published in recent years. In the early days the favourite means of adopting a foreign word was by imitating its sound as nearly as possible, though, because of the language's poverty of sounds, the result was rarely like the word translated. (*Ai ti mei tun* 哀 的 美 敦, ultimatum, is an example.) Later on, the creation of new characters to express an idea was resorted to. This was done by new combinations of radicals and phonetics. A more common method of expressing new ideas was to add some classifying suffix to existing word or phrase. As an example of the latter process Evan Morgan instances the addition of 力, strength, to certain words as an ending to form abstract nouns. Hence 記 力, remember-strength = memory ; 智 力 = wisdom-strength = intellect. 力 as a suffix carries the idea of power and generally marks an abstract noun. 化, to transform, used as a suffix was another helpful discovery as the need of such a suffix had long been felt. A difficulty had been experienced in translating English words ending in *ize* and *ization*. Now 化 answers the purpose both for the transitive and intransitive senses. There is 外國化 foreignize, 農業化 agriculturize, 赤化 red-ize = bolshevize. Sometimes old phrases were revived to convey a new idea, such as hunger strike (不食周粟), plural voting (騎藉選舉權), etc. The most common method of all was to place two or more existing characters in juxtaposition to form a new phrase, such as 進化, progress. Many of these new coinages are borrowed from the Japanese.

The neglected fashion of rendering a foreign word by its equivalent sound in Chinese is now returning. Instead of 新法, etc. for "modern", 摩登, *Mo-têng* (Cantonese *Mo-tang*), is much more used in the papers, and 羅只 *Lo-chih* (Cant. *Lo-chik*) is a strong competitor to 論理, logic. This practice is to be preferred for the reasons given at the end of the article on "socialism" below.

The principal works referred to in the following descriptive studies of words and phrases are :—

1. *Chinese-English Dictionary*, by H. A. Giles. Kelly and Walsh, 1912, referred to as (G.).

2. *Webster's Collegiate Dictionary with Chinese Translation*. Commercial Press, Shanghai, 1928. Referred to as (W.).

3. *The Oxford Dictionary*. Referred to as (O.).

4. The 辭源, *Tz'ŭ Yüan*, two vols. Commercial Press, Shanghai, 1927. Referred to as (T.).

5. *Analytic Dictionary of Chinese and Sino-Japanese*, by B. Karlgren, Paris, 1923. Referred to as (K.).

6. 新術語辭典 (*Hsin Shu Yü Tz'ŭ Tien*). Nan Chiang Book Co., Shanghai (two vols.), 1932. Referred to as (H.).

7. *New Terms for New Ideas*, by Mrs. Mateer, Shanghai, 1922. Referred to as (M.).

8. 新文化辭書 (*Hsin Wên Hua Tz'ŭ Shu*), (Encyclopædia of New Knowledge). Commercial Press, Shanghai, 1923. Referred to as (HS.).

9. *Dictionnaire Chinois - Français*, by P. Séraphin Couvreur, S.J. Ho Kien Fu, 1890. Referred to as (C.).

10. *San Min Chu I*, the Three Principles of the People, by Sun Yat-sen, various editions from 1925 onwards. Referred to as (SMCI.).

(T.) is a gold mine to the student of incommensurable meanings for it explains Chinese meanings *in Chinese words*. It also gives the sources of its quotations which the otherwise invaluable Giles does not condescend to do. But there is a great need for a Chinese dictionary on the lines of the O.E.D.

The articles appended to the descriptive analysis do not pretend to be authoritative or in any way complete discussions of their subjects but finger-posts pointing to the probable hiding place of a host of incomplete translations and misunderstandings. The examples are arranged under " general " and " sociological ". It is in the latter class that the widest divergences of meaning are apparent.

The complete dictionary meanings of the Chinese words are usually given, for although many of them are excluded by the context, it is thought advisable to indicate the possibilities of associative influence.

General

Abstract Idea.

Abstract. From Latin *abstractus* p.p. of *abs* + *tractus* (*trahere*, draw). Separated from matter, practice or particular examples, not concrete; ideal, not practical... (Concise (O.)).

Idea... a. Greek ἰδέα, look, semblance, form, configuration, species, kind, class, sort, nature (in Platonic philosophy) a general or ideal form, type, model, f. root ἰδ-, ἰδεῖν, to see: the word being thus analogous in derivation and original sense to Latin *species* from *spec-ere* to see, behold. So It. Sp. Pg. *idea*, F. *idée*.

The original development of the word took place in Greek; and it was in the developed Platonic sense that the word was first adopted in modern languages. . . .

1. In Platonic philosophy: A supposed eternally existing pattern or archetype of any class of things, of which the individual things in that class are imperfect copies, and from which they draw their existence.

. . . 1563 Vale *Institutes of Chirurg.*

2. Figure, form, image 1594 Blundervil *Exerc.*

. . . .

3. Mental image, conception, notion, 1589 Greene *Menaphon.*

. . . .

4. Modern philosophical developments . . . (O.). Chinese, 抽象觀念 (H.).

抽 = 扌, the "hand" radical + 由, from, by, to permit (phonetic) (K.).

= to pull up; to take out. To divide up; to allot. To levy; to exact (G.).

抽矢 (Mencius) to draw an arrow from its quiver (C.).

象 = 象, picture of an elephant (K.).

= the elephant . . . ; ivory. A figure: an image: form; objectivities; the Platonic idea (noumenon) as an entity, as opposed to 形 (phenomenon). Stars; constellations. [One writer says the elephant subsists by virtue of its trunk and not of its mouth; the stars subsist by virtue of 氣 vitality and not of words; therefore they have the same characters. Others say that in ancient days the *form* or *figure* of a living elephant was inferred from inspection of its bones.] The visible figures of the Diagrams; the illustrations of the 周公 Chou Kung. The elephant or

THE LANGUAGE PROBLEM

" bishop " of Chinese chess ; the game itself. . . . A visible sign or counterpart of something, such as a force or influence ; an omen, or prognostic . . . (G.).

象數 the religion of images, Buddhism (G.).
各物象數 the inherent characteristic of things (G.).
體無形象 without form ; immaterial (G.).
(T.) explains the character in its senses of image, figure, etc., by 形狀 and 法.
觀 = to gaze at ; to view ; to inspect (G.).
觀覽 peruse, examine (G.).
觀音, the Goddess of Mercy, the hearer of the prayers of the world (G.).
念 = have 今 *present* to 心 the mind (K.).
= to think ; to reflect ; to ponder on ; to study ; to remember ; to repeat from memory ; to read aloud. Twenty (G.).
思念 to think, to ponder on (G.).
無以爲念 to have no cause for anxiety (G.).
念佛 to repeat the name of Buddha (G.).
念根 the organ of memory (G.).
念頭 a thought (C.).
(T.) explains the main sense as 思想 (see p. 131), (SMCI) also 觀念 is the modern phrase for " idea ", the " see-think ".

Therefore the complete phrase 抽象觀念 means " Drawn off image-y idea ".

The most important meanings of idea in the West are those that refer to generalizations, viz., species, kind, class, sort, nature. But, as we have seen, Chinese does not generalize or summarize readily and when it does its classification is different from ours. The argument quoted from (G.) above for placing elephants and stars in the same category is a not too far-fetched example of Chinese associative classifications. It is possible, too, that Europeans, in forming ideas and in thinking generally, utilize their sense of hearing as much as their sight. The Chinese depend almost exclusively on sight, and the peculiar nature of their written language tends to tie them to this process. An examination of the difference in thought due to this possibility would be a profitable line of research.

The difficulty of rendering the word "thought" has already been referred to. 念 is bound up with the emotions.

Philosophy . . . ME a. OF. filosofie twelfth century in Hatz- Darm.) philosophie (thirteenth century) . . . L. *philosophia* a. Gr. φιλοσοφία noun of condition from φιλόσοφ-ος philosopher. . . .

1. (In the original and widest sense.) The love, study, or pursuit of wisdom, or of knowledge, and their causes, whether theoretical or practical. . . .

1340 (Germ.).
1430 Lydgate *Minor Poems.*

2. The more advanced knowledge or study, to which, in the mediæval universities, the seven liberal arts were recognized as introductory; it included the three branches of natural, moral, and metaphysical philosophy, commonly called the three philosophies. . . .

1387–8 T. Usk *Test. Love.*

3. (= natural philosophy) the knowledge or study of nature, or of natural objects and phenomena " natural knowledge ": now usually called science. Now rare and obsolete.

4. (= moral philosophy.)
5. (= metaphysical philosophy.)
6. Sometimes used of knowledge obtained by natural reason, in contrast with revealed knowledge.
7. . . .
8. A particular system of ideas relating to the general scheme of the universe; a philosophical system or theory.

THE LANGUAGE PROBLEM

1390 Gower *Conf*....
. . . .

9. The system which a person forms for the conduct of life ... (O.).

Chinese. 哲 學 (H.), (W.).

哲 = break off, break up; fold, bend; to curb, repress, maltreat, judge, decide ... diminish ... barter, etc. (= 扌 (手) hand + 斤 axe) (K.) + 口 mouth (often omitted).

= Wise; discerning. To know intuitively (G.).

哲 人 wise men (G.).

濬 哲 profoundly wise—said of the Emperor Shun (G.).

聖 哲 intuitive wisdom—said of sages or prophets. Also used of the Emperor (G.).

(*N.B.* 哲 is sometimes written 悊.)

知 之 曰 明 哲 (書 說 命). He who knows things well is called intelligent and enlightened (G.).

學 = 爻 and 冂; below 子 (a son); interpretation doubtful (K.).

學 文 learning (G.).

大 學 the *Great Learning* (G.).

= To learn, to teach (cf. apprendre); to study. To imitate. (G.). Hence 哲 學 wisdom-learning.

Philosophy, when the word was first used, covered the whole range of knowledge; Plato considered it to be concerned with the ideal alone; and nowadays scarcely two writers are agreed as to its boundaries. Kant defined philosophical knowledge as knowledge through conceptions, and Herbart divided it into three compartments—logic, metaphysics, and æsthetics (including ethics). It is not difficult, as we have seen (p. 49), to find in China the counterparts of the numerous European systems (in sense 8) if one fixes on the superficial identity of the general conclusions. Yang Chu's egoism might be twisted to make him appear a Chinese Nietzsche; Hsün Tzŭ with his belief in the evil nature of men and his advocacy of physical force in government might be set up as a rival to Hobbes; Chou Tzŭ with his primordial ether and supreme ultimate might be coupled with Spinoza. In fact the lack of any necessary coincidence of European words and phrases makes it possible for the ingenious or interested to do exactly what he likes.

The speculations of European metaphysicians into the nature of reality have all been conducted with *logic*; that is a technical apparatus depending largely on language. We can only understand our philosophers in so far as we can penetrate into the meaning of language. This point is reserved for discussion under the heading *Logic* below. Chinese philosophy was concerned almost entirely with morals, with little metaphysics and less logic.

Logic . . . a. French *logique* (thirteenth century) ad. Med. L. by *ars logica* ad. Gk. λογική (first found in Cicero); elliptical for ἡ λογικὴ τέχνη rendered in Med. L. by *ars logica* (fem. of λογικός . . . pertaining to reasoning. f. λόγος word, oration, reasoning, reason, etc. . . . The word is current in all the modern Romance and Teutonic languages . . .).

1. The branch of philosophy that treats of the form of thinking in general, and more especially of inference and scientific method.

. . . .
1362 Langl. *Piers Plowman.*
1386 Chaucer.
. . . .

2. A system or a particular exposition of logic; a treatise on logic. Also, the science of art or reasoning as applied to some particular department of knowledge or investigation.

1377 Langland.
. . . .

3. Logical argumentation; a mode of argumentation

THE LANGUAGE PROBLEM

viewed as good or bad according to its conformity or want of conformity to logical principles . . .

4. Attrib. of or pertaining to logic.

5. Comb. . . . (O.).
Chin. 論理學 (H.), (W.), and 名學 (T.).

論 = 言 to speak, words (derivation uncertain) + 侖, arrange (亼 = 集) to collect 冊 documents) (K.).

= to discourse; to discuss; to reason; to argue; to consider; to estimate. Theory, as opposed to 行, practice; a view, a postulate . . . The *shastras* or philosophical works of Buddhist literature (G.).

談論 to converse; to discuss in conversation (G.).

詳論 to discuss critically (G.).

論語 the Discourses or Analects of Confucius (G.).

天論 (王禮制) natural law (C.).

理 = 里 phonetic + 王 jade (K.).

= abstract right; . . . the eternal fitness of things; principle; *rationale*; rule. To arrange; to attend to; to settle up; to manage . . . streaks; veins, as in minerals [original meaning]; the grain of wood; the lines of the hand (G.).

理宜 natural, reasonable (G.).

道理 right principle; doctrine; reason; argument (G.).

天理 nature; natural right; the reason of a thing's being; justice; equity; duty (C.).

Hence the phrase means $\left.\begin{array}{c}\text{discussion}\\\text{reason}\end{array}\right\}$ principle learning.

We have seen that the essence of Chinese prose style is balance and rhythm. At all costs the passage must scan. It is a matter of " take care of the sounds and the sense will take care of itself ". If the ordinary antithesis (*tui*) is not employed (see p. 21) the chances are that the familiar "house-that-Jack-built" construction will be. The sections are linked together by the repetition of a word or phrase occurring in the preceding section, and when the apex of the parabola has been reached the argument subsides through a similar series of linked arcs (probably the same series) back to the base of the figure where the passage is completed and at rest. For this reason the logical devices of deduction and induction are rarely employed and analogy is stretched as far as it will go. There are thousands of examples in Chinese literature to choose from, but the well-known passage in the *Ta Hsüeh* referred to by Professor Duyvendak is as good as any to take as an illustration :—

> "Those of old who wished to make illustrious illustrious virtue throughout the empire, first ordered well their states. Wishing to order well their states, they first regulated their families. Wishing to regulate their families, they first cultivated their own characters. Wishing to cultivate their own characters, they first rectified their hearts. Wishing to rectify their hearts, they first made their intentions sincere. Their intentions being sincere, after their hearts were rectified. When their hearts were rectified, their characters were cultivated. When their characters were cultivated, their families were regulated. When their families were regulated, their states were well ordered. When their states were well ordered, the empire was at peace." [1]

The construction of this passage is exactly suggested by the English nursery story of the old woman whose pig would not leap over a stile. The uphill work of effort, "Water won't quench fire," etc. is continued through the first half but when the key is found there is an easy procession of success. Sometimes the thinker climbs up section by section to the apex of the parabola and then slides down

---

[1] Translated by T. L. Bullock in *Progressive Exercises in the Chinese Written Language*, Shanghai, 1923.

the other side as down a slippery pole and at once starts off from the same base on another climb, e.g. :—

" The superior man must cultivate his character ; if he desire to cultivate his character, he must serve his parents ; if he desire to serve his parents, he must acquire knowledge of men ; if he desire to know men he must acquire knowledge of God (天), if he knows by what means to cultivate his character, he will know by what means to govern men ; if he knows by what means to govern men, he will know by what means to govern the empire, its states, and its families."

These examples are taken from the classics and are not offered as first rate examples of Chinese cogency as it was developed under the Sung ;[1] they are merely typical of the prose style which was maintained for two milleniums, and is still maintained. It can be seen that repetition and analogy took the place of syllogism. Completeness is not obtained by a process of logical inevitability but by a rhythmical rounding off. The reader may have travelled in something like a circle, but he feels that he is at rest and last and not left in an uncomfortable state of becoming.

Whatever the achievements of individual logicians or writers like Chu Hsi, it is fair to say that the genius of the language did not favour the growth of the logical faculty. The " eight-legs " essay given in Chapter I is a fair example of the average Chinese reasoning. By the date of the essay (1879) scholasticism had deprived the argument of any practical bearing it might have had in earlier times. The aim is to distinguish the abstract of the Holy Man from the equally hypothetical completely Humane Man, without any recognition of the practical consideration, namely that if mankind can be aided it is of secondary importance whether

---

[1] I have (except for a casual reference to Chu Hsi) not referred to the Sung thinkers because their writings did not have any permanent effect on the Chinese method of thought. Nor have I referred to the Chinese " Sophists " who came as near to " logic " as the language would allow.

the benefactor be holy or merely humane. Theology is not involved, merely terminology.

The well nigh irresistible force of traditional thought is splendidly illustrated in the following passage from Sun Yat-sen's *San Min Chu I* (People's Livelihood, Lect. 3, last para.) :—

> " If we want to solve the food problem, first of all we must ensure adequate food production, and secondly [we must have] a very equitable distribution of the food supplies. Once the problems of production and distribution of food are solved, it will be necessary for the citizens to fulfil their obligations. If all the citizens fulfil their obligations towards the state, we shall naturally reach the point where the family supplies man with plenty. The food problem will truly be solved, and if the problem of food is solved, the other problems will also readily be cleared away." [1]

The method of argument is exactly that of the *Ta Hsüeh*.

Of course, it does not follow that Chinese is incapable of logical arrangements. It is only that tradition and style are against it. If the immediate reaction to the proposition " rain falls " instead of being " crops grow " or a questioning " Why ? " is the completing but irrelevant antithesis " wind blows ", there is little encouragement to the building up of a causative edifice. The Chinese thinker is always executing the complementary steps of a contredanse. In the hands of the scholar translating logically arranged matter, Chinese can be made to assume a close mimicry of form to the original. If there is not complete equivalence it is due to vocabulary and to the difference in the nature of the union of consecutive Chinese and consecutive English words. This must be the final subject of our attention.

Science . . . a. French *science* . . . L. *scientia* . . . from *scient-em* present part. of *scire* to know.

---

[1] Translation of Father Pascal d'Elia.

1. The state or fact of knowing; knowledge or cognizance of something specified or implied; also, with wider reference, knowledge (more or less extensive) as a personal attribute. Now only theological, in the rendering of scholastic terms. ...

1340 Hampole *Psalter* . . :

...

4. In a more restricted sense. A branch of study which is concerned either with a connected body of demonstrated truths or with observed facts systematically classified and more or less colligated by being brought under general laws, and which includes trustworthy methods for the discovery of new truth within its own domain.

1725 Watts *Logic* (O.).

Chin.

In sense 1, 知 識.

知 = " To 口 speak so as to 矢 hit the mark," says the scholastic commentary (K.).

= To know; to be aware of. To perceive; to feel; knowledge; sensation. To have experience of. To inform. To administer; to manage ... (G.).

知 = savoir, connaître (C.).

識 = 言 words + 戠 (the man with 戈 a lance [phonetic] who 音 commands) (K.).

= To know; to be acquainted with; to understand ... (G.).

舊 相 識 an old acquaintance (G.).

見 識 過 人 of more knowledge and experience than men in general (G.).

In sense 4 科 學 (W.).

科 is from 斗 (peck, graduated measure) signific and 禾 grain (phonetic.) (K.).

= A class; series; the classification of graduates of the second degree; a course of study. A hole. Used of the " business " of the stage.

(T.) explains 科 as 程 (rule, pattern) and as 品 (kind, class).

力不同科 people's strength is not equal (G.).

科甲 the classes of graduates of the second and third degrees (G.).

主科 compulsory subjects (G.).

科則 a rate or classification (G.).

說科 (Mencius) to establish different classes; to divide by classes (C.).

學 = To learn. Teach (see entry under "Philosophy" above).

Hence 科學 means systematic learning. (T.) gives an explanation translated from a European source and makes no claim to any anticipation in China.

Science does not consist in facts or even in useful knowledge, but in the method in which any facts are dealt with. To decide, then, how far the scientific idea is present in Chinese investigation we should have not to make a list of the Chinese inventions of printing, paper, gunpowder, the compass, porcelain, sericulture, and the like, but to find what methods have been utilized for the correlation of phenomena. Bacon tried to classify knowledge on the analogy of a tree; Comte recognized mathematics, astronomy, physics, chemistry, biology, and sociology and the science of morals, whilst Spencer classified sciences as abstract and concrete. Recently Rudolf Carnap and others have sought to show that the branches of science are fundamentally of the same kind and are all branches of the unified science of physics.[1] The cataloguing of the Imperial Library of the Manchu Dynasty is some sort of a guide to the Chinese ideas of the classification of knowledge—namely " literati, military, legislation, agriculture, medicine, astronomy and mathematics, cyclopædias, essayists, Taoism,

[1] *The Unity of Science*, London, 1934.

THE LANGUAGE PROBLEM 127

Buddhism ". Ch'ên Yüan-lung (陳 元 龍), whose history of the physical sciences (格 物 鑑 源) was published in 1723, divides astronomy into Heaven, Sun, Moon, Stars, Wind, Thunder and Lightning, Clouds, Dew, Frost, Snow, Hail, Rainbow, and Fog and Mist ; Geography he classifies under Earth, Mountains, Ocean, Water, Wells, Bridges, City, Graves, etc. ; in Zoology he places cats in the same group as dogs and pigs because they are domestic animals, and tigers with wolves and foxes because they are wild animals.[1] In spite of Ch'êng-tse (tzǔ), Chu-tse (tzǔ) (i.e. Chu Hsi) and Lu Hsiang-shan of the Sung Dynasty (A.D. 960–1277) who enumerated extensive study, accurate enquiry, careful thinking, clear discrimination, and firm action as the requirements of method, Chinese science progressed no further than Ch'ên Yüan-lung until the present day.[2] But we must bear in mind that Sir Thomas Browne wrote his observations on the disparate length of a badger's off and on legs about forty years after the death of Bacon. As regards scientific method we are safe in saying that experiment, as distinct from the deductive and inductive processes of reasoning, has been responsible for the great Chinese discoveries. Scientific method, depending so intimately on the language machine available, has for the reasons elsewhere given, not been at hand for the Chinese investigator. The idea of science and the scientific method[3] is a new one to China and upon the success of the Chinese language in adapting itself to scientific needs depends the future of the country.

Evolution . . . ad L. *ēvolūtiōn-em* (recorded in the sense " unrolling of a book "). Noun of action from *ēvolvēre* . . .

---
[1] *A Study in the Chinese Principles of Education*, by Monlin Chiang, Shanghai, 1925, p. 68.
[2] The methods of Chinese science have been compared with the empiric ones adopted in Lamb's *Dissertation on Roast Pig*, but Mr. Carter's *Invention of Printing in China and its Journey Westward*, does not bear out this view.
[3] Except, perhaps, in philology.

1. The process of unrolling, opening out, or disengaging from an envelope.

. . . .

5. The process of evolving, developing, or working out in detail. What is implicitly or potentially contained in an idea or principle; the development of a design, argument, etc.

6. Biol. *a.* of animal and vegetable organisms and their parts; the process of developing from a rudimentary to a mature or complete state.

. . . .

b. Theory of Evolution: the hypothesis (first propounded under that name by Bonnet 1762) that the embryo or germ, instead of being brought into existence by the process of fecundation, is a development or expansion of a pre-existing form, which contains the rudiments of all the parts of the future organism. Also called the theory of Pre-formation to avoid confusion with the following sense.

c. The origination of species of animals and plants as conceived by those who attribute to it a process of development from early forms and not to a process of "special creation".

Chin. (W.) gives 展開, but the ordinary Chinese translation of evolution (sense 6*b*) is 進化論 (sometimes rendered by 天演論).

進 = To advance, as opposed to 退; to be promoted. To enter. To send in; to offer (G.).

進入 to enter (G.).

進達 to advance; to be promoted (G.).

進士 an "advanced scholar"—a graduate of the third or doctor's degree. Instituted A.D. 606 (G.).

化 = 亻 man + 匕, the seal graph has two senses for 匕; 1, picture of a spoon; 2, a man turned in opposite direction to ordinary (K.).

THE LANGUAGE PROBLEM

= to change; to alter; to influence; to transform; to civilize, to melt; to die (G.).

化工 God; creative art (G.).

教化 to teach and transform—to reform (G.).

造化 to create and transform—the operations of nature (G.).

赤虹化玉 (幼學) the empurpled rainbow has been changed to precious stone (C.).

SOCIOLOGICAL

Right(s) ... 9. A legal, equitable, or moral title, or claim to the possession of property or authority, the enjoyment of privileges or immunities, etc. ... (Bill of Rights, the Right of Man.).

900 Cynewulf ... 1300 *Cursor Mundi* ... 1375 Barbour, *Bruce* 1491. Act 7. Hen. VII ... (O.).

Chin. 權 (W.), (H.).

= 木 wood + 雚 (the 吅 crying 隹 bird with tufts on its head) heron. (K.). Here 雚 is the phonetic.

= The weight or balance of a steelyard; hence that which is variable, as opposed to 經; to weigh. Direction; authority; power; influence ... 主權, sovereign rights; sovereign power (G.).

See (*SMCI*), part ii, Democracy.

平權 to adjust; equalize (G.).

權勢 power; influence—usually in bad sense (G.).

平權 equal rights; sovereign power (G.).

變權 to modify or interpret generously laws or rules, because of circumstances, in a particular case (C.).

Mr. Frank W. Price says in the preface to his translation of Sun Yat-sen's *San Min Chu I* ... " I have tried to make the translation faithful to the original and yet clear to the English reader. This is not an easy task ... Ch'üan

(權) sometimes means sovereignty, sometimes rights, and at other times power or authority."

This word, perhaps better than any other, makes clear the enormous problem of translation. Bentham in chapter xvi of *An Introduction to the Principles of Morals and Legislation* [1] writes (Powers) :—

" though not a species of rights (for the two sorts of fictitious entities termed a *power* and a *right* are altogether disparate) are yet so far included under rights that wherever the word *power* may be employed the word *right* may also be employed. The reason is, that wherever you may speak of a person as having a power, you may also speak of him as having a right to such a power ; but the converse of this proposition does not hold good ; there are cases in which, though you may speak of a man as having a right, you cannot speak of him as having a power, or in any other way make mention of that word."

It is scarcely remarkable that a word which it took Bentham about a chapter to define and as to the strict sense of which the West is in lasting doubt (though it has a lively sense of the reality of the idea) should have caused so much misunderstanding in Sun Yat-sen's work. In Chinese there is only 權 to do duty for the two English words. The use of the word 權 in traditional literature is nearly always in the strict sense of " power ", e.g. 權勢 power, influence (usually in a bad sense) ; 英國利權, the power of England.[2] It is not that the idea of rights is new to China. The people have always had distinct ideas as to how far authority should be allowed to go and at what point it should be resisted. Even an emperor was theoretically only to be tolerated so long as he ruled justly. But the abuse of authority or power could go a long way in China without arousing any feeling that it was

[1] Quoted by C. K. Ogden, op. cit., p. xxiii.
[2] In the School of Law the word was very important. See J. J. L. Duyvendak, *The Book of Lord Shang*, pp. 100 and 260.

THE LANGUAGE PROBLEM

encroaching wrongfully on the rights of the community or of any particular section of it. Thus when, in transported Western moral and political theory, all sorts of new claims for the people are put forward, the confusion is inevitable. For instance, the student body (and " student " includes school boys and girls), greedily imbibing new doctrine, has distinguished itself by indiscipline and excess. The relaxed central authority and the decay of the family together with the innate respect for learning now transferred to the new learning, have conspired to give the students a great deal of power of a certain kind which they have readily identified with their " rights " in the Western sense.

Freedom ... O.E. fréodóm : see Free and -dom.

1. Exemption or release from slavery or imprisonment, personal liberty ... *Letter of freedom* ; a document emancipating a slave.

1230 *Hali. Meid.*
1382 Wyclif. *Deut.*
1596 Spenser *Fairy Queen.*
....

2. Exemption from arbitrary, despotic, or autocratic control ; independence ; civil liberty.

1375 Barbour *Bruce* Fredome all solace to man giffis
                          He levys at ese that frely levys.
....

4. The state of being able to act without hindrance or restraint, liberty of action. ...

5. The quality of being free from control of fate or necessity ; the power of self-determination attributed to the will.

888 King Aelfred *Bœthius.*
[and other senses].

Liberty ... a. F. *liberté* (14th c.) ... a. L. *Lībertāt-em* f. *līber*, free.

1. Exemption or release from captivity, bondage, or slavery.

1386 Chaucer . . .

2. Exemption or release from arbitrary, despotic, or autocratic rule and control.

1484 Caxton . . .

. . . .

4. Free opportunity, range, or scope to do or of doing something, hence, leave, permission.

. . . .

5. Unrestrained action, conduct, or expression; freedom of behaviour or speech, beyond what is granted or recognized as proper; licence (O.).

Chin. 自由 (自由之理) is given by (W.) as a translation of the senses 1, 2, and 4 above, of both freedom and liberty.

自 = ᛒ a picture of the nose in the human face (and means "nose", e.g. in 鼻, breath > self cf. Sanscrit *ātmán*—breath and self (K.).

= The nose. . . . From, with reference either to time, place, or person. Self . . . ; oneself; personally. Naturally; spontaneously; as a matter of course. According as. To use . . . (G.).

自行 moving of one's own accord, automatic (G.).

自持 self-control (G.).

自言自持 to soliloquize (G.).

不由自 not within one's own control (G.).

由 = Symbol for the idea "protrude, proceed from" (G.).

= Cause; means; instrument; motive; source; origin. From; by; by way of; because of; proceeding from. To follow; to walk in; to allow (G.).

由來 cause; means; source (G.).

不知其由 I do not know its cause (G.).

由於 arising from (G.).

自由之理 freedom in the abstract (G.).

THE LANGUAGE PROBLEM

Hence 自 由 = proceeding from oneself (i.e. action directed solely by the light from within oneself).

(H.) gives 自 由 主 義 as a translation of liberalism lit. freedom-ism. (T.) gives 自 由 意 志 in the sense of free will. 自 由 權 also occurs.

Freedom, though it has been claimed as the natural right and the natural state of the human being, is an essentially European conception. It has developed and grown very much during the last four centuries. Because of social, economic, and other limitations it has never been realized in anything like its theoretical formulation. In political theory anarchism is the extreme claim to individual freedom. In recent years the idea of the supreme good of the state transcending that of the individual has modified that of complete individual freedom and several peoples have been induced to surrender much of their freedom for the supposed good of the nation as a whole. In the nineteenth century the unpossessing classes were brought to realize that liberty in the face of economic disabilities could not be a reality, and liberty, equality, fraternity, was displaced by other popular slogans. Yet after the Revolution in China, under the Minister of Education, Ts'ai Yüan-p'ei, these three principles were adopted as the aim of the revolution and of education, being considered appropriate guiding stars for a new-born republic. In its real sense freedom has not yet been approached by the peasantry under conditions imposed partly by nature and tantamount to serfdom, by the unorganized wage earners in the cities, the victims of a growing industrialism, or by the merchants subject to arbitrary taxation, but in its sense of licence it has been a demoralizing stimulant to thousands of young Chinese. In China, society has always been authoritarian. The son deferred unquestioningly to the father, the father deferred to the head of the clan, the head of the clan deferred to the official, the official to the emperor, and official and emperor deferred alike to the sages of antiquity, however arbitrary their teaching might be. In a society where the unit was the family, "self-instigation" had very little place. The tradition of the Chinese people has been submission to a code and to a ritual. Docile in ordinary, the people, subjected to undue pressure, have burst into a violent but temporary turbulence which has not resulted in the growth of the idea of freedom, but has acted only as a safety valve to relieve the pressure. "The Chinese do not understand freedom" (SMCI.).

Democracy . . . a. F. démocratie (in thirteenth century Latin translation of Aristotle, attrib. to William of Moerbeke) a. Gr. δημοκρατία popular government, from δῆμος the commons, the people + κρατια in comb. = κράτος, rule, sway, authority. . . .

1. Government by the people; that form of government in which the sovereign power resides in the people as a whole, and is exercised either directly by them (as in the small republics of antiquity) or by officers elected by them. In modern use often more vaguely denoting a social state in which all have equal rights, without hereditary or arbitrary differences of rank or privilege.

1531 Elyot Gov . . .

2. That class of people which has no hereditary or spiritual rank or privilege; the common people (in reference to their political power).

1827 Hallam *Const. Hist.*
. . . .

Chinese, 民主政治 (W.) for sense 1 above (sense 2 is translated by a sentence, not by a phrase).

民 = character analogous to 氏 clan, family, both of doubtful analysis (K.).

= Mankind, including all classes; the people; the unofficial masses (G.).

民人 the people; Chinese as opposed to Manchus (G.).
良民 law abiding, harmless people (G.).
軍民人等 you soldiers and people in general (G.).
民夫 labourers employed in Government works (G.).
民情 the popular feeling (G.).
民部 literary designation of the Board of Revenue, adopted A.D. 650 (G.).
萬民 all the peoples (C.).
民以君爲心君以民爲體 (禮緇衣) the sovereign is like the heart; the people are like the body (C.).

主; the signific is 王 king; as the first stroke of this happens to be curved (⌣) in the seal, the commentaries consider the whole as a picture of a lamp with the flame rising up, symbol of a prince—a typical scholastic interpretation (K.).

= A host; president of a feast. A master, as opposed to 役; a lord, a sovereign, a ruler, a manager . . . To preside over; to have to do with . . . (G.).
自主 self-governing; free; independent (G.).
主治 to govern (G.).
主意 intention; plan; decision; leading idea (G.).
政 = Same word as 正 enlarged by 攴. 正 = a foot walking in — a straight line (K.).
= Government; administration of affairs (G.).
政 the administration of government (G.).
政人 government officials (G.).
治 = 台 I, myself; name of certain stars in Ursa Major; (the character is now mostly used in conventional abbreviations for 臺). (K.) + 氵water.
治國 to govern a country (G.).
= To govern; to manage; to arrange. To cure... to treat... (G.).
民權 is the phrase used for democracy in *San Min Chu I* (see Rights *supra*), i.e. rights or powers of the people.

It can be said that until the abolition of the examination system in 1905 China's institutions had not been materially affected by the West. In the administration of the foreign settlements, in the exercise of extra-territorial jurisdiction, and in the foreign control of their Maritime Customs and Salt Gabelle, the Chinese saw not the extension of a remote democracy but the hand of the conqueror operating according to the recognized rules of conquest. The powers the Chinese saw were the foreign gunboats, the Legation garrisons, and the less apparent but equally potent economic power of the foreign banks, not the executive of a popularly elected parliament at Westminster or Paris. China continued under a loose absolutism tempered by the patriarchal organization of society. At the revolution the reformers, Sun Yat-sen and others of the revolutionary party, were responsible for adopting the republican and democratic form of government. Because of the constant civil wars and the influence of the forces of conservatism what resulted for years was the fluctuating control of the military commanders. Foreign diplomacy and banking policy, too, played a part in this. The rise to power of the Kuomintang has meant a party dictatorship, but one subject to the influence of the military and of the separatist tendencies of various provinces. The Kuomintang programme provides for an indefinite period of military tutelage to be succeeded by a directly representative and democratic system. The National Government at Nanking derives its mandate from the Central Executive Committee and the Central Advisory Committee of the Kuomintang. An elaborate provisional constitution based on the Three Principles of Sun Yat-sen, devolves the administration on the Executive, Legislative, Judicial, Examination and Control *Yüans*, or bodies. Discontent with the Kuomintang régime, and its failure to function effectively during the Japanese crisis of 1932, has resulted in the adoption of various devices, such as the establishment of the National People's Assembly and the alteration of the organic law of the constitution to introduce a democratic check on the Kuomintang during the period of political tutelage.

Mr. H. N. Brailsford says of the Kuomintang, " In so far as it is spontaneous, its policy is that of a nationalistic middle class struggling to establish a native capitalist state within a framework of privileged foreign penetration." [1]

The Chinese attitude through the centuries towards the " people " can be divined from the apparently, but not actually, contradictory sayings " The people can be made to follow, but not to understand ", and " The people are the most important element in a nation, then the spirits of the land and grain, and the sovereign is the least of all ". China takes up the European idea of democracy at a curious stage in its history and it will make something different of it from the thing we understand. The great obstacle to the spread of democratic institutions is the uneducated state of the great mass.

State ... 29. The body politic as organized for supreme civil rule and government ; the political organization which is the basis of civil government (either generally and abstractly, or in a particular country) hence the supreme civil power and government vested in a country or a nation.

1538 Starkey *England*.

30. A body of people occupying a defined territory and organized under a sovereign government. Hence occasionally the territory occupied by such a body.

Chinese. In sense 29 above 政 治 團 體 (W.).

政 = Government ; administration of affairs (see entry under Democracy above).

= To govern ; to manage ; to arrange (see entry under Democracy above).

---

[1] *Property or Peace ?*, London, 1934.

團 = A round mass; a sphere; a lump; an agglomeration; to collect; to coil; to surround. Trainbands; volunteers. The female of crabs (G.).

體 = The limbs; the trunk; the body; thickness, as a dimension ... to be incorporated with; to embody. To treat with consideration, to sympathize with. Form or embodiment; style in literature, as opposed to 用 substance, practical outcome; also in painting.

四體 the four limbs of the body (G.).

夫婦一體 husband and wife are one flesh (G.).

大體 principle; scope; real interests; proprieties (G.).

Hence 政治團體 = government-collected-body, body politic.

In sense 30 = 國 (W.).

國 = A nation; a kingdom; a state; a country; the capital of a country; a dynasty; a house or line. ...

國號 (title) the name of a ruling house or dynasty (G.).

國家 The social family; the state; the government; the reigning family (C.).

國家 nation; state (SMCI).

外國 the outside nations (G.).

開國 to found a state (G.).

三國 the Three States into which the Empire was divided at the fall of the Han Dynasty (G.).

The Chinese have always had a strong sense of themselves as a cultural entity, though never as a nation in the modern sense of the term. The written language included the " Black Haired Race " in Chekiang, Yunnan or Chihli in a universal brotherhood rather as the Catholic Church did Europe in the Middle Ages. The parts of the Empire, however, were bound politically only by common allegiance to the throne. There was no cohesive political or economic structure to unite the people in one interest. The feeling was purely local. It is this which modern nationalism is

THE LANGUAGE PROBLEM 139

trying to correct by intensive propaganda in the schools and by bringing the separatist provinces together under the only banner which has ever rallied them—namely anti-foreignism. (T.) explains 國 as " that which has territory, people and sovereignty ". As a translation of " country " it is adequate, but not of " nation ".[1]

Nationalism . . . from National + ism.

Nation . . . An extensive aggregate of persons, so closely associated with each other by common descent, language, or history, as to form a distinct race or people, usually organized as a separate state and occupying a definite territory.

Nationalism. 1. Theol. The doctrine that certain nations (as contrasted with individuals) are the object of divine election.

1836 Fraser's Magazine.

2. Devotion to one's nation; national aspiration; a policy of national independence.

. . . .

Chin. (W.) translates these meanings by explanatory periphrases. Sun Yat-sen in *San Min Chu I* uses 國家 as the equivalent of " nation " and 民族 for " race ".

民 = People (see Democracy *ante*).

族 = To collect together, a tribe ; a clan ; a family ; agnatic relatives . . . To destroy.

民族 race. (SMCI.) Nationalism, Lect. I.

百族 all living creatures (G.).

宗族 clan ; family ; kindred (G.).

---

[1] The use of 國 in names for China has given it limited frontiers. Before it was 天下 which was a universalistic term claiming allegiance from the " outside barbarians ". Historically 國 were the feudal units within the 天下; in the Chan Kuo Period, when the 國 became self-conscious, they were conceived of in a military aspect. See *The Book of Lord Shang*, Introduction.

Couvreur describes 族 as those who are descended from a common branch and bear the same family name.

(Nationalism in China is discussed in Chapters V and VI. See also State *ante*.)

Public ... M.E. publike, -ique, a. French *public* (1311) ad. L. *pūblicus*; from *poplus* (later *popul-us*) People. The change to *pūblicus* appears to have taken place under the influence of *pūbes*, in the sense "adult men", "male population."

In general, and in most of the senses, the opposite to private. The varieties of sense are numerous and pass into each other by many intermediate shades of meaning. The exact shade often depends upon the substantive qualified, and in some expressions more than one sense is vaguely present; in others the usage is traditional, and it is difficult to determine in what sense precisely the thing in question was originally called "public".

I. Pertaining to the people of a country or locality.

1. Of, or pertaining to, the people as a whole; that which belongs to, affects, or concerns the community or nation; common, national, popular.

1513 *Bradshaw's St. Werburge Another Balade to auctour.*

2. Phrases from 1.
... public good, weal.

1436 *Libel Eng. Policy.*
. . . .

Public opinion.
. . . .

4. That is open to, may be used by, or may or must be shared by, all members of the community; not restricted to the private use of any person or persons; generally accessible or available; generally levied (as a rate or tax). Also (in narrower sense), that may be used, enjoyed,

THE LANGUAGE PROBLEM

shared, or competed for, by all persons legally or properly qualified.

. . . .

6. Of, pertaining to, or engaged in the affairs or service of the community; esp. of a person: occupying an official or general influence or authority.

. . . .

8. Devoted or directed to the promotion of the general welfare; public-spirited, patriotic.

119 ... With extended, international, or universal reference.... Of, or pertaining to, the nations generally, or to the Europeans, Christian, or civilized nations, regarded as a single community; general; international; esp. in *public law*.

... (O.).

Chin. In sense 1. 屬於民的 = what belongs to or pertains to the people (W.).

For sense 4. (W.) gives an explanatory sentence ending with 公衆之享樂的 = that which is enjoyed by the public.

(H.) uses 公 for the various senses of " public ". It also uses it in the phrases 公平地租 Fair rent, 公平貿易 Fair trade, 公平價格 Fair price, and 公母 Common denominator. 公民 is given for Citizen, 公社 for Commune and 公海 for Open (*id est* High) Sea. 公司 = Company (trading).

公 = Public; common to all; as opposed to 私 ... hence just, equitable ... the highest order of nobility " duke "; gentleman; sir; esquire. Male as opposed to 母 (G.).

以國家爲公

以國滅私 (書周官) to make individual interest yield to the public interest (C.).

秉公審訊 (京報) to examine a matter with all justice (C.).

不入公門 (禮曲禮) not to enter the palace (C.).

公事 public business; public affairs (G.).

公署 a public office; a yamen (G.).

公正 just and upright; impartial (G.).

(T.) merely explains 公 as "not private" (私).

The absence of municipal organization and of public works on a large scale has been a great obstacle to the Chinese understanding of "public". Even in the cities the provision of common necessities such as watchmen, roads, or street lighting, has been left to the individuals immediately interested. Smith, in *Chinese Characteristics*, tells of a farmer whose top soil was removed by a flood on to the public road and who, without a thought that he was interfering with the property of the community, recovered his soil at the expense of removing a portion of the road. Eleven years ago I groped at night through the rich *Saikwan*, or Western Suburbs, of Canton without encountering a single street light. But there has been a vast change in China in the last few years, or rather in some parts of China. Municipal government has been adopted in many centres. The idea that a person had a personal financial interest in everything he did or touched was so engrained in the Chinese that even the postman in many parts received a commission on every letter he delivered. But the idea of what is "public" as distinguished from what is "private" is gradually gaining ground in China.

Loyalty . . . a. French *loialté* (mod. *loyauté*) from *loyal* ad. Latin *lēgal-em*, from *lēg-lex*, law.

1. Faithful adherence to one's promise, oath, word of honour, etc. Conjugal faithfulness, fidelity.

1400 *Romaunt de la Rose.*

. . . .

2. Faithful adherence to the sovereign or lawful government. Also, in recent use, enthusiastic reverence for the person or family of the sovereign.

1531 Elyot *Gov.* . . .

Chinese. Here again (W.) translates the idea by a periphrasis, but in senses 1 and 2 involving the use of 忠.

忠 = 中 centre (picture of an arrow in the centre of a target) (K.) + 心 heart.

= Loyal, patriotic, faithful, as opposed to 奸 (G.).

爲下克忠 (書伊訓) a subject, he was noted for his fidelity and devotion towards his prince (C.).

私臣不忠, 忠臣不私 a selfish minister is not loyal; a loyal minister is not selfish (C.).

(T.) explains 忠 as 竭誠 " to display utmost sincerity ". " To exhaust the capacity of one's heart " is to be loyal (忠). A quotation from Mencius is given as an illustration 教人以善謂之忠 = " To teach men to be good is called loyalty."

There are many stories in Chinese history of loyalty to a principle, to a clan, or to an individual. The idea of filial piety has been extended or transferred.[1] But the makers of the New China find that the localized loyalty to a small group is a great obstacle to national unity. They wish to create what China has never had before, a sense of loyalty to the nation as a whole. In achieving this they are handicapped by the huge area of China, the diversity of peoples, Mohammedanism, Thibetan Buddhism, Communism, the lack of national organization, and by the decay of classical education. There is, moreover, no emperor as the visible object of loyalty, and the National Flag which has been changed twice since 1911 has yet to capture the Chinese imagination as the symbol of the nation.

[1] See M. Granet, *La Pensée Chinoise*. M. Granet thinks that in ancient Chinese social thought 孝, " filial piety " is less important than 忠 " loyalty."

Socialism. Social (L. *socius*, companion) + ism. F. *socialisme* 1832 employed in contrast to *personnalité*. In its modern sense it is variously claimed for Leroux or Reybaud, writing within three or four years after this time. *Encyc. Britt.* (1887) assigns priority to England, says that word originated in 1835 in the discussions of a society founded by Robert Owen.

1. A theory or policy of social organization which aims at or advocates the ownership and control of the means of production, capital, land, property, etc., by the community as a whole, and their administration or distribution in the interests of all.

Quarterly Review, Dec. 1840. " The two great demons in morals or politics, Socialism and Chartism " ... 1881 Stevenson, *Virginibus Puerisque*. " I do not greatly pride myself on having outlived my beliefs in the fairy tales of socialism ... " (O.)

The word " socialist " occurs earlier.

1833 *Poor Man's Guardian* (Letter signed) a Socialist. 1833 *The Crisis*. The Socialist who preaches of community of goods, abolition of crime, of punishment, of magistrates, and of marriage. 1853 " Jordan ". " He was a socialist in the best sense of the term." 1889 Shaw. *Fabian essays on Socialism.* " The young socialist is apt to be catastrophic in his views." (O.)

Chin. 社 會 主 義 (W.), (H.).

社 = the 示 religious rites for 土 the land (K.).

= The Earth, divinely personified ; the spirit of the land ; the god of the soil (= 土 神), generally associated with a tree, and sometimes apparently the tree itself ; the sacrifices to this spirit, of which every 里 group of twenty-five families had its own, corresponding in some senses to the worship of the god Terminus ; also the altar which symbolizes the god ; a clan, a society ; in Formosa, a savage village or tribe (G.).

社所以神地之道也 she is the personification as a God of the energies of the earth (G.).

社稷 the spirits of land and grain; one's country; the commonwealth (G.).

文社 a literary club (G.).

同社諸君子 (張溥) all the sages of the same society (C.).

會 = to 亼 meet (ancient form of 集) round the fire (cf. 黑) and 曰 chat (K.).

= To meet together; to collect; to unite; to co-operate; a guild; a society. To understand; mental possibility.... To be able, in reference to acquired knowledge or skill.... A moment of time; just at that time (G.).

三合會 the Triad Society (G.).

In 主 the signific is 王, king; as the first stroke of this happens to be curved in the seal (⌒) the commentators consider the whole as a picture of a lamp with the flame rising up, symbol of the prince—a typical scholastic interpretation (K.).

= A host; a president of a feast. A master, as opposed to 役...; a lord; a sovereign; a ruler; a manager. To preside over; to have to do with (G.).

義 = from 羊 sheep (good-natured, kind) signific and 我 phonetic (K.).

= That which it is right to do, as opposed to 利 that which is profitable; duty towards one's neighbour; loyal; patriotic; heroic; faithful. Common; free; open to all. Meaning; purport (G.).

主義 is a modern phrase coined to represent the suffix "ism". It can perhaps be analysed as ruling-thought and means policy, principle, doctrine, platform of party; advocacy of, spirit etc., and is interchangeable with 思想. Sun Yat-sen defines "ism" at the opening of *San Min Chu I*.

L

The whole phrase, then, is village-society-ism. (Giles gives the phrase 社會 as meaning " sacrificial spirits ".)

Socialism as a word and as an idea has only a 100 years of history, though it has, subsequent to its invention, been used to describe elements in the Mosaic Law, in Hosea and Isaiah, certain mediæval social experiments, and the ideas of some eighteenth century reformers. It is essentially a creation for conditions arising from the industrial revolution and the growing articulateness of the working classes. The early socialism of Robert Owen was not addressed to the working classes in particular, though they were the only ones to whom, at that time, it had any appeal. At first the word was used as much as a term of dislike or fear of Jacobinism or Radicalism as to describe a new social movement, but it acquired a more precise denotation with the growth of socialist parties in various countries. Mr. G. D. H. Cole says, " The communist manifesto of Karl Marx and Engels in 1848 is generally regarded as the starting point of modern socialism." The Marxists condemned the pioneers —Owen, Saint-Simon, etc., as unscientific utopia builders. Instead they maintained the " materialistic conception of history " by which the objective would be attained by a series of class struggles. New socialist parties—the Social Democrats, the Christian Socialists, the Fabians, the Indpendent Labour Party—have come into being at various stages. All parties, even those of the Right, have been influenced in their programmes by socialist theory. " We are all socialists now," said a Tory spokesman at the beginning of the present century. It was not true, but it showed that " socialist " had ceased to be regarded as a mere term of disapproval.

Socialism, though a modern idea, did not originate in a vacuum. The medieval guildsmen, the philosophers of the eighteenth, and the revolutionaries of the eighteenth and nineteenth centuries, developed ideas that were latent in our civilization. Socialism utilized and developed those ideas to fit a new set of conditions. We, our fathers, and even our grandfathers have lived with the idea, and our opposition or support has modified the nature of the movement. We accept nowadays as axiomatic certain things that were immoral or subversive to our immediate predecessors. The process continues. Socialist theory and practice takes shape from the functional municipal, national, and other organizations of our society. *Socius*, a companion, we apply in our modern sense to the man who has the same employment as ourselves, in a different sense to the neighbour with whom we share our gas and water mains, in a third sense to the Hebridean whom we regard as a fellow national and, maybe, an ex-comrade in war, and *socius* is latent in socialism.

The principles which socialism seems logically to imply have been thought by European socialists to apply as a matter of course beyond the society in which the doctrine has had its growth, often, I think, without sufficient understanding of what this extension means. Socialism, translated into Chinese or applied to the Chinese must, by the very circumstances, mean something very different from what it does in Darlington or Bordeaux.

It happened that when the impact with Europe caused, or precipitated the break-up of the ancient Chinese system, an alien dynasty was on the Dragon Throne. For this reason reform movements tended to be republican and socialist-republican because the reformers were influenced by the more advanced of the theories of the West. If there had been a native emperor on the throne it is more than likely that the reform movement, as in Japan, would have been monarchist. Anti-foreign feeling was the mainspring of reform action, and were not the Manchus as alien as the Europeans ? Sun Yat-sen, the revolutionary whose party and ideas influenced the course of the revolution for many years and finally triumphed after his death, lived in America and Europe and became imbued with socialistic ideas. It was therefore his interpretation of socialism in *San Min Chu I* and elsewhere, and its application by himself and his followers, which decided the meaning of 社會主義 in Chinese.

社 denoted a clan, a small group of families with common worship at the local shrine of the Earth. It was much later used for other social combinations such as 弓箭社, an archery club,[1] and 文社, a literary club. Frequently in a village the inhabitants had the same surname and a common ancestor and their life centred round the ancestral temple. Disputes between neighbouring villages were common, leading sometimes to serious disorder (as a typical instance the one in 1895 in Kwangtung over water rights). The rise of secret societies in the Straits Settlements has been traced to the clan system. The District Magistrates, through the village elders and local gentry (紳耆), maintained a loose sway over the villages,[2] being usually more interested in tax collection than in administration. It was perhaps appropriate that 社 should have been chosen to play the same part as *socius* with us, but unfortunate, too, because the clan system has been the subject of the denunciation of reformers including Sun Yat-sen himself.[3]

會 was a character with a curious history. It was used by the dreaded secret societies—the *San-ho Hui*, or Triad, the *San Tien*, etc.—which for centuries disturbed the quiet of China. For this reason it was proscribed by the government. When towards the end of the nineteenth century revolutionary societies came into being, the word *hui* (會)

---

[1] Occurs in Sung History (*Tz'ŭ Yüan*).
[2] "They (the villages) are extremely jealous of external interference." Y. K. Leong and L. K. Tao, *Village and Town Life in China*, 1915, p. 40.
[3] *San Min Chu I*, trans. Price, 1929, p. 5. "The Chinese people have shown the greatest loyalty to family and clan, with the result that in China there have been family-ism and clan-ism but no real nationalism."

was employed by their founders to describe them, though the *T'ung Mêng Hui* of Sun Yat-sen later became the *Kuo Min Tang* (國民黨). Note the etymology of "meeting round a fire and chatting".

Altogether the phrase 社會主義 denotes to the native reader something very different from "socialism" as we understand it. In the Treaty Ports and other big cities industrialism and capitalism are sufficiently developed to produce conditions in some way comparable to those of the West, but in the village communities (80 per cent of the country), where agriculture is on the small-holding scale, there can be little understanding yet of terms such as the "nationalization of the means of production". When the largest social unit he can comprehend *is still* the *shê* (社) (though the word in spoken usage is only understood in its sense of "guild, society") it is clear that the rustic Chinese composing the bulk of the people can have as yet but a vague notion of "nation", "state", "class", "capital".

Those responsible for introducing "socialism" into the language had two alternatives. They could have rendered it by its nearest phonetic equivalent or could have coined a phrase with existing words. The former course would have meant the representation of the idea by a pure symbol, one untrammelled by the meanings of Chinese words. Its significance would, however, have had to have been explained to the people in terms of existing words and knowledge, which is the prime objection to all translation. We speak of a Chinese "shoe", "chair", or "bed", although in each case the English equivalent of these notions is different. The latter course, on the other hand, had the advantage of offering a partial explanation of the idea which the phrase was coined to convey. In the case of "socialism" the renaissance leaders chose to coin a phrase. There is evidence, however, that the phonetic equivalents of foreign words are coming back into favour.

Capitalism . . . Capital (commerce). The stock of a company, corporation, or individual with which they enter into business and on which profits or dividends are calculated; in a jointstock company it consists of the total sum of the contributions of the shareholders + ism. The condition of possessing capital; the position of a capitalist; a system which favours the existence of capitalists.

1854. Thackeray *Newcomes*.

" Capitalist " occurs first in 1792. A. Young, *Travels in France*.

Chin. 資本主義. (W.), (H.).

資 = Property; valuables; fees; subscriptions; means of living. To help; to protect; to trust to; to depend on. (G.).

本 = The root, as opposed to 末; the origin; point of departure; hence, native as opposed to foreign; personal; one's own; used for " I ", " We ", etc. Capital or principal of money. Numerative of books, documents, paintings, plants, etc. (G.).

主義 = " ism." (*Vide* Socialism above.)

When the Treaty of Nanking opened up China to foreign trade her economic system was self-contained. She exported a small percentage of her native produce, accepting silver, opium, and woollens in return for it. She had no essential need of what the foreigner could produce. She even exported manufactured cotton goods (nankeens) to England. In the course of the century the whole position changed. The demand for foreign articles was gradually stimulated, and the machines of Europe and America turned out articles which the Chinese had formerly produced for themselves. One consequence was the practical ruin of domestic spinning and weaving and other industries. The whole foreign trade in 1833 was valued at £10,000,000, in 1845 at £13,000,000, in 1902 at £26,000,000, and in 1931 at £117,000,000, the

THE LANGUAGE PROBLEM 151

proportion of imports to exports in the latter case being fourteen to nine. With the foreigners came banking on the modern scale and in the sense which the modern world understands it, and the modification of commerce due to the nature and requirements of finance. Industries have sprung up in the Treaty Ports and their neighbourhood but they are unevenly balanced and distributed. The number of industrial workers in the twenty-nine principal cities in the nine provinces where industry is centred was estimated at only 1,204,347 in 1930. China is still mainly agricultural. The land, too, is still largely in the hands of the peasant cultivator. The percentage differs in various parts of the country, but on an average it seems safe to say that over 50 per cent of the peasants own their own land, about 20 per cent are part owners and cultivators, and the remainder are tenants.[1] Yet in various periods of Chinese history there have been large land-owners, and at the present day the " land-lordism " attacked by Sun Yat-sen is an evil in China. The price of surplus agricultural produce, too, like that of all other things, is regulated by the world economic system, i.e. " capitalism," but for some time to come capitalism must mean a very different thing in China than it does in an industrialized country like England or the United States.

Class . . . In seventeenth century, *classe*. French *classe*, fourteenth century ad Latin *classis* (which was in earlier use).

6. Gen. A number of individuals (persons or things) possessing common attributes, and grouped together under a general or " class " name ; a kind ; sort, division. (O.)

Chin. (W.) translates the sense by a long periphrasis. (M.) says,

" the two following are used as suffixes as we use -ers, -ors, -ists, or -kind, to designate a class or from a generic. They

[1] But see p. 184.

may be used interchangeably, 家. Its use in this sense is not new, but the number of new combinations now coming into daily use seems unlimited. This word is often used to denote one of a class. 派 A class, a tribe, similar in use to the above, but does not, like that, imply any special qualifying preparation, but simply an aggregation of individuals of the same stamp. It is not used in the singular. 界 Sphere—wider in its meaning than the above, and not used in the singular. It may also be translated *sphere, circle, world*, or by some distinctive generic as 女 界, *the female sex*. Or the definite article before an adjective may make it generic, as 青 年 界, *the young*."

The following are examples from Mrs. Mateer's work:—
美 術 家, artists; 厭 世 家, pessimists (fed-up-with-the-world class); 笑 罵 家, satirists (laugh-scold-ers); 農 界, farmers; 家 = lit. family; 派 = lit. a section, party, school; and 界 = lit. a boundary.

In China there was disparity of wealth, but nothing like that which in the West has created the gulf between social classes. There was much community of living and no complex differentiation of function among the people. The four social classes of traditional China (四 民) were the officials, the farmers, the mechanics, and the merchants (士, 農, 工, 商).[1] This was their classical order of precedence. The revolution in economic conditions now taking place, the growth of the Treaty Ports, and the rise of industrialism and capitalism are creating new classes in China. The rise of new classes is calling into being new terms to describe them.

International (Inter + National).

Existing, constituted, or carried on between different nations; pertaining to the relations between nations.

---

[1] The ancient division was into 士 and 庶, the nobles and the masses.

1780 Bentham *Principles of Legislation* ... (O.).
(Bentham invented the word.)

Chin. 國際的, etc. (W.).

國 = country (see entry under "State" ante).

際 = A border; a limit; the boundary line between two times, state, conditions, etc. A juncture. (G.).

的 = possessive (but see p. 98).

Hence the phrase = That which appertains to the boundaries or intercommunications of countries or nations.

(SMCI.) translates "internationalism" by 世界主義 (i.e. world-ism).

The national, says Sun Yat-sen, must precede the international. Mazzini said the same thing a 100 years ago, but there are no distinct signs so far of internationalism emerging from the belligerent and daily more water-tight nationalism of Europe.

There is no Western word or phrase, however, esoteric which modern Chinese cannot deck out with a closely imitative native dress. How far it can digest the idea it stands for into its system is another question. The following are chosen to illustrate the ingenuity of the translator :—

Romanticists 傳奇派 (H.) lit. the " relating-wonders school" (*ch'uan ch'i* is a term taken from the drama). For " Romanticism " (W.) has 浪漫主義 lit. waves, billows (unrestrained, extravagant) + water overflowing (will, reckless) + ism.

Axiom is translated 公理 (H.) or " common to all principle ".

Irony is translated by (H.) as 反語 or "turning-back words". Irony, as we understand it, is not to be found in Chinese.[1]

---

[1] Professor Duyvendak remarks : " A good example of the difference between the Western term and the Eastern translation is 反對 used for (parliamentary) opposition. The old T'ang Shao-yi quoted this expression to me, in 1926, as an example of a translation that conveyed an entirely

I have concentrated on examining new terms and I have only touched on the more general problems of translation. Behind the problem is not only the question of comparative structure, but also that of vocabulary. Apart from new terms manufactured expressly to convey European ideas, the Chinese language consists of characters which generations of translators have identified with words in Latin, English, French, German, and the like. Dr. Richards in his study of Mencius [1] reveals the lack of real equivalence between the Chinese and English vocabularies and he urges the development of a technique for comparative studies. With the efficiency of a diathermic knife he dissects the meanings of a number of key words in English like Truth, Beautiful, Knowledge, Order. His system for the plotting of the ramifications of meaning goes far beyond that of the Oxford Dictionary and his methods promise us a leap towards understanding our own meanings when we use our words. He does not lay down a definite technique for the manipulation of meanings, English and Chinese, but he brings home the need for it. A solution that seems to arise tentatively from his study is that when English has been subjected to a multiple definition analysis, similar steps shall then be taken with Chinese and the translator will then have at his disposal two graduated scales of meaning which can be slid against one another till the point of exact equivalence is found.

I spent some time experimenting with the table in which Dr. Richards analyses " Beautiful " into ten " senses " and

---

different idea, 反 having always been associated with the idea of 'revolution', something done with armed force. In this connection he quoted to me the old Confucius adage, that the most important thing was to 正名, 'to satisfy the names.' Another example is 帝國主義 'imperialism'. In Chinese it sounds as if the idea were to establish an empire (under an emperor) ! "

[1] *Mencius and the Mind*, London, 1932, p. 186 seq. See also " Preface to a Dictionary," by the same author, in *Psyche*, 1932.

THE LANGUAGE PROBLEM

six " gestures ". A fairly exact equivalence can be obtained for a number of the senses and gestures of Beautiful by the use of the character 美, others can be matched by characters like 優, 高, some require a phrase, and a number cannot be translated at all. But even if complete analogies were available for all the senses and gestures it yet appears that the translation would be nothing but an exact mimicry in another plane of reality. 美 (etymologically a 大 large 羊 sheep and suggesting thereby a biblical standard of beauty-riches) denotes Yang Kuei-fei, a good " eight legs " essay, a landscape by Wu Tao-tzŭ, the flavour of pickled eggs. It is likely that many of the things to which "beautiful" applies could be described by 美, and vice versa, but there would still be a region in which one would apply and the other would not. " The Nike of Samothrace is beautiful " is undoubtedly true in all European languages: its translation into Chinese is probably untrue. Where words are conditioned by racial experience, by local conditions, and by the emotions, translation is bound to go wrong. This is particularly so with sociological terms. It is true, in fact, of nearly everything except the mathematical and physical sciences. It is likely that the properties of manganese dioxide are the same in China as in Canada, that the laws of gravity are constant in Peking and in Paris, and that (subject to relativity) two and two make four throughout the world.

Yet the terms for the physical elements and compounds, usually not corresponding to observable or isolated substances, have to have special terms manufactured for them in Chinese. Manganese, for instance, is denoted by the word 錳 *mêng*, an obvious coining from 金, metal, an 孟, *mêng*, phonetic. Chinese can manufacture these words without any difficulty. But the creation of new terms, even if they are equivalent to the thought, is not enough: it is still necessary to formulate propositions concerning them. It is doubtful whether Chinese is capable of the exactness of expression requisite for scientific purposes. It is not, as Professor Heinrich Hackmann suggests, due to its lack of inflection, for English in which inflection is decayed is at least as efficient a medium for scientific purposes as German.

Argument based on philological theories must be idle: practical experience alone must be the guide. There is a woeful scarcity of data. Mr. L. G. Morgan who has had a number of years' experience teaching science to the Chinese, in a valuable book published not long ago,[1] considers that Chinese cannot convey the exactitudes of science, and advocates the adoption of some Western language, thus avoiding many possibilities of misunderstanding which must result from the looseness of Chinese expressions.

Mr. Morgan gives what is worth an age of speculation—an example. It is an extract taken " almost at random " from a recent science textbook in *Kuo Yü* which is in common use in Middle Schools " 空氣 (air) 遇 (meets) 熱 (heat), 體積 (substance) 即 (immediately) 脹 (swells), 遇 (meets) 冷 (cold) 即 (immediately) 縮 (shrinks) ". It is the equivalent of " When air is heated it expands, when it is cool it contracts ". After giving the meanings of the separate characters as they are explained in Eitel's *Cantonese Dictionary*, Mr. Morgan says:—

" The term used in the sentence for air is 空氣 which is somewhat misleading in that 空 commonly means empty or void. There is no single character in Chinese meaning ' to heat ' but only a noun meaning heat.[2] The expression ' is heated ' is put 遇熱, which means literally ' meets heat '. This is a most unfortunate expression as the character 遇 is often

[1] *The Teaching of Science to the Chinese.* Kelly and Walsh, 1933.
[2] 熱 is also an adjective, and Professor Duyvendak remarks that all Chinese adjectives are in reality verbs.

used in the sense of meeting people or things and thus tends to convey the idea that heat is some material thing. The two characters 體積, which have been translated by 'substance' would in general convey nothing like such a definite idea. The actual meaning given them depends to some extent on the context and it also depends on the discrimination of the reader. They present certain rather floating ideas to the reader which he can within certain limits construe as he will. Here the meaning can be taken from a compôte of ideas, such as 'bodily Form', 'whole vital substance', 'whole general appearance', 'complete massed up material of the whole,' 'the essential matter of composition'. The character 體 tends to introduce some idea of life or vitality into the meaning. The character 脹, is by no means so suitable as the English word 'expand', which is free from associations, whereas 脹, owing to its association with dropsy, may very likely lead to the impression that expansion is due to some actual growth or chemical change taking place in the nature of the substance."

Let us consider this criticism in detail. The use of 空 is not essential; 氣 can stand alone. 熱 is used as an adjective as well as a noun, but it is true to say that it is not used as a transitive verb. 遇 is used in the sense of meeting persons but it is also used in the sense of meeting abstract things, such as 遇險, meet danger. 體積 does not, I think, mean "substance", but is a new coinage for "volume". I am inclined to suspect a misprint here for 體質. But actually no word or phrase for "substance" seems required. 脹 has the disadvantage of being associated with dropsy, as Mr. Morgan points out. A better word would be 漲. 即 seems out of place, 則 would be better.

The idea, at any rate, could be better expressed. I tentatively suggest 空氣受熱則漲, 受冷則縮. Professor Duyvendak considers that *pai hua* is really better suited to this sort of thing and he suggests 空氣一熱就伸張一令就縮小. To translate scientific textbooks, experts with a knowledge of both science and Chinese are required.

Dr. W. W. Yen admits that Chinese is very defective from the standpoint of clearness, accuracy, and logical sequence. He says, " Chinese is a language more appropriate for the expression of poetic and literary fancies than for the conveyance of legal and scientific thought." [1]

To this I may add, for what it is worth, an observation based on my own experience of the language as an administrative officer and as a magistrate in Hong Kong and Malaya. I should mention, perhaps, that I speak Cantonese fluently and Mandarin fairly, and that I have some knowledge of Hokkien and Hakka. I have found that although skilful manipulation may twist Chinese to express almost anything, the colloquial as ordinarily used is often incapable of rendering the temporal and conditional constructions essential for English administrative and legal purposes. It is not merely a question of education, for I have found that the Chinese who has a good literary knowledge of his own language is less open to receive these ideas than is an illiterate coolie. The spirit of Chinese is against it. I can best illustrate this conclusion by an example.

I am hearing a civil suit. The evidence so far shows that A. has contracted to build a wall for B. The wall is faulty and B. has refused to pay. A. is suing B. for the agreed price. B., giving evidence, is asked by the solicitor in English, " If he had promised to put the wall right, would you have paid him the money ? " The suit turns on the intention of B. at a certain moment. Now, in Chinese (Cantonese in this instance) it is quite possible to form a conditional question, e.g. *K'u hai ying shing sau ching hō ko fuk ts'eung nei hang ch'ut ts'in ni ?* But although the question is put in this way the witness takes it as two separate ones, " Did he promise to repair the wall ? " and " Did you pay him ? ", and when it is put to him again he understands it as, " if he promises to repair the wall *now, will* you pay him ? " The

[1] Quoted in *Debabelization* by C. K. Ogden, p. 132.

THE LANGUAGE PROBLEM

witness, like most of his countrymen, is not accustomed to think in terms of contingent happenings. And many other examples might be given.

I once gave a competent Chinese Court interpreter the exercise of finding in literary Chinese (or colloquial for that matter) the translation for a well-known petrol advertisement. A man watching a passing motor car exclaims, " That's Shell—that was ! " The exclamation is a humoristic but quite legitimate variation of the sentence that contains a repetition for the sake of emphasis. The point in this case lies in the contrast of tense. The interpreter's first effort was to render it as " This is Shell ; that is ! " The English however, retains the same demonstrative pronoun in both clauses. When afterwards he employed words like 今 and 往 denoting passage of time he could not use the demonstrative pronoun as well.

To revert to the problem of language *vis-à-vis* education. The Chinese pupil who is a native of the non-Mandarin-speaking provinces and who is receiving instruction in *Kuo Yü* not only has the shortcomings of the language to contend with ; he is also dealing with what to him is a foreign language. I have observed that Cantonese, Hailam, Tiuchiu, Hakka, and Hokkien children having been put through a course of *Kuo Yü* with the aid of *Kuo Yü* or National Language textbooks, go on to learn geography, history, etc., with the aid of other textbooks written in *Kuo Yü*. As often as not what they now learn is not geography, history, etc., but a little more *Kuo Yü*. Owing to the incompetence of teachers and other reasons the pupils from the south-eastern maritime provinces (and there are many thousands of them) have rarely sufficient command of *Kuo Yü* to enable them to use it as a medium for learning other subjects. In Canton province, for this reason, they are reverting to the literary medium for instruction, though *Kuo Yü* is still taught as a special subject.

It seems certain that for the purpose of teaching Western ideas, especially Western scientific ideas, the best course would be to adopt a Western language as a medium. But what Western language ? The answer can only be English, for English in addition to its very strong claims on other counts, is the only Western language at all widely spoken in China. It is taught in all Middle Schools and schools of a higher standard. But the results are very poor. Few students ever attain to a knowledge of English which would allow them to use it as a medium for learning other subjects. With an allowance of only five hours a week no other result can be expected. But even in schools (such as the government schools of Malaya) Chinese scarcely ever become thoroughly at home with English. It seems that English is too hard for most Orientals to acquire in addition to their native tongue.

But there is a solution which, if adopted on a large enough scale, and systematically, has in my opinion every chance of wide success. I refer to Basic English. This international language with 850 words instead of 30,000 or 40,000 is not just an ingenious *tour de force*. It is a scientific language derived from root principles of logic, physics, and geometry, and yet designed with a strictly practical object. From the examples I have read, and from the judgment of many authorities of eminence it seems suited to all essential purposes. It is claimed that it can be mastered in a few weeks by a person unacquainted with a Western language. My present concern, however, is with Chinese.

Tremendous developments are taking place in the Chinese language. It is expanding daily. The written ideographic script remains universal. " The day that the Chinese discard their written script," says Karlgren, " they will surrender the very foundations of their culture." I cannot prophesy whether with the increased incidence of Western ideas this event is bound eventually to supervene.

CHAPTER V

SAN MIN CHU I

On 15th May, 1928, the first National Educational Conference, called by the *Ta Hsüeh Yüan*,[1] opened in Nanking. The Conference lasted for two weeks and was attended by seventy-eight delegates, including the Commissioners of Education of different provinces, the Presidents of Government Universities, eighteen experts appointed by the *Ta Hsüeh Yüan*, and representatives of the Central Headquarters of the Kuomintang and the National Government. Many resolutions for the reform of education were passed, including one that henceforth the educational aims of the Government should be in accordance with the Three Principles of Dr. Sun Yat-sen. The resolution then went on to set out the intention in detail:—

(1) To promote Nationalism, education shall seek to instil into the minds of youth the national spirit, to keep alive the old cultural traditions, to raise the general level of moral integrity and physical vigour of the people, to spread scientific knowledge, and to cultivate æsthetic taste.

(2) To attain Democracy, education shall seek to teach such civic virtues as law-abidingness and loyalty, to train for organizing ability and spirit of service and co-operation, to disseminate political knowledge, and to inform the people of the true meaning of liberty and equality.

(3) To realize Social Justice, education shall seek to

[1] The organization of the *Ta Hsüeh Yüan* is explained in Chapter VI.

train for habits of labour and productive skill, to teach the application of science to everyday life, and to enlighten the people on the interdependence and harmony of economic interests of various classes.[1]

In 1929, the National Government officially announced the following as the educational objectives of the country :— (a) the realization of the Three Principles, (b) the satisfaction of the wants of the common people, (c) the improvement of the livelihood of the people, (d) the continuance of the separate existence of the Chinese race, (e) the achievement of national independence, (f) the universal extension of the rights of the people, (g) the promotion of the commonweal of the whole world. In primary education it was still considered important, (1) to improve the mind and to develop the body of the pupil, (2) to cultivate virtue, and (3) to teach the rudiments of knowledge and craftsmanship so that the pupil might be enabled to earn a living.

The " Three Principles " referred to is the collection of lectures delivered by Dr. Sun Yat-sen not long before his death and published as *San Min Chu I*. In 1918 he had published three volumes of his *Plans for National Reconstruction*, consisting of Psychological Reconstruction, National Reconstruction and Social Reconstruction, and his intention had been to complete the series with a final definitive work called " The Reconstruction of the State ". The work was to consist of eight parts—the Principle of Nationalism, the Principle of Democracy, the Principle of Livelihood, the Quintuple-Power Constitution, Local Government, Central Government, Foreign Policy, and National Defence. Most of his manuscripts were destroyed when Ch'ên Chiung-ming revolted in 1922 and Dr. Sun had to fly from Canton.[2] When, two years after, the Kuomin-

---

[1] *China Year Book*, 1931.
[2] Dr. Sun's preface to *San Min Chu I*, trans. F. W. Price.

tang was reorganized, Dr. Sun delivered a series of lectures in Chinese on the subjects that were to be contained in his final great work. These lectures were taken down in shorthand, corrected by Dr. Sun himself,[1] and published as the *San Min Chu I* or " Three Principles of the People " (三民主義).[2] In his will Dr. Sun enjoined on his comrades that they should follow the principles laid down in his works together with the " Manifesto " issued by the First National Convention of the Kuomintang.

The Kuomintang was faithful to its dead leader's wishes, and with the progress of nationalism these extemporaneous lectures were elevated into the Bible of the New China. In his preface to the first edition, Dr. Sun hoped that his comrades would take his book as a basis or as a stimulus, expand and correct it, supply omissions, improve the arrangement, and make it a perfect text for propaganda. But his disciples have chosen rather to follow the unaltered gospel as it was taken down from the prophet's lips and they have done nothing towards systematizing it or correcting it.

To give force to the resolutions of the First National Education Conference, a curriculum committee consisting of thirty-seven experts was appointed by the Ministry of Education in October of the same year to draft new curricula. After four plenary sessions and eighteen sub-committee meetings and with the co-operation of seventy outside specialists in education the work was completed, and, on 14th September, 1929, the new curricula were officially promulgated by the Ministry of Education.[3]

In the primary schools higher grade curriculum, of 1,530 minutes per week, 90 minutes per week were allotted to

[1] But see *The Chinese Recorder*, 1928, p. 47.
[2] Father Pascal d'Elia translates *San Min Chu I* as the " Triple Demism of Sun Yat-sen ".
[3] *China Year Book*, 1931.

the study of the " Three Principles ". The remainder of the time was given up to History, Geography, Hygiene, Nature Study, Arithmetic, Industrial Arts, " Form Arts ", Physical Education, and Music. But the 90 minutes by no means represents the time occupied with the " Three Principles " and connected political subjects. Since 1925 the textbooks issued with the approval of the Chinese Ministry of Education and otherwise, had already been systematically permeated with political lessons designed to cultivate political, especially anti-foreign, feeling. These textbooks continued to be used under the new curriculum, and in fact they anticipated the resolution of the 1928 conference in disseminating much of the doctrine of the " Three Principles ".

A casual examination of any of the many series of primary textbooks will show the arbitrary way in which the original subject matter has had the anti-foreign teaching introduced into it. For instance, a textbook on sociology published by the Commercial Press, and intended for children of about 11 years of age, has introduced into it a full page picture of the " massacre " at Shanghai on 30th May, 1925, in which British and Sikh police are shown as shooting down defenceless Chinese.

It had been my intention to include in this account an examination of Chinese textbooks. I had, in fact, collected much material to this end. But since then Mr. Cyrus H. Peake has covered the ground so thoroughly in his *Nationalism and Education in Modern China* that it would be redundant for me to attempt the same task. I have, however, included as an appendix an analysis of Chinese textbooks which I made at the request of the Royal Institute of International Affairs for its survey of the school textbooks of the entire world. This analysis is set out in the framework devised by the Institute to facilitate comparative study, and the books analysed are those selected by the agents of the Institute in China as being representative of those used in Chinese schools.

In 1931 the Sokikusha (Press Association) of Tokyo issued a handbook called *Anti-foreign Teachings in New Textbooks of China* (182 pages) giving a long series of extracts from Chinese textbooks, both in the original and in English. The selection of books is naturally not on the impartial principle of the Royal Institute of International Affairs, but the extracts, nevertheless, are all from existing books in use in Chinese schools. The preface to this handbook says :—

> "The present compilation is a rough English version of examples taken at random from typical paragraphs of a strong anti-foreign nature which are enormously abundant in the textbooks at present extensively used in the elementary schools of China. In many instances the paragraphs represent an exposition or a construction of facts so distorted as to put foreign nations and individuals in a light altogether unfair and undeserved. In other instances the compilers resort to an astute art of telling half-truths; that is, what they tell about foreigner's doing is quite true, but there is gross omission of the truth as to the real cause that necessitated foreign nations or individuals taking steps, which taken singly apart from the circumstances, do not fail to appear very unreasonable. Or again, incidents calculated to discredit foreigners are dwelt upon so constantly, and to such a degree as to obliterate foreigners' merits and to create a totally wrong impression. In some cases tendencious statements of the above character are not conspicuous to casual readers, yet an analogous effect is produced, chiefly by giving full play to the hyperbolical style or the subtle metaphorical style which is a characteristic of Chinese literature. Thus there are employed not only *suppressio veri* but *suggestio falsi.*"

Mr. Peake deplores the tendencies shown in Chinese textbooks and concludes his introduction by saying :—

> "It is easy to understand why and how the Chinese have imitated the West in this respect, but to understand in a case does not mean to condone. Indeed, it seems but the more

tragic that this should have come about when one reflects upon the richness of certain universal conceptions set forth by Chinese philosophers through the centuries. The author cherishes the belief that the present period, marked by the expression of an intolerant form of nationalism, may pass and that the Chinese will yet contribute constructively to the realization of the World Community."

The compilers of the textbooks have faithfully interpreted the resolutions of the educational conferences, and at the same time have gone a good deal further than Sun Yat-sen in the expression of intransigent nationalism. The result is that in 1935 eleven million school children are imbibing the doctrine of the " Three Principles " every day of their lives, not only from the special *San Min Chu I* textbooks, but from the textbooks on geography, history, sociology, and even arithmetic.

Considering its enormous and increasing influence on the minds of a fourth of the human race, it is remarkable that the *San Min Chu I* has received such scant attention at the hands of foreign scholars and publicists. The books on Karl Marx and " Das Kapital " would fill a large library, yet in the course of a considerable search I have discovered only two or three foreign books which treat of the *San Min Chu I* at any length. There is, in particular, Professor Holcombe's *The Chinese Revolution* ; a phase in the regeneration of a world power, *The Triple Demism of Sun Yat-sen*, by Pascal M. d'Elia, in which the " Three Principles " are examined from the Catholic point of view, and a chapter in *China and England*, by Professor Soothill. Beyond this there is very little but references in articles in newspapers and other journals.[1]

Of the two above-mentioned books, *The Triple Demism of Sun Yat-sen* is a translation and expansion of the author's *Le Triple Demisme de Suen Wen*, published in 1929. It is

---

[1] I understand that there is a Dutch Summary.

an enormous work of 800 pages, and contains a mass of valuable matter. Nevertheless, as a criticism of the " Three Principles " from the point of view of the educationalist, it is almost without value. Its sole concern is to prove that the " Three Principles " are not irreconcilable with the teachings of the Catholic Church, and it does this at whatever cost.[1] Since the Catholic Church has condemned socialism, Sun Yat-sen's socialism is not socialism at all but " Demism ", a word coined by Father d'Elia. The Nanking government ordered 5,000 copies of the book for distribution, so it apparently fits in with Kuomintang orthodoxy.

Professor Holcombe's approach, on the other hand, is that of optimistic idealism and American democratic conviction. His book is written in a tone of quiet reasonableness and sympathy which must have been balm to Chinese eyes after the too numerous journalistic diatribes couched in terms of scorn. He is not concerned with the tenability or otherwise of individual parts of the text, but with the soundness of the general policy. Dr. Sun himself, he points out, had in his preface directed that his text should be corrected and amended, and " those who are duly forewarned should be sufficiently armed against the error of permitting the book's imperfections to blind them to its real significance ". " Economic fallacies concerning international trade and credit are too familiar among protectionist writers in all countries to attract special attention when adopted by a Chinese." Thus Sun Yat-sen's inconsistencies and errors are not mentioned in Professor Holcombe's book, and he concludes that the principles set out in Dr. Sun's works are fundamentally sound. But one cannot help feeling that the fact that the " Three Principles " are

[1] Mr. J. O. P. Bland in *China, the Pity of it*, London, 1932, p. 44, speaking of Father d'Elia's work, says " whenever it (*the San Min Chu I*) seems wholly irreconcilable with the Christian faith, its errors can be explained away ".

suggested by American models, plays quite a part in softening his approach. Also one feels that it would have been a friendly act on the part of such a great authority on political science to have pointed out to his friends in New China that their leader's text was in sore need of amendment, correction, deletion, systematizing, and rearrangement, if it is to be proof against criticism and to be a satisfactory text for political salons and for schools.

The business of examining the *San Min Chu I* obviously belongs to the political scientist and to the economist. I have addressed myself to a number of political scientists and economists of the highest standing, and of different political opinions, without eliciting anything except a general interest in the subject. I am therefore driven to undertake the task on my own account, for in a review of education in modern China a work which is the acknowledged fountain of educational principle cannot be passed over with a mere reference.

To venture to criticize the *San Min Chu I* at all is to incur the resentment of Nationalist China. The text is sacred, and must not be referred to except in terms of reverence and eulogy. Even the orthodox nationalist who dared to criticize would, like Bishop Colenso, be liable to excommunication. Moreover, since Dr. Sun has professed adherence to socialist and other advanced doctrine, it is difficult in criticism of his work to avoid giving the impression that one is inspired by hostility to socialism, communism, and the like. All I can do is to disclaim any feeling of this sort, in fact I claim in several essential respects to have strong affinities with these schools of thought.

The commentary I propose to offer is not intended to have political or economic authority but merely to be a consideration of the *San Min Chu I* in its character as the testament of Chinese education.

Those who wish to test the validity of my remarks are

SAN MIN CHU I

recommended to the translation by Mr. Frank W. Price, Shanghai, 1927, or to that given in *The Triple Demism of Sun Yat-sen,* and to any of the standard Chinese editions. The Chinese edition I have used is that published by the *Kwong Chau I Man T'ong Yan Mo Shu Kwun,* Canton (no date). For the convenience of those who have not time to do this, I give below a complete summary of the work with Dr. Sun's own phrases for key ideas bracketed in Chinese. A summary cannot be an entirely fair means of presentation, but an endeavour has been made to omit nothing that Dr. Sun considered essential for his argument. In point of fact the summary reads much more cogently than the full text, for in the former a mass of irrelevant digression is dispensed with, and the verbal illustration, sometimes (from a European point of view) failing in taste as well as in logic, is omitted.

I give to begin with, a summary of Sun Yat-sen's life in which an attempt is made to reconcile the sometimes conflicting accounts of Morse and MacNair and Father d'Elia.

LIFE OF SUN YAT-SEN

Kuomintang doctrine represents Dr. Sun Yat-sen as both the Marx and the Lenin of the Chinese Revolution, whereas up to his death at any rate he appears rather in the character of its Kerensky.

Dr. Sun was born on 12th November, 1866, in the Heungshan (Hsiangshan) district of Kwangtung province.[1] He attended the village school, and in 1877, at the age of eleven, he went to Honolulu where he remained five years and completed a high school course at the Protestant Episcopal School. Returning from Honolulu he spent a year at the Medical School at Canton and then entered

[1] *Far Eastern International Relations,* by H. B. Morse, and H. F. MacNair, New York, 1931, says 1867.

Queen's College, Hong Kong, passing thence to the Medical College where he graduated as licentiate in 1892.[1] He then practised for a while at Macao. China's defeat in the Sino-Japanese War of 1894 decided him in his course as a revolutionary, though he had joined the " Young China Party " (少年中國黨) in 1892. After sharing in an attempt at insurrection in 1895 he was forced into exile where he remained for many years. First of all he fled to Japan, then to America, pursued by the agents of the Manchus. In Amercia he read the Gettysburg oration which suggested the " Three Principles ". In October, 1896, he was kidnapped in the streets of London and held captive in the Chinese Legation. After ten days he was released on the intervention of Lord Salisbury, moved thereto by Dr. Sun Yat-sen's former medical instructor, Dr. (afterwards Sir James) Cantlie.

The upshot of the Boxer trouble in 1900 gave momentum to the cause of the Revolution. Many who had been inclined to the more peaceful methods of K'ang Yu-wei, the " Erasmus of the Reform Movement "[2] now transferred their faith to the insurgent party. At a conference of revolutionaries held in Tokyo in 1905 the T'ung Mêng Hui (同盟會) was formed. In October, 1911, the Revolution came. It was, by Western standards, more like a general strike than a revolution. Dr. Sun was in London[3] at the time, but he returned to China at once.

A revolutionary National Assembly in session at Nanking at the end of December, 1911, elected Dr. Sun " President of

---

[1] Biographical Sketch prefacing Mr. Price's *San Min Chu I*. Father d'Elia says, " Bachelor of Medicine and Surgery," p. 14, op. cit.
Speaking in 1912, he said, " I am afraid I have forgotten most of my medical work. I practised for about two years immediately after I was qualified, but have not done so since." Mr. A. H. Crook, in foreword to *The Teaching of Science to the Chinese*, by L. G. Morgan, Hong Kong, 1933.

[2] *Far Eastern International Relations*, by Morse and MacNair, p. 444 et seq.

[3] Morse and MacNair, but Soulié de Morant says Colorado.

the Provisional Government of the United Provinces of China ". It was agreed that he should soon retire in favour of Yüan Shih-k'ai,[1] for the Manchu Emperor had stipulated as a condition of his abdication that Yüan should become president[2] and should retain the provisional presidency until a permanent government could be organized. According to Father d'Elia, Dr. Sun was already tired of his responsibility. On 12th February, 1912, the Emperor Hsüan T'ung abdicated, and three days later Yüan was elected provisional president. But the apparent accord between the Sun and Yüan factions did not last long. Yüan's financial arrangements with the Five-Power Group acts caused a rupture and a second revolution was attempted in 1913 by Sun's Kuomintang (國民黨) which had succeeded the T'ung Mêng Hui, but it was crushed. Dr. Sun fled to Japan. His position now strengthened, Yüan Shih-k'ai purged the new parliament of its Kuomintang members. In January, 1914, he dissolved parliament altogether and established a dictatorship. Yüan's schemes for the re-establishment of the Empire in his own person ended abortively, and he died of acute chagrin in 1916. But the power of the Kuomintang was not sufficient for it to establish a government. Sun Yat-sen returned from exile to Canton, to be the leader of the malcontents, the " parliamentarians ", who had taken refuge there. On 10th September, 1917, a " military government " was proclaimed with Sun Yat-sen as generalissimo.

Even in Canton (and he never ruled the complete province) Dr. Sun's control was only intermittent. He was ousted from time to time by military groups. In 1918 he was a refugee in the French Concession at Shanghai. He returned

[1] *Far Eastern International Relations*, by Morse and MacNair, p. 556 et seq.
[2] Father Pascal d'Elia, op. cit., p. 24. R. F. Johnston, *Twilight in the Forbidden City*, London, 1934, p. 96.

to Canton again and managed to keep some sort of control from 1920 to 1922. In 1922 he was driven out by General Ch'en Chiung-ming. In February, 1923, he was restored. During his period of refuge in Shanghai he had come under Russian influence. Hence the new government of Canton worked in close co-operation with Russia. To keep himself in power Dr. Sun was compelled to employ large numbers of mercenaries from Yunnan, Kwangsi, and Hunan. This meant the imposition of crippling taxation on the merchants and people. The merchants raised a sort of army of their own for police purposes, but on 15th October, 1924, it was crushed by means of labour bands organized by the left wing of the Kuomintang with much brutality, bloodshed, and looting.

In spite of his alliance with Russia Dr. Sun was in communication with Tuan Ch'i-jui, the chief executive of the provisional government in Peking, and with Marshal Chang Tso-lin, who were both anti-Russian. In November, 1924, fearing for his personal safety, Dr. Sun again forsook Canton and went north to take part in the reorganization of the government. He was now a sick man, and on 12th March, 1925, he died of cancer in Peking.

Mr. Nathaniel Peffer, whose article I shall have occasion to refer to in a moment, says that in 1923 Dr. Sun was a disappointed, frustrated, and for all practical purposes repudiated leader. He was in a constant state of setting up provisional governments at Canton and flying in a hurry. Yet the lectures which he began to deliver in 1924 were later made into a book which has since become the Bible of Revolutionary China. I must endeavour to explain how this happening came about.

For six months or more before his death the close followers of Dr. Sun had been making preparations to elevate his memory when he died to a level with that of Lenin in Russia. One message to Moscow soon after his death read, " We the heirs of Sun Yat-sen, greet you, the heirs of Lenin."

There is no space here to do more than briefly outline the complex of events which led to the ascendency of the Kuomintang. Anti-foreign propaganda, the rise of the power of the labour unions, strikes, all played their part in consolidating the country under the leadership of the party whose platform had as a main plank the elimination of foreign control. The incidents on 30th May, 1925, in Shanghai, and of 23rd June of the same year in Canton brought this anti-foreign feeling to a fever point. The provisional government in the north, weakened by the jealousy of rival commanders, was, by reason of its geographical position, more subject to Japanese influence and therefore less and less acceptable to the daily increasing nationalism of the country. The Kuomintang was, in any case, the only party with a programme at all, though there was a conflict developing within it between the left and right wings. At the right moment the Kuomintang found its military leader in Chiang Kai-shek who was guided by a German military adviser. He was able to lead his army northward and succeed where the expeditions sent out by his old superior Sun Yat-sen had failed at the outset. He and his forces were assisted everywhere by the spread of nationalism and anti-foreignism. In the north the students, as elsewhere becoming politically more powerful every day prepared the way for the Kuomintang by their intensive propaganda, especially against the government's acceptance of the Taku Ultimatum delivered by the protocol powers in connection with the Kuominchun's interference with navigation on the Tientsin River. By June, 1928, the opposing forces were hopelessly divided amongst themselves and Peking capitulated to the forces owning allegiance to the Kuomintang.

Subsequent events have shown that the unification

174 PROBLEMS OF CHINESE EDUCATION

achieved by the great Kuomintang drive was largely illusory, in fact, to use the words of Bismarck in another connection, it had only " papered over the cracks ". But in one respect the establishment of the government at Nanking did result in a more lasting community of view, and that was in the matter of educational aims. The Ministry of Education has so far not succeeded in keeping financial control over all provincial schools, but its influence is certainly more widely extended than that of the government itself.

Summary of the " Three Principles "

1. *The Principle of Nationalism*

Lecture 1.—The " Principle of Nationalism " begins with defining " race " (民族) and " nation " (國家). The greatest force is common blood. Chinese belong to the yellow race because they belong to the blood stock of the yellow race. China is the only country where " race " and " nation " are the same. In other cases race or nationality has developed through natural forces, while the state has developed through force of arms (霸道). (The forces leading to the formation of a race are described and those leading to the formation of a state.) Concerning the law of survival of ancient and modern races, if we want to save China and preserve the Chinese race, we must certainly promote Nationalism. The Chinese people are of the Han or Chinese race with common blood (一 血), common language, common religion, and common customs—a single race (一 個 民 族). But the Chinese have no national spirit; they only know their family and clan groups (家 族, 宗 族). Thus China is only a loose sheet of sand. Our position is extremely perilous—if we do not promote nationalism and weld together our four hundred millions into a nation, we face a tragedy—the loss of our country and the destruction of our race.

Dr. Sun develops an argument conjuring up a "White Peril". At the present moment China has perhaps four hundred million people but the population has not increased since the time of Kien Long. The population of Europe and America on the other hand is increasing by leaps and bounds. The U.S.A. has increased 1,000 per cent in a century, England 300 per cent, Russia 400 per cent. A hundred years hence if their population increases and ours does not the more will subjugate the less and China will eventually be swallowed up.

Lecture 2.—The population ratio is not the only danger to China; a more immediate and pressing one is foreign political and economic domination and oppression (政治力, 經濟力, 之壓迫). During the past century China has suffered enormous territorial loss but the loss from economic encroachment though invisible, is even more severe. Through military victory the foreign Powers gained control of China's customs and used this control to sacrifice native industries to foreign ones. There has been in addition the invasion of foreign paper money, foreign bank exchange, foreign freight charges, concession profits, and speculation business.

Lecture 3.—For centuries China has lost her national spirit (民族的精神). The truth of this is shown in her subjection to alien races. The seeds of decay, too, were in China's ancient imperialism and theory of cosmopolitanism. Nowadays cosmopolitanism (世界主義) is developing in the West to camouflage imperialism. There is a danger of China being seduced by this. Nationalism must precede internationalism.

Lecture 4.—In the last century the white race has expanded enormously. Before the European war all the European nations had been poisoned by imperialism (受了帝國主義的毒). What is imperialism? It is the policy of aggression upon other countries by means of political force (政治力).

As all the peoples of Europe were imbued with this policy; wars were continually breaking out. The cause of war between England and Germany was first the rivalry for the control of the sea, and second the struggle of both nations for more territory. When America realized that England, of her own race, was in danger of being destroyed by Germany, an alien race, she threw in her lot with England to defend the existence of the Anglo-Saxons.[1] Moreover America tried with all her might to arouse all the neutral countries of the world to join in the war to defeat Germany. [President] Wilson enunciated the rights of " self determination of peoples " (民族自決). But after the war England, France, and Italy realized that freedom for nations conflicted too seriously with the interests of imperialism. The result was a peace treaty with most unjust terms; the weaker, smaller nations not only did not secure self-determination and freedom but found themselves under an oppression more terrible than before. One hopeful result (大希望) of the war was the Russian Revolution. The one hundred and fifty million Russians, when their revolution succeeded, parted from the other white races and condemned the white man's imperialism (反對帝國主義); now they are thinking of throwing in their lot with the weaker, smaller peoples of Asia in the struggle against the tyrannical races. We are the wronged races (受屈民族). The struggle is coming between the tyrant nations and the oppressed nations. The world is divided into two camps. The ancient imperialism of China was far more benevolent than modern imperialism. Nations paid tribute to ancient China through respect for her culture (仰慕中國的文化), not through force of arms. It is only on the material side (物質的文明) that European civilization is superior to China's.

[1] Elsewhere Dr. Sun says the U.S.A. is composed of Englishmen, Frenchmen, Germans, Italians, and Southern European peoples (Lecture 1, Nationalism).

Lecture 5.—To revive China's nationalism we must awaken the people to an understanding of China's position. We are the slaves (奴) of all nations. The destruction of the nation by political force may happen any day. China may be destroyed (滅) by political as well as by economic force, by military power or through diplomacy (外交). China must face the facts and build her new national sentiment on the foundation of existent family and clan loyalties (家族的觀念). If India can unite on a programme of non-co-operation, China should also be able to unite. Both positive (積極的) and negative (消極的) opposition must be offered to foreign aggression.

Lecture 6.—China's ancient greatness was due above all to her high moral standards (道德). We must recover and use the best in our past. The ancient morality—Loyalty (忠), Filial Devotion (孝), Kindness (仁), Love (愛), Faithfulness (信), Justice (義), Harmony (和), and Peace (平) must be preserved. The ancient Chinese had a profound political philosophy. The poor impression that a Chinese makes on the average foreigner is due to the Chinese lack of personal culture (修身). We must learn the strong points of the West, scientific knowledge and methods. Only the most advanced science should be brought to China, e.g. electric rather than steam power.

2. *The Principle of Democracy*

Lecture 1.—Any united and organized body of men is called a " people " (民). " Sovereignty " (權) is power and authority extended to the area of the State. When " people " and " sovereignty " are linked together we have the political power of the people (民權). The functions of sovereignty are protection (保) and subsistence (養). In order to exist mankind must have protection and sustenance. Protection means self-defence (自衛); sustenance means food-seeking (覓食).

But while man is maintaining his existence other animals are also trying to maintain theirs ; while man is defending himself, other animals are also defending themselves ; while man seeks food, other animals are also seeking food ; and so the protection and subsistence of man comes into conflict with the protection and subsistence of other animals, and struggle ensues. To keep alive in the midst of struggle man must fight, and so mankind has not ceased to fight since the beginning of life. There have been several periods in human history (Dr. Sun here gives a summary of early human history as derived from his study of geology and other sciences. He says *en passant* that in the study of all kinds of knowledge China has depended solely on books ; but foreign countries make use of actual investigation as well). The rise of the Chinese race is described and the lecture illustrates human history by miscellaneous references to foreign nations. The first period of government was the theocratic (神權), then came the autocratic (君權), now we have the democratic (民權). In summing up, the first period of human history was one of the struggle between man and beast in which man employed physical strength rather than any other kind of power ; in the second period man fought with Nature and called divine powers to his aid ; in the third period men came into conflict with men, states with states, races with races, and autocratic power was the chief weapon. We are now in the fourth period—the war within states, when the people are battling against their monarchs and kings. The issue now is between good and evil, between right and might (可以說是善人同惡人爭, 公理同強權爭), and as the power of the people is steadily increasing we may call this the age of the people's sovereignty —the age of democracy. The essential question is this : Is China to-day ripe for democracy ? If we ask history whether autocracy has really been a good thing for China or not we find that its effects have been about half advantageous and half disadvantageous. But if we base our argument on the intelligence and ability of the Chinese people we come to the conclusion that the sovereignty of the people would be far more suitable to us. Foreigners, because they look down upon the Chinese, express strong disapproval when we talk to them of democracy. But thousands of years ago the Chinese were discussing democracy. The democratic ideas appeared, it is true, only in theoretical discussions (言論) and did not develop into reality (事實). We Chinese must now follow world tendencies (潮流); nevertheless we must avoid false theories like Rousseau's (盧梭) "natural rights" (天賦的權利) of men. Facts must precede theory. In Chinese history there was a ceaseless struggle for imperial power: democracy is the only safeguard against this.

Lecture 2.—The watchword of the French Revolution was "Liberty (自由), Equality (平等), Fraternity (博愛)" just as the watchword of our Revolution is "People's Nationalism, People's Sovereignty, People's Livelihood". We may say that liberty, equality, and fraternity are based upon the people's sovereignty. As revolutionary ideas have spread through the East, the word "liberty" has come too. But the Chinese do not yet understand what liberty really is. Since the revolutionary element of the West has lately spread to China, the new students and many earnest scholars have risen up to proclaim liberty. These Chinese have not applied themselves to the study of democracy or liberty and have no real insight into their meaning. The "Three Principles" should be the basis of the Revolution, not "liberty". If one's liberty is incompatible with another's sphere of liberty, it is no longer liberty. In the West the people came to say, "Give me liberty or give me death" but the Chinese do not know "liberty" they only know about "getting rich" (發財). The fact is that personal liberty has been taken for granted in China like fresh air, so no one is concerned about it. The Western doctrine of liberty is out of place in China to-day and generally misapplied. The idea of liberty has been abused in schools and in the Kuomintang. The aim of the Chinese Revolution should be unity and freedom for the nation.

Lecture 3.—Equality (平等) is not a natural endowment. Artificial inequalities of rank etc. accentuate natural inequalities. Equality, too, is an artificial, not a natural, thing and the only equality we can create is equality in political status. Because of the nature of her civilization China does not need personal liberty and equality as Europeans did. The " Three Principles " in any case will give China liberty and equality. The theory of " equality " was proposed in Europe to counteract the theory of " divine right " (天賦之特權). The democracy advocated in the " Three Principles ", upon which the Kuomintang Party proposes to reconstruct China, is different from Western democracy. When we use Western history as material for study, we are not copying the West entirely or following its path. We will use our Principle of the People's Sovereignty and re-make China into a nation under complete popular rule, ahead of Europe and America. To realize this aim we must first study democracy till we understand it with perfect clearness.

Lecture 4.—A century of struggles brought but scanty results even in countries regarded as pioneers of democracy. (Democracy's rise in America is discussed at length ; then democracy in France.) In France people wanted full political rights without any limit or restriction, hence the " Reign of Terror ". In England the claims of democracy were met with concession (退讓的手段); in Germany the government sought to deprive the working classes of grievances that would lead to extended claims. (The Constitution of Switzerland and of other European countries and the U.S.A. are referred to.) Parliamentary representative government (代議政體) has not solved the question of democracy. China must find her own solution, and if she does she will find herself above Europe and America.

Lecture 5.—The Chinese people's ideas of political democracy have all come in from the West, but mere imitation is not enough. The defeat of the Boxers in 1900 showed China the superiority of Western material civilization (物質文化) and was followed by excessive faith in the imitation of the West. But Western material sciences have progressed far beyond the Western science of Government (政治社會科學). The foundation of the government of a nation must be built up on the rights of the people, but the administration of government must be entrusted to experts (專門家). We must not look upon these experts as stately and grand presidents and ministers, but simply as our chauffeurs, as guards at the gate, as cooks, physicians, carpenters, or tailors.

Lecture 6.—(This lecture is a lesson on the machinery of government and its control and Sun Yat-sen propounds his solution.) The people can exercise the controlling powers of suffrage (選舉權), right of recall (罷免權), right of referendum (複決權), and right of initiative (創制權). The five administrative powers of the government are the legislative (立法權), judicial (司法權), executive (行政權), examination (考試權), and censorship (監察權).

3. *The Principle of Livelihood*

Lecture 1.—The principle of Livelihood (民生) is Socialism (社會主義), it is communism (共產主義), it is collectivism (大同主義). The problem of Livelihood is now rising like a tide in every country. Yet it is comparatively new, with a history of not much over a century. The cause of it is the rapid progress of material civilization all over the world, the great development of industry, and the sudden increase in the productive power of the human race. Following the introduction of machinery great numbers of men suddenly lost their occupations and were unable to get work or obtain food. This is why a social problem has come into existence, and the result has been an effort to relieve mankind of suffering. But, although Socialism has been a growing force for several decades, Western nations have not yet found a solution for the questions involved in it, and a severe dispute is still raging over them. Marx was the first Socialist to rely on the facts. He founded scientific socialism. The scientific socialists (科學派) were henceforth to be distinguished from the utopian socialists (烏託邦派). Marx considered class war essential to social progress—the driving force of social progress. Since the interests of capitalists and workers inevitably conflict and cannot be reconciled, he said, struggle ensues and this struggle within society is what makes for progress. But the actual facts do not bear this out. The development of socialized distribution has done much to destroy the monopoly of the tradesman. Heavier taxes upon the incomes of the capitalists increase the wealth of the state and enable it to take over the means of transportation and communication, to improve the education and health of the workers, and increase the productiveness of society. When the capitalists improve the living conditions of the workers, and the workers can produce more for the capitalists, this means both increased production and higher wages. Here surely is a reconciliation of the interests of capitalists and workers (資本家和工人的利益相調和) rather than a conflict between them. Society then progresses through the adjustment of major economic interests rather than through the clash of interests. Class war (階級戰爭) is a disease of social progress. Marx was a social pathologist (社會病理家), not a social physiologist (社會生理家). His three essential conditions for increasing surplus value have been flatly contradicted by history. Marx said that the capitalist would have to lengthen the working day; the Ford factories have shortened the working day. Marx said that the capitalist would have to reduce wages; the Ford factories have raised wages. Marx said that the capitalist would have to raise the price of the manufactured product; the Ford factories have reduced the price of their product. And how can the workers in the factories say that surplus value (盈餘價值) is created entirely by their own labour? Surplus value is the fruit not only of labour within the factories, but of many useful and powerful factors in society working directly or indirectly towards the production or consumption of the manufactured commodities. We can no longer say that material issues are the central forces in history. We must let the political, social, and economic movements be focussed upon the problem of livelihood.

Lecture 2.—The different countries of the world, because of varying conditions and varying degrees of capitalistic developments, must necessarily follow different methods in dealing with the livelihood problem. We cannot imitate the West, because even the Socialist parties in the West are not agreed on the right course of action. The Kuomintang some time ago settled on its party platform that the principle of Livelihood was to be carried out by the equalization of landownership (平均地權) and by the regulation of capital. If we follow those two methods we can solve the livelihood problem in China. In the West both revolutionary and evolutionary socialism are opposed by the capitalists. The tyranny of the capitalists has reached the limit and people are finding conditions unbearable. Modern capitalists use all sorts of tyrannical methods to protect their own private gains. The socialist parties in the West may in the future be forced by circumstances to adopt Marxian methods for the solution of economic problems—who can tell? The class struggle is only possible in highly industrialized states. The difference between the principle of Livelihood and Communism is one of method rather than of principle. In China there is no extremely wealthy class. In the West the problem of land value, and unearned increment is a serious one; it is beginning to be so in China. If we want to solve the land question we must do it now; if we wait until industry and commerce are fully developed we shall have no way of solving it. Our policy is that the government shall buy back the land, if necessary, according to the amount of land tax and the price of the land. The landowners will be allowed to assess the value of their own land and will pay taxes accordingly, but as a safeguard against under-valuation the government will have the right to buy back the land at the amount of the owner's assessment. After the land values have been fixed a law will be passed that all increase in land values (所漲高的地價) shall revert to the community. In China to equalize landownership is practically to regulate capital. But, whereas other countries are rich, China is poor; other countries have a surplus of production whilst China is not producing enough. So China must not only regulate private capital, she must also develop state capital (國家資本). We must develop waterways and open up mines. We must promote industry. To begin with, we shall certainly have to borrow foreign capital (借用外資) to develop our communication and transportation facilities, and foreign brains and experience (外國有學問經驗的人材) to manage them. We are not hostile to Marxism; it is merely that our own problem must be met according to our own circumstances.

Lecture 3.—The food problem is the chief problem of livelihood. China has not an adequate food supply and has to import food. Yet if China, twenty times the size of France, were to follow France's example, develop intensive agriculture and multiply productions, we should certainly produce twenty times as much food as France. In China every year tens of thousands die of starvation. Because of foreign economic domination China is losing rights and privileges worth $1,200,000,000 every year. Part of this loss is in food. China has not sufficient food for her own people, yet sends it to other countries. For instance, a billion eggs a year are sent to the U.S.A. In China, although there are no big landlords, nine out of ten farmers do not own their own fields. The landlord gets 60 per cent of the production whilst the farmer gets 40 per cent. We must study methods of liberating the peasants. We must also improve agriculture by the use of machinery and fertilizers, rotation of crops (換 種), eradication of pests, by manufacturing, transportation, and the prevention of natural disasters. Afforestation must be practised. In the U.S.A. and Europe the food problem is not yet solved because profit is still the only aim. We in applying the Principle of Livelihood must make the aim of food production not profit but the provision of sustenance for all the people. We must store up the surplus production every year and if after three years the food supply is still short we must stop shipment of food abroad. But in applying the principle of Livelihood for the solution of China's food problem we can only make gradual changes in the capitalistic system; we must not try to overthrow it immediately.

Lecture 4.—The second problem of livelihood is clothing. With the development of civilization the problem has come. The sources of clothing material are silk, hemp, cotton, and wool. China's ancient silk industry is now outstripped by the silk industry in other countries. Improvements in sericulture are needed in China. China's silk is chiefly for export. She produces a large quantity of cotton, but it is exported and bought back as cotton goods. Because we do not know how to stimulate our industries and to recover our rights we have to wear foreign cloth and send a great deal of our money away to foreigners. The reason that native mills fail is because of the political domination over China by foreigners through the unequal treaties signed by the Manchus. The foreigners control the Maritime Customs. When foreign countries send cotton yarn into our ports the Maritime Customs collect a 5 per cent duty; when the yarn circulates in the interior of China $2\frac{1}{2}$ per cent more of *likin* (octroi duty) is charged. Altogether foreign yarn or textiles pay only $7\frac{1}{2}$ per cent duty. In the Manchu dynasty the Chinese people foolishly listened to foreigners and imposed a 5 per cent duty upon native manufactured cloth But when Chinese cloth goes into the interior it does not, like foreign cloth, pay only one *likin* tax, it has to pay a *likin* tax at every station. The Customs and *likin* are not free to raise the tax on foreign cloth, but they can do it at will on Chinese cloth.[1] In order to compete with other countries we must imitate the tariff policy of the Western nations. China must champion native goods and boycott foreign goods. We must first abolish the unequal treaties and secure control of the Maritime Customs. The clothing needed by our people must protect the body, it must be good-looking, and it must be convenient and not hinder work. The State should establish clothing factories on a large scale. Everyone should be provided with clothing. All the people must fulfil the obligations of citizenship to the State or disqualify themselves as citizens. Those who disqualify themselves as citizens disqualify themselves as masters of the State. Lazy vagabonds are parasites upon

[1] The *likin*, however, is a purely native " squeeze ".

the State and upon the people. The Government should force them by law to work and try to convert them into honourable labourers, worthy to share in the rights and privileges of the nation. When loafers are eliminated then there will be enough to eat and wear, homes will be comfortable, and the people will be content and the problems of livelihood will be solved.

(Here the lectures end off suddenly)

A SOURCE OF DR. SUN'S INSPIRATION

Anyone who has read even this summary with attention cannot fail to perceive a wide divergence in attitude and tone between the early and late lectures. The Lecture 4 of Nationalism the author is telling us of the coming struggle between right and wrong, between oppressing and oppressed races, with the capitalist-imperialist nations using military and economic force to subjugate the rest of the world, whereas in Lecture 1 of Livelihood we are told that China, to develop her industries, will certainly have to borrow foreign capital. We are not to be surprised by this, for the Marxian class-war is now discredited, " The capitalists on one hand benefit by greater production, the workers on the other hand get higher wages. There is a reconciliation of the interests of capital and labour; not a conflict between them." (Lecture 1, Livelihood.)

By reason of a curious discovery this and other phenomena can now be explained, and it is better to dispel the mystery before we go any further. The facts are set out by Mr. Nathaniel Peffer in an article in the July, 1932, number of the American periodical *Current History*.

It appears that in 1920 a book called *The Social Interpretation of History* was published in America. The author was Dr. Maurice William, a New York dentist. In 1924 this book was read by Dr. Sun Yat-sen and it converted him from Communism. This was shortly after he had made what was tantamount to an alliance with Soviet Russia. Dr. William has recently published another book *Sun Yat-sen versus Communism* in which he claims the credit for Sun Yat-sen's conversion. Mr. Peffer says " the claim is corroborated from Sun Yat-sen's own writings and is indisputable ".

Dr. Sun refers more than once to two distinguished Occidental scholars, Marx and Williams. What Dr. Sun was doing was to confuse Maurice William with Mr. Whiting Williams, an American welfare worker and lecturer on labour problems.

In Dr. William's *Sun Yat-sen versus Communism* the proof of the influence of *The Social Interpretation of History* on Dr. Sun is set out in detail.

> " In some way—how, no one knows," says Mr. Peffer,[1] " the volume had come into Dr. Sun's hands. The lectures on the principle of livelihood not only reflected it, but were based on it. In *Sun Yat-sen versus Communism* are a hundred pages of quotations in parallel columns from Sun's lectures, and *The Social Interpretation of History*. On crucial points Sun quotes William almost verbatim. In other words, the most important part of what was to become the testament of revolutionary China was the product of an unknown dentist on the other side of the world, who had written an obscure book having no reference to China, who never had been in China, knew nothing about China, and was probably not in the least interested in it. History abounds in irrational and fantastic episodes inseparably interwoven into great events, but no episode is more fantastic than this."

In 1923, just when he had again been evicted from Canton, Dr. Sun met Joffe the Soviet diplomatic repre-

---

[1] Father Pascal d'Elia, op. cit., p. 423, says that the work was privately printed and circulated by the author the world over, with a request for criticism.

sentative in Shanghai. Joffe converted him to communism.[1] In consequence, when Dr. Sun returned once more to Canton, Borodin, as Soviet representative, was there to advise him.

" Fired by initial successes, as he always was when entering on a new campaign, Dr. Sun again planned grandiosely. Early in 1924, he began to give his lectures which later were embodied in the volume called *San Min Chu I*, or the Three Principles of the People. . . . In the first two sections, covered in lectures delivered from January to April, 1924, Dr. Sun enunciated what could at least have been construed as Russian doctrine. Dr. Sun appeared to be converted, and with the prestige thus conferred, communism began to make rapid strides within the Kuomintang and more particularly among the student classes."

Yet three months later when lectures on livelihood were given, Dr. Sun announced a complete reversal. He repudiated the class struggle and the dictatorship of the proletariat. " In other words," says Mr. Peffer, " he threw Russia overboard."

Mr. Peffer concludes,

" He (Dr. Sun) starts with an enunciation of his philosophy and programme on which, as leader of New China, he will build the regenerated society. Personally he has thought them out. Then midway in the course of their pronouncement he reads one book, a book by a man of whom he knows so little that he takes him to be somebody else, and then he turns a complete about-face and simply adopts a new philosophy and programme. He had already done the same thing. In fact, only three years before he was espousing Communism and inveighing against the capitalistic, imperialistic powers he had

[1] The only reply to Mr. Peffer I have seen is an article by Mr. Li Yinglun, in *The China Critic*, for 6th December, 1934. Mr. Li characterizes Mr. Peffer's statement that Dr. Sun was converted to communism by Joffe as " not only a falsehood, but also a malicious slander ". He says that Dr. Sun was never a communist, which may be true, but unfortunately Mr. Li relies for his proof on showing that the *Min Shêng* lectures (People's Livelihood) contain no communism, which is exactly Mr. Peffer's own argument.

published a book outlining a plan for the economic reconstruction of China with foreign loans. Thus, in four short years, he had travelled between two opposite extremes in social philosophy. . . ."

It is clear that Dr. Sun had no very stable political or economic convictions, and that he was easily swayed by new influences. But to prove him guilty of inconsistency, or even of plagiarism, is not by that fact alone to discredit his doctrines. At the same time we are entitled to expect from a work offered as the *vade mecum* of the Chinese people, and used to replace the whole body of classical thought, that it should be of one piece, and that the facts stated in it should survive the strictest tests. Do we find this to be the case with the *San Min Chu I* ? [1]

Commentary on the "Three Principles"

"Nationalism," says Dr. Sun Yat-sen, "is that precious possession by which humanity maintains its existence," but the history of nationalism in Europe in the last hundred years does not encourage the belief that the cultivation of the intense individuality of peoples, with the resultant wards and economic rivalries, is likely to promote the cause of cosmopolitanism except by way of reaction. But Dr. Sun is only advocating that China should copy the rest of the world, and this he is entitled to do.

Dr. Sun fears not only the disintegrating force of modern imperialistic oppression, but also the force of "natural selection" that may cause a people to disappear. "It is natural" he says, "for one to desire the perpetuation of one's race." Though he condemns the oppression of foreigners as unethical, he, we suspect, is concerned more

---

[1] "To refute its false history, its pathetic economics, its bitterness of spirit, is almost hopeless." Professor Soothill, *China and England*, Oxford, 1928, p. 216.

with China's lack of the means to oppress, even if she were willing, than with any absolute evaluation of conduct. He laments the loss of Burma and Thibet, though China's possession of them was pure imperialism.

Dr. Sun's alarm at the increase of the white races is quite without foundation. He is apparently unaware of the declining birthrate in the West, and the tendency to a static and even diminishing population.

The claim that surrounding nations paid tribute to China through respect for her culture and not through force of arms [1] is not borne out by the history of the innumerable wars undertaken by the Chinese to bring neighbouring barbarians into subjection. These wars, too, have usually been conducted with barbarity and wholesale slaughter. At the same time it must be allowed that many of these barbarians paid spontaneous respect to the only civilized state known to them. But China's position is not unique in this. The tribute paid to Rome or, in modern times, to the Western civilization by the thousands of Asiatics, Chinese included, who elect to be educated wholly under European or American systems rather than to partake of their own native culture, is a tribute of a similar nature, even if due discount must be made for economic motives. This, too, has come about when the native and the foreign cultures are competing for favour and not, as in the case of China's outer barbarians, when the Middle Kingdom had no peer or competitor. Dr. Sun's assertion that imperialism (and by this he means British imperialism in particular) has succeeded by the force of arms alone is one that would not be supported even by the most anti-imperialist of historians.

In the last lecture on the " Principle of Nationalism " Dr. Sun touches on the fundamental problem, the synthesis

[1] " This is a statement that will not bear the least examination, and which he utterly contradicts later," Soothill, op. cit., p. 187.

of cultures. The best of China's past must be recovered and combined with those methods of the West that tend to power. (Here it is necessary to repeat that the ancient Chinese qualities of loyalty, filial devotion, kindness, love, faithfulness, justice, harmony, and peace, do not correspond closely to their Western equivalents.) Dr. Sun complains that in abolishing the old régime the New China wished to abolish with it the old morality. Loyalty, for instance, was now more needed than ever it was. The question remains: can China naturalize Western civilization and at the same time retain the essentials of her own? Many think that she can. But even if she can, it is first of all necessary for her to comprehend what the main ideas of Western civilization are. So far she has failed to do so in any large measure, and her language and her past history obstruct her path.

The first lecture of the " Principle of Democracy " contains a general review of human history based on the evolutionary theory. Dr. Sun accepts " Huxley's Cockpit " as the state of nature and he concedes that up to the present the history of mankind has been the history of strife. Yet he concludes, rather surprisingly, that the struggle for existence has in this age given place to a final great battle in which the forces are dualistically arranged. " The issue," he says, " is now between good and evil, between might and right— between the people and the oppressors of the people." Reference to other parts of his text show that the " oppressors of the people " are capitalists and imperialists. This is, as I have said above, difficult to reconcile with his chapter on Livelihood when he favours the gradual reconciliation between capital and labour. There is a marked divergence between his acceptance of an evolutionary development of society and this pitched battle between good and evil, might and right. The reason for this muddle of ideas is that Sun Yat-sen is describing social progress from an evolutionary point of view, and at the same time trying to be Marxian.

Dr. Sun infers the readiness of the Chinese for democracy from the intelligence and ability of the people. At the same time intelligence and ability are notoriously incomplete without education, and 80 per cent of the Chinese people are illiterate. Dr. Sun says that the Chinese were discussing democracy ages ago, but the fact remains that it is only yesterday that they gave up their age-old system of loose autocracy, patriarchal and clan government in favour of a system that has yet to prove itself in the West. What is more the Chinese have so far not understood the meaning of the idea. Dr. Sun himself says so—" The Chinese have not studied democracy and liberty and have no real insight into their meaning." But self-determination is an accepted principle in modern political ethics and we must leave democracy as a domestic question which the Chinese alone can decide.

Dr. Sun is sympathetic to the Bolsheviks but in the end disagrees with Marx. His Socialism, at least in the final lectures, is of the moderate labour variety. In China, he says, the co-operation of capital and the aid of foreign experts must first of all be sought. The shortage of food and clothing in China, on the other hand, he attributes to foreign economic domination, and he advocates direct and indirect methods, including the boycott of foreign goods, to regain control of the customs. (Since Dr. Sun wrote this the Chinese have succeeded in regaining customs autonomy). In Lecture 2 he says that the foreign control of the customs and the huge surplus realized revealed the rottenness of Chinese officials. It has been a great dilemma for recent Chinese ministers to decide how China could devise terms which would retain Chinese economic sovereignty and yet offer enough security to attract foreign investment.

The extra-territorial system whereby foreign nationals

in China were subject to their own law arouses the indignation of Dr. Sun. But the " Three Principles " gives none of the historical data that would enable the reader to judge how far this system was the inevitable outcome of conditions and was necessitated by the imperfections of the Chinese judicial system. Indeed, the reader who relies on the " Three Principles " solely for his information would conclude that the imposition of extra-territoriality was an inexplicable act of tyranny, whereas a study of books such as Morse's *International Relations* [1] would conduce to a more philosophical attitude.

But even if Dr. Sun's arguments are not judicial he advances a legitimate claim of the Chinese to intact sovereignty. Since 1925 great strides have been made in removing the grievances of which the " Three Principles " has been able to make capital. For instance, by a series of agreements, the last of which came into effect on 18th November, 1930, China has achieved complete tariff autonomy. She is now at liberty to protect her own industries. This advance has been made possible by the comparative unification of China under the Nationalist government in 1926. Again in the matter of rendition of concessions by the British, great progress has been made. The Hankow, Amoy, Chiukiang, and Weiheiwei concessions have already been returned. Moreover the day of unilateral treaties has disappeared. Since 1929 three powers that had no previous treaties with China have concluded treaties with her on a basis of absolute equality and reciprocity—which, of course, can be said to prove that Dr. Sun's contentions in this respect were right.

Dr. Sun has discussed and analysed the actions of the Powers at inordinate length. The impression that one cannot fail to receive from the " Three Principles " is that the troubles of modern China are to be ascribed to the foreigner.

[1] See section on " The Opium War ".

The natural inference is, then, that prior to the invasion of the foreigner the unequal treaties and the foreign control of the customs China suffered from none of the ills that she does to-day. Yet in 1840 China was as subject to famine and to pestilence as she was in 1924, the standard of living of her millions was as low if not lower than it was then. Writers on China have uniformly ascribed the hardship of the great agrarian population to several main factors :— (a) the ignorance of scientific agriculture which prevents the peasant getting the most out of his land, (b) the lack of organization for distributing surplus to famine areas, (c) the terrible floods due to the deforestation, neglect of dykes, and want of drainage, (d) the Confucian morality which encourages the breeding of children without any regard to their future sustenance.

According to Dr. Sun the way of the natural force that formed the race is the " way of right ". " The way of might " is the evil way. A race may, by dint of procreation, cover the face of the earth—this is the way of nature, the right way— but an organized people that uses its initiative, its enterprise, its superior organizing ability, its will to achieve, and its military force, to contest the claims of numbers or priority to monopolize the earth, is following the way of evil. " Armed force (武力) is *pa-tao*, the way of might, the group formed by way of might is the ' nation '."

It is difficult to follow Dr. Sun's arguments about " race " and " nation " because he often uses the latter word (國家) for " state ". A race is a blood-group, a nation is a culture-group, and a state is a law-group. What is formed by *pa-tao* in Dr. Sun's text is apparently the law-group. China is a blood-group, and perhaps a culture-group, but to survive she must be also a law-group. To achieve this it may be necessary to follow *pa-tao*—a thing of evil except as the tool of Chinese nationalism.

The main reason for Dr. Sun's muddle of theory is this.

He is in the first place a nationalist, and argues that China has evolved naturally and organically, unlike the Western nations which have grown by armed force. At the same time he is, in the " Nationalism " period at least, under the influence of the materialistic interpretation of history which makes the battle to come (i.e. the class war) an essential condition of progress. In point of fact Marxism quarrels with Nationalism and the idea of the National State. The array of forces for the class war cuts across the divisions necessary for Dr. Sun's nationalism. The coming battle he visualizes is not really a class war ; it is a fight between the good and bad nations. Even his nationalism is of a low order since it relies mainly on anti-foreignism.

The " Three Principles " gives ample evidence that its author is not unaware of the existence of defects in his countrymen, but in accounting for the present state of China he refuses to allot a fair share of the responsibility to the Chinese and attributes too much to " foreign oppression "—in itself too strong a word. For instance he says, " The Chinese psychology now is one of distrust towards the native banks and of extreme confidence in the foreign banks. Some people are even willing to store up foreign paper currency in preference to Chinese silver currency." An observer of the facts might conclude that this state of affairs was due, in part at least, to the efficiency of the organization of these foreign banks and to the way they honour their obligations, and Dr. Sun's case would be greatly strengthened by admitting this. But Dr. Sun says, " And when we study the reason of it we find it is because the people are poisoned by the foreign economic domination." This and no more. Dr. Sun refuses also to be impressed by the efficiency and integrity of the foreign customs officers : he is interested only to describe " foreign oppression ".

Another complaint is that foreigners in the concessions

take advantage of a weak point, avarice, in the Chinese character and provide daily opportunities for speculation, and every few years some big opportunity which arouses the gambling passion of the Chinese to fever heat. " On each occasion of speculation over the mark or the rubber market Chinese have lost tens of millions." The word " oppression " is evidently susceptible of unexpected extensions.

Nearly everything that Dr. Sun advocates for the salvation of China is to come from the West—the science, the agriculture, the scientific sericulture, the electric power systems, the political theory, and the experts who shall teach China how to prosper; but Dr. Sun is never betrayed into any expression that may be interpreted as appreciation, or even qualified approval, of Western peoples or their civilization. He refers to the *English* proverb " might is right " as if this were a piece of popular wisdom in England and, more than that, the avowed principle of English policy. Europeans belong to the race of oppressors: they are of an inferior civilization. Every act, every voluntary gift, of the Powers, whether it be the foregoing of the Boxer Indemnity or of a concession is seen as meanness or hypocrisy. " After the European War," he says, " the Powers thought to return some of the more recent cessions and give back Tsingtau and just lately Weihaiwei. But these," he adds depreciatingly, " are only small places."

The description that Dr. Sun gives of the Chinese people is flattering to their self-esteem. " One generation has succeeded another and we are still the world's most cultured people." Speaking to the British Consul-General at Canton during the War, he said, " Our civilization has already advanced two thousand years beyond yours." " All European people are more hairy than the Chinese and the reason is that they have not developed so far in the process of evolution as the Chinese."[1]

[1] See Schneider, *History of Civilization*, for the opposite view.

Repeated reference is made to the loss from economic oppression; the expressions "robbed from us" and "stolen from us" are invariably used. As we have seen, a principle grievance is the foreign control of the customs. An interesting, but inaccurate, account of how this control came about is to be found in Lecture 2 of the "Principle of Nationalism". "The Manchu government calculated that it would take a long time to pay the war indemnity in full, but the British, after securing control of the customs for this purpose, surprised the Manchus by paying themselves all the indemnity in a few years; the Manchu government then realized how rotten their own officials had been." The officials are referred to as "Manchu" but in point of fact they were Chinese, and, as far as one can estimate, not widely different from their successors of the present day.

The animus of the "Three Principles" is against the British. Dr. Sun is determined that they shall be belittled even at the expense of praising the Germans. "When the European War raged most fiercely," he says, "Germany was victorious. Whatever opposing forces met—infantry, artillery, or cavalry on land, torpedo destroyers, submarines, and all kinds of battleships on the sea, airships or aeroplanes in the sky—Germany always triumphed. From first to last Germany never lost a battle." She was defeated by the blockade alone. Elsewhere he says that the United States won the War. Sun Yat-sen, we may remember, was the son of a mission-convert, obtained his medical training and general education from the British in Hong Kong, in 1896 he was rescued from certain death by the British when his compatriots imprisoned him in the Chinese Legation in London, he twice escaped from Canton in a British gun-boat, and hid several times in the foreign settlements at Shanghai.

China, Dr. Sun claims, exceeds all other nations in virtue. She is beyond the West in filial piety, kindness, and love.

"Since our foreign intercourse began," he says, "some people have thought that the Chinese ideal of kindness and love was inferior to the foreigner's because foreigners in China, by establishing schools and carrying on hospitals to teach and relieve the Chinese, have been practising kindness and love. In the practical expression of the fine qualities of kindness and love it seems as though China were far behind other countries, and the *reason is that the Chinese have been less active in performance.*" The italicized sentence is an achievement in naïvety.

Dr. Sun continues his comparison of Chinese and Western virtue. " In my estimation the quality of faithfulness is practised better by Chinese than by foreigners." He illustrates this by saying that the Chinese do not use written contracts ; " the word of a Chinese is his bond." This may be true, but it does not explain why Chinese would not trust Chinese banks or why the customs officials " squeezed " the customs receipts. The Chinese, too, are superior to others in their sense of justice. A study of the administration of the Ch'ing Penal Code suggests that though *Kung tao* and justice stand for one another in translation they have no blood relationship.[1] " China's ancient virtues of Loyalty, Filial Devotion, Kindness, Love, Faithfulness and such," Dr. Sun concludes, " are in their very nature superior to foreign virtues ". Nevertheless he cannot bring himself to claim loyalty as an outstanding virtue of Modern China, a quality in which she is too plainly deficient.

Sun Yat-sen exalts his race beyond all others, but behind his claims for the excellence of his race one cannot fail to detect an acute lack of confidence, a misgiving of his people and himself. He castigates the Chinese for faults that are inconsistent with the high claim he makes for their virtue, though he is careful to explain that the shortcomings are only superficial and not radical. In fact, he denies to the Chinese

[1] Wade's collection of dispatches illustrates this point.

as an individual what he claims for the race as an aggregate. " The Chinese are still the most cultured people in the world but foreigners can see that we are much lacking in personal culture. Every word and act of a Chinese," says Dr. Sun, " shows absence of refinement ; one contact with Chinese people is enough to reveal this. The ordinary foreigner's impression of the Chinese is that they are uneducated and quite uncivilized ". He then proceeds to give a piece of constructive advice—namely that a Chinese when in public should not break wind audibly and then say " Pardon " (Lecture 6, Nationalism). " Chinese do not understand patriotism (忠). For the nation there has never been an example of the supreme spirit of sacrifice." " A Chinese weakness is avarice." " The Chinese do not know ' liberty ' but only about ' getting rich '."

It is clear that whilst Dr. Sun is extolling his country as if her ancient virtues still lived in her and her people, he is really thinking of these virtues as residing in her past. " If we want to restore our race's standing, besides uniting all into a great national body, we must first recover our ancient morality " (Lecture 1, Nationalism).

The " Three Principles of the People " is the product of the miscellaneous reading of Dr. Sun in Western literature, and to a lesser extent in Chinese literature. The facts of Dr. Sun's personal history must be borne in mind in reading his work. He himself was never able to realize the ambitions he had set out in the " Three Principles ". He was in intermittent control of a small part of South China, often very little more than the city of Canton, where he had restricted liberty to apply his theories. During this period Canton was bled white by taxation, largely to support mercenaries and an expeditionary force with the name of " Punish the North Army ". When he was driven out of Canton on one occasion, in a spirit of pique he bombarded his own city from his gunboats. It was only after his death in 1925 that a movement founded on the "Three Principles" obtained any measure of success.

It is quite possible that somewhere in the *San Min Chu I* are to be found stated the principles on which China must rely for the solution of her difficulties. It seems likely that if China is to retain her sovereignty she must become economically autonomous. She will have to improve and extend her banking system and, in the end, provide credits for her industry and agriculture on her own account. It is also to be conceded as a legitimate aspiration that she should aim at complete territorial sovereignty. It may even be that to achieve unity and a solid front against the remainder of the world she must cultivate nationalism with the aid of anti-foreign propaganda and teaching in the schools. It may be that she must conscript her subjects and turn herself into a strong military nation in order to avoid foreign encroachment, though one may be forgiven for questioning whether the moves made so far to this end have resulted in an increase of strength or improved her position amongst the nations. It may be that China should adopt Communism and throw in her lot with Russia against the oppressing nations of the world. On the other hand her right course of action may be to create a middle-class capitalistic and nationalistic oligarchy under the leadership of the Kuomintang. But Dr. Sun has not in his "Three Principles" bequeathed to his country a closely reasoned argument and a definite programme for it to follow out. After his death there was a split between the left and the right wings of the Kuomintang followed by the victory of the right and the purging of the party, by drastic and even brutal action, of its communistic elements. Thereafter, under Chiang Kai-shek, the Kuomintang advanced to victory. But Communism is by no means dead in China. On the contrary it has control of large areas of the country and its guerilla armies are well organized and disciplined. The struggle between Communism and nationalist capitalism is one of the main sources of misery in modern China.

Criticism of the " Three Principles " is not to be construed as support for the die-hard section of foreign opinion, which ridicules not only the extravagant ideology and the insincere proposals of nationalism, but also every genuine attempt of the Chinese to improve their methods of government and to put their house in order. This attitude is partly responsible for the ultra-sensitive condition of modern China and its refusal to believe that criticism can be anything but hostile in intention.

If China decides that nationalism is the path to progress, there can be no valid objection from outside; if she considers democracy feasible, she cannot be prevented from adopting it; if she thinks she can ensure the livelihood of her people by the measures Dr. Sun outlines, she is entitled to make the experiment. But, considered as the foundation of the education of a race, the book has grave deficiencies. Above all it gives no guidance to the Chinese whereby they may discover the source of their own weakness and correct it.

It is regrettable that Sun Yat-sen compiled his lectures when he was a sick man and when he was embittered by the intrigues against him and by the action of the Powers in depriving his government of a share of the Customs surplus. We catch no sight of the man who earlier in life had so impressed Sir James Cantlie and other Europeans. The tone of the lectures is unworthy of the revolutionary who for more than thirty years had followed his object relentlessly, who had not been deterred by the ever-present possibility of assassination, and who had proved his disinterestedness beyond doubt by his refusal to make use of unequalled opportunities to acquire a private fortune. The lectures bear everywhere the marks of the failing power of a man suffering from an incurable disease.

Inconsistencies and errors of fact are as frequent as pips

in a pomegranate. The Chinese are of the pure bloodstock of the yellow race (Nat. Lect. 1). The Americans are more heterogeneous than any other race, consisting of English, French, Germans, Italians, and peoples of Southern Europe (Nat. Lect. 1), yet (Nat. Lect. 4) America entered the Great War " merely out of racial considerations " because she was of the Anglo-Saxon Race and did not want to see the Anglo-Saxon Race destroyed. The reason for the two versions is that in the first case Dr. Sun wishes to show that the Americans are not " a single pure race " like the Chinese; and in the second case he wishes to show what a strong thing race can be. In ten different places the population of China is given as 400,000,000, in five other places as 310,000,000 or less; at other times, and sometimes on nearly the same page, it is given as both, " according as to whether it must be proved that China is the greatest in the world, or that she is the innocent victim of foreign exploitation " (Father d'Elia, op. cit., p. 556). At the Revolution of 1776 America had thirteen states, each with 200,000 inhabitants, total 3,000,000 (Dem. Lect. 4); at the Revolution a third of the population left to colonize Canada yet there were still 3,000,000 left. The story of the origin of the foreign control of the Maritime Customs (Nat. Lect. 2) is not accurate. During the occupation of Shanghai by the T'ai P'ing the customs ceased to function, and at the request of the Chinese themselves, foreigners were appointed to take control of them. This was in 1854. Science does not support the notion that the Chinese are further removed from the apes than other peoples because they are without beards, or because they are vegetarians (P. L. Lect. 4), and although the inhabitants of India are being exterminated by Imperialism (Nat. Lect. 4) the present population of India, after two hundred years of Imperialism, is 350,000,000, the highest in its history. Pottinger did not go to Nanking to negotiate with the T'ai P'ing, as is stated in Democracy, Lecture 1.

Great Britain is not composed of three islands (Nat. Lect. 4, Dem. Lect. 4, and P. L. Lect. 3). We are told on many occasions that Chinese antedates European civilization by several thousands of years, yet the cradle of human civilization is the Nile and Mesopotamia (Dem. Lect. 1). If both these statements are true then civilization must have travelled a path unknown to historians and pre-historians.

Some of the above inaccuracies (and there are dozens more [1]) are due to carelessness or hurried writing, others are due to a piecemeal and obsolete education, but most are due to a lack of a sense of logic. None of them need any special refutation but it is interesting to note the present state of opinion as to the identity of the Chinese race :—

> "The modern Chinese people is an amalgamation of many elements originally different from one another ... In colour, in stature, above all in cephalic indices, there is an enormous range in China ... about 43 per cent are brachy-cephalic, about 42 per cent mesocephalic, and about 42 per cent dolicho-cephalic. Even these classes are distinctly sub-divided into dolicho-leptorrhinic and dolicho-platyrrhinic. There is also a low-headed type, and, in the South, a trace of a dwarf element.... Prehistory points to a race already mixed in the basin of the Yellow River...." [2]

Dr. Legendre argues that the Chinese are the mixture of Aryan and Negroid.[3]

Accuracy in fact is not indispensable in a political declaration. The "Social Contract" of Rousseau was not less of revolutionary influence because its historical basis was

---

[1] e.g. "Lecture XVII (People's Livelihood) opens by saying that 'China under foreign economic pressure is deprived of some 1,200,000,000 dollars to 1,500,000,000 dollars every year'. This is really an increase during the lectures of a mere 300,000,000 dollars. Of this sum, 300,000,000 dollars is represented by 'foreign cotton cloth'. How happy the merchants, Chinese and foreign, if it were true! The total amount is actually less than 75,000,000 dollars, or less than a quarter." Soothill, op. cit., p. 213.

[2] *China Year Book*, 1934.

[3] *Modern Chinese Civilization*.

fictitious. The important thing is to offer as true something which the audience addressed wishes to believe. What the declaration must do is to sound a clear, distinct, blood-rousing clarion call; it must denounce recognized abuses in the dignified but uncompromising terms of an ultimatum; it must offer a remedy with unswerving conviction. The " Three Principles " is no clarion call—its tone is that of complaint; and the abuses, though mainly arising from the foreigner, seem to alter their identity in different places in the book; its remedy is, first, out-and-out Socialism, and then, alliance with foreign capital.

Sun Yat-sen enjoined upon his followers to " expand and correct " his text. His followers have shown a blameworthy neglect. As we know, the Kuomintang has long ago purged itself of communist influences; its battle to-day is a death struggle with communist forces. Yet the text of the *San Min Chu I* in all the published editions remains as its author or his secretaries left it; the " Three Principles " incorporated in the modern textbooks is, as the Appendix A clearly shows, drawn from the original text. The errors have been left as they were.

It is quite possible that Nationalism, Democracy, and Livelihood will yet prove the keys to China's salvation. The Kuomintang and its successors, though they do not dare to tamper with the inspired words of their Leader, are yet perhaps in practice amending and sytematizing his doctrine. If so, the Bible of Modern China will have earned this lofty designation. But just as modern theologians lament the discrepancy between the Synoptical and the Fourth Gospels, so will Chinese of a latter day regret that the statistical, historical, ethical, economic, political, and other errors in the imperfect text of the *San Min Chu I* were not early corrected by the intellectuals of the nationalist movement.

The great disadvantage of the *San Min Chu I* as the foundation of education in China is that it is a textbook as well as a credo. Its errors of fact, its unscientific and uncritical attitude, find their way into the curriculum and make it muddy. Friends of the Chinese must assuredly recommend to them that, even if the *San Min Chu I* is considered an adequate substitute for the Four Books of the Five Canons, it should be rendered by the innumerable experts whose services are available to the National Government, a connected, consistent, homogeneous, and accurate guide for the generation now at school.

Chapter VI

THE PRESENT PERIOD

The year 1928 opened with the entire educational system threatened with collapse. The main cause was the lack of funds due to the unceasing demands of the military authorities. Salaries were months in arrears and grants were not forthcoming. Mission schools were closed owing to the pressure of nationalist requirements. Students made extravagant demands to elect and dismiss their teachers, to decide the school hours, to fix the fees.

Educational policy was directed by an extreme nationalism. The mandates of the Kuomintang were to be followed in every particular. The Ministry of Education and the Provincial Governments, in the midst of the chaos, continued to legislate for the conduct of schools and the qualifications of teachers, though their detailed regulations were in no great measure obeyed. Schools, too, were to be registered.

With the removal of the National Government to Nanking there was established a new University of the Republic of China or *Ta Hsüeh Yüan* (大學院) with Dr. Ts'ai Yüan-p'ei as its Chancellor. This University was more than a university, for it took the place of the Ministry of Education. It had five departments—Secretariat, Higher Education, General Education, Social Education, and Cultural Enterprises. Its name was sometimes translated " Ministry of Education and Research ". The idea was in origin a French one. The new system did not last long, for at the end of 1928, on the promulgation of the Organic Law of the National Government, the *Ta Hsüeh Yüan* was changed back into the Ministry of Education (教育部). Dr. Monlin Chiang became the Minister.

The *Ta Hsüeh Yüan* provided for a commission of education in each province, except in Kiangsi, Chekiang, and Peking (now Peiping) which had a university district system. This university district system was similar to the *Ta Hsüeh Yüan* system, for the President of the University was also in charge of the education of the province. In addition he was the head of an academic body with the functions of a university proper. In every district (*hsien*) of both the " commission " and " university " provinces there were several school districts with an officer in charge. The system functioned according to the ability of the provincial governors, the school organization of Shansi being the most efficient.

The university district system, after two years trial, was abandoned in June, 1929, as a failure.

The present organization of the Ministry of Education is practically as it became in 1928 on the cessation of the *Ta Hsüeh Yüan*, though in 1932 the Central Political Council adopted a resolution providing for the revision of the rules of the Ministry. The administration is divided into departments of Higher Education, Elementary and Secondary Education, Social Education, and the Committee on Textbooks. The conferring of degrees is a function of the first-named department, and overseas education comes within the care of the Department of Elementary and Secondary Education. The Department of Social Education is concerned with the development of adult and civic education, including the teaching of *San Min Chu I* and Tang Principles, vocational training in continuation schools, and multifarious activities such as the provision of libraries and parks and popular literature for the masses. The Committee on Textbooks, with the Bureau of Publications has charge of editing and translating educational books, texts and works of

THE PRESENT PERIOD

reference, and the standardization of technical and scientific terms. It also examines textbooks compiled by publishing firms.

It is difficult to exaggerate the importance, actual and potential, of the last-named bodies. Under the Empire the Hanlin Academy had undertaken the work of writing and compiling books, though on a much smaller scale, but on the disappearance of that body at the end of the Ch'ing Dynasty, the work had been left to a " handful of traders and charlatans ".

In each province there is a Department of Education. At the head of this there is a commissioner, assisted by three or four heads of divisions and four to six inspectors. In each *hsien* there is a Bureau of Education with a director who is appointed by the provincial Department of Education. The *hsien* is subdivided into several school districts each of which has an education officer and sometimes an assistant. The organization, however, is said to be loose and inefficient and the authorities are not vested with sufficient power to deal with local situations. Shansi, as before, is in advance of the other provinces.

The academic functions of the *Ta Hsüeh Yüan* were, on the reorganization in 1928, transferred to the *Chung Yang Yen Chiu Yüan*, Academia Sinica, or National Academy. The founder and head was Dr. Ts'ai Yüan-pei, and his Secretary-General at the present time is Dr. V. K. Ting,[1] the geologist and publicist. The research activities of the Academy include astronomy, meteorology, geology, physics, chemistry, engineering, psychology, history and philology, and social sciences, and it maintains a museum of natural history.

Such is the bare outline of the Chinese educational organization. On paper it is imposing, but the political and economic circumstances of the last few years have meant that

[1] Dr. Ting died in January, 1936.

at times the machinery creaked stridently and at moments slowed down almost to a standstill. At the end of 1931 the educational anarchy and the student problem had reached such a pitch that a special Education Committee was instituted with a membership of various Ministers, the Garrison Commander at Nanking, and the Chief of Metropolitan Police, and presided over by the veteran Ts'ai Yüan-p'ei. However, the committee did not function satisfactorily, and, with the subsidence of student agitation and the reorganization of the National Government at the end of 1931, the Committee ceased to be.[1]

Primary School Curriculum

On 14th September, 1929, the standard curriculum for primary schools was promulgated. It was as follows (the numbers refer to minutes per week spent in the classroom excluding preparation) [2]:—

Subject.	Lower Grade. 1st and 2nd Year.	Intermediate. 3rd and 4th Year.	Higher. 5th and 6th Year.
San Min Chu I	30	60	90
Kuo Yü (including conversation, reading, composition, penmanship)	330	360	390
Social Studies, history, geography, hygiene	90	120	150
Nature Study	90	120	150
Arithmetic	120	150	180
Industrial Arts	150	180	210
Form Arts	60	90	90
Physical Education	150	150	180
Music	120	90	90
Total Minutes per Week	1,140	1,320	1,530

In May, 1932, the Ministry of Education drafted a programme for moral training in primary schools, laying particular stress on the practice of self-denial, and the cultivation of a strong personality.

[1] The *China Year Book*, Peake, op. cit., and the *Official Gazette of the Ministry of Education*.
[2] *China Year Book*, 1934, p. 315.

THE PRESENT PERIOD

CHINESE INEFFECTIVENESS

Chapter III contained a warning. It was there said that the documentary material for the study of Chinese Education was very great indeed, but unless the proper allowances were made for the curious Chinese tolerance of a very large discrepancy between programme and performance, the person studying these documents would receive a false impression. In reading over the summary of Chinese educational organization which appears above I realize the necessity of bringing home this warning in a more effective way. This, I think, can very well be done by giving some account of the schemes for universal education.

In 1920 it was proposed to set up a scheme of universal instruction of four years primary schooling all over China within the following eight years. The scheme was scheduled to come into operation as follows [1] :—

1921—provincial capitals and open ports.
1922—country seats and centres.
1923—towns with over 500 families.
1924—towns with over 300 families.
1925-6—towns with over 200 families.
1927—villages with over 100 families.
1928—villages with below 100 families.

Now, what was it that the Chinese proposed to do? The League of Nations' experts,[2] referring to the year 1931, say that the number of pupils in all schools in relation to that of children from 6-15 years of age in the U.S.A. is over 120, in England, Prussia, Czechoslovakia, about 90-100, in Poland and Bulgaria about 70, in Russia about 40, in China about 10 only. Even in 1931, after the above scheme was scheduled to have been completed, the League experts,

---

[1] *The Reorganization of Education in China*, by the League of Nations' Mission of Educational Experts, Paris, 1932, p. 85.
[2] Ibid., p. 77.

basing their opinion on official figures, estimated that China would have to augment the number of its pupils at least five to ten times to bring her anywhere near the countries "which take a lead in education", i.e. that have among other things established compulsory education. The number of children in Chinese primary schools in 1920 was under six million. In a space of eight years it was planned to bring this number to not less than forty-five or fifty million, whereas the actual figure for 1928 was rather over eight million.

China, at the time when the scheme was promulgated, was in no settled condition. The amount of money likely to be available for education was very small. In 1931, it was estimated as 15 Mexican cents per head of population, and in 1920 it was, if anything, smaller. It was not surprising, then, that by the end of 1928 not a twentieth of the programme had been translated into fact.

"In 1930," say the educational experts of the League,[1] "As this project had not been realized, a new project for universal instruction on a four-year basis was introduced. It was to apply to all China and twenty years was allowed for its realization. The first five years were to be devoted mainly to the establishment of normal schools, and fifteen years being allowed for the development and spread of the four years primary instruction scheme. *During the period that has to elapse before the ratification of this project, no essential action has been taken with a view to its realization.*"

I have supplied the italics.

The experts continue :—

"Doubtless a great hindrance to the execution of both these projects has been such incalculable factors as political disturbances and armed struggles in the country and misfortunes like flood or famine. Nevertheless, in the very initiation of these projects certain drawbacks are perceptible and grave doubts may be entertained as to their chances of realization."

[1] Op. cit., p. 85.

It may be thought that an over-ambitious programme is no great disadvantage, because even if it is not realized much will have been accomplished in the attempt to carry it into effect. Those who favour this argument may have in mind the Russian Five Year Plan. But there is a great difference between a Russian Five Year Plan and a Chinese Compulsory Education Scheme. The former is devised with relation to Russia's capacity; the latter scarcely takes China's capacity into consideration at all. The result is that a Russian Five Year Plan is considered all along as a practical programme, whereas no serious attempt is made to carry out a Chinese Compulsory Education Scheme. Whatever has been accomplished in primary education has been quite apart from these schemes.

We must always bear in mind that paper schemes, reports, and the like, mean very much less in China than they do elsewhere in the world. I have often noticed that even the most inefficient schools have posted up on their notice boards the most elaborate timetables and graphs analysing the supposed activities of the pupils. A year or so ago I was connected with a joint examination of certain Chinese schools conducted by a public body. There were numerous officials, committees, and sub-committees, but the effectiveness of the examination may be gathered from the following fact. To test the candidate's knowledge of English they were not asked to compose an essay, or even a single sentence, or even to do a piece of translation; they had merely to fill in a word that was left blank in an English sentence, e.g., "The boy was going ... the road." The standard of the Chinese papers was higher, but not very much. Yet the examination was voted a great success, and no sign of any misgiving could be discerned amongst those responsible for holding it.

This serious defect lies deep in the Chinese character. The dispatches of the mandarins in the eighteenth and nineteenth centuries reveal a strange belief in the magic of words. When a disaster takes place we always hear of the Provincial Governor reporting that he has given strict instructions to the Intendant of Circuit to take action, the Intendant of Circuit reports that he has given instructions to the District Magistrate, the District Magistrate reports that he has given instructions to the village headman and local gentry. But we rarely hear of anyone taking direct action to relieve the effects of the disaster or to prevent its recurrence. The attitude of the mandarin and of the modern administrator and committee member can be compared to that of Sheridan when he signed an I.O.U.—" Thank God that is off my mind ! "

COMMENTS IN THE CHINESE PRESS

I have insisted that the Chinese at large are indifferent to any discrepancy between programme and performance, and for that reason programmes are devised with the wildest optimism, and in the few lucid intervals when their authors see how little relation they have with the facts there are moments of abject pessimism. But it is true at the same time that there are many Chinese who see the position clearly all the time, and their note of warning sounds in the Press and on the platform.[1]

In giving the gist of native opinion, it is important to exclude mere propaganda devised to encourage and urge on the country to greater effort, and to exhibit instead the critical views of those who wish to profit by past errors and discover the road to improvement. This, however, is not a task of great difficulty.

A leader writer in the *Ta Kung Pao* (Tientsin) of 27th March, 1934, puts his finger on the most vital point of all :—

[1] Sir Herbert Goffe's valuable *Summaries of Leading Articles in the Chinese Press*, published fortnightly by the Royal Institute of International Affairs, are quoted from in this section.

" We have pointed out that in education there are always two things to be considered; what is to be taught and how it is to be taught; and the ideals to be arrived at are of infinitely greater importance than the method of inculcating them. In the past we have made the mistake of thinking that the best paid more attention to the art of teaching. Now we must reverse our ideas . . ."

The article goes on to say that unless the objective of their education is fixed by the Chinese themselves, it will fail.

The *Hsin Wên Pao* (Shanghai) of 27th and 29th December, 1933, stresses the lopsided nature of Chinese education. Education in China to-day is for the few. In Russia, at the end of her first Five Year Plan, 92 per cent of the population were able to read. In China the most crying need is for teachers, especially for primary schools. But teaching does not attract as a profession; it is badly paid, and pay is often in arrears.

The *Tung Kung Pao* of Tientsin, of 9th October, 1934, takes the nation seriously to task :—

" The great defect with us Chinese—young as well as old—is that we are decadent, decrepit; we talk a lot, yet allow ourselves to be fooled and refuse to face facts; we commit the same fault over and over again without setting ourselves to correct it; our hearts do not flutter and our blood does not circulate . . ."

In Chinese newspapers there are dozens of articles in the same strain.

A typically critical view is taken of primary education in China in a leading article in the *I Shih Pao* (Tientsin) of 21st June, 1934. It is commenting on the recently published Ministry of Education statistics regarding primary education for the year 1930 :—

" Chinese children are surely amongst the unfortunate ones of the world ! In 1930, the attendance at the primary schools throughout the country was just under eleven millions, equal to twenty-three per thousand of the population ; and even if we put it at 10 per cent, that should be a hundred children in the primary schools for every thousand of the population. That there are only twenty-three means that out of every hundred persons at least seventy-eight are unacquainted with Chinese characters, and know nothing of China outside their own villages and nothing of Chinese history beyond what they pick up in their homes. China has a population of four hundred millions, but only eleven million budding citizens. The education of each child in the primary schools costs eight dollars odd a year—a somewhat niggardly expenditure ; but a teacher has on an average only nineteen in his class—and this can only be considered an extravagance. If twenty children were added to each class it would not be too much, and twice the number of scholars could be accommodated without incurring any extra expense. In these straitened times this is a point worth considering.

"Hopei province is included in the above figures for primary education ; and it may afford Hopeiites some satisfaction to learn that in the years 1929–30 the attendance in the primary schools increased by two hundred thousand and the expenditure on primary schools increased by two million—of course not provincial money. But the expenditure cannot be considered as lavish, as each child only cost six dollars eighty cents; neither can it be looked on as economical, for a teacher only has an average of fifteen in his class. This Province is, therefore, the worst offender in these respects. This is due to various causes—such as fluctuation of prices, local organizations, village distribution, etc. ; but whatever they may be it is to be hoped that the newly-arrived commissioner of education will take steps to effect some improvement.

"In 1930 China spent some thirty-six million dollars on the higher education of fifty thousand students, and only eighty-six millions on the primary education of eleven million children. This works out at eight hundred dollars for each university student and eight dollars for each child in the primary schools. The cost of educating citizens is only twice the cost of higher education ; but the amount spent on a university student is a hundred times as much as that on a child in the primary schools. In no country in the world is there so great a discrepancy between the amounts spent on higher and primary education; and it shows the predilection for the former and the reluctance to spend money on the latter—a failing common to the public as well as to the Government. There are reasons for this; one is that returned Boxer indemnities are devoted exclusively to higher education; another is that a university brings fame and influence to a province which stimulates emulation in other provinces, whereas primary schools add nothing to a province's prestige. Hopei is also an offender in this respect."

We can see from the extracts from the Chinese vernacular Press that there are a number of Chinese quite alive to the situation, but the surest commentary of all comes, as we might expect, from Dr. Hu Shih. Dr. Hu Shih made a speech at the Yen Ching University on 9th October, 1934, which was published as a leading article by the *Ta Kung Pao* of 14th October. This is a small part of Sir Herbert Goffe's summary of the article :—

> " At this time we may well ask ourselves what we have done in the past twenty-three years, and what achievements we have to our credit worth commemorating. It is easy to be pessimistic and depressed, if we just feel that not one of our aims has been achieved, that culturally we have nothing to offer the world, and that we have been unable to prevent invasion of our territory by a powerful neighbour; and many people are wondering why we have these annual commemorations. But we who refuse to be downhearted feel it our duty to present to the country an honest statement of our gains and losses during this period, with due regard to the short space of time we have had at our disposal.
>
> " The worst pessimists to-day are those who were most optimistic in the early days of the Republic. They did not realize what it was they were hoping for. They dreamt of a state that was independent, and on a footing of equality with other countries, a state that was both prosperous and powerful; and they imagined that they were going to get all this in a very short space of time. They foolishly expected a miracle,

and now that there has been no miracle they have fallen from the heights of optimism to the lowest depths of pessimism.

"This pessimism is due to a lack of 'historical perspective'. Thanks to this they have underrated the difficulties with which we were confronted; they have not realized how badly equipped we were to meet those difficulties; they have not grasped the fact that we were late in entering on our task; they have not considered how short a space of time twenty-three years is; and finally, they have failed to recognize that even in this short space of time we have some definite achievements to our credit.

"If people had any historical perspective at all they would realize that in these twenty odd years, without any miracle, we have made such progress as should fill us with confidence in ourselves. Progress is all relative, and, in order to judge whether we have progressed or not, present conditions must be compared with those of past days.

"Last week Mr. Wang Shih Chieh, the Minister of Education, in a broadcast speech, told us that now we had four times as many primary schools, ten times as many middle schools, and a hundred times as many universities and technical schools, as in the first year of the Republic. The disproportion in the rate of increase in the three classes of educational establishments needs to be corrected; but these figures show what astounding progress has been made in these twenty-three years, a period, moreover, when the country was wracked by poverty and unrest.

"But our progress has not been limited to the numerical increases recorded by Mr. Wang; other improvements have been made that are not revealed in statistics. Twenty-five years ago when I was in a middle school at Shanghai, trigonometry, the calculus, advanced algebra, were all taught in such schools by Japanese. At the Government normal schools in the principal provincial capitals, science and technology, even painting and handicrafts, were taught by Japanese; teachers for foreign literature, as well as geography and history, were drawn from the Y.M.C.A. or St. John's College. I remember that at my school foreign history was taught from Pailey's World History, an American book dating from before the nineteenth century. It began by saying that God created

THE PRESENT PERIOD

the world in seven days, and went on to speak of the Flood; at the end there were a few paragraphs on China with a picture of Confucius in a cap with a red tassel and wearing a pigtail! This is what schools were like five and twenty years ago. Now, in our hundred and eleven universities and colleges, the staffs, with few exceptions, are entirely Chinese, and the value of the work done by the students is generally recognized in the universities of the world. This is some progress in twenty-five years.

"Twenty-five years ago the books in use in primary schools were written in the classic script and had to be expounded—literally translated—character by character and sentence by sentence. After 1917, Pai Hua (vernacular) came into use, and since 1921 the 'national speech' has been in general use in primary and middle schools. This saving of drudgery and expenditure of brain-power to millions of children must surely be accounted as progress.

"It is a historic fact that in 1911 we had not a single centre of scientific research. Now we have research centres for every kind of work, and they are all doing work that is worth while. And these have all been set up during a period of financial stress and widespread unrest . . ."

Dr. Hu Shih goes on to describe the improvements in transportation, and the greatest achievement of all—the emancipation of women. He concludes :—

"Despite many objectionable features, in many respects definite progress has been made. After all, a revolution is a revolution, and is bound to produce some pernicious influences; at the same time it can get rid of many systems and influences that ought to be got rid of. For many of the objectionable features the upheavals subsequent to the revolution are responsible, and for this reason I subscribe to the slogan 'the revolution is not yet accomplished'. But in all fairness we cannot but admit that much of the progress we have made is the work of forces liberated by the 1911 revolution. A right understanding of the result of our efforts of the last twenty years should dissipate any pessimism and stimulate us to make further progress. Facts tell us that we are not yet in a position to resist a powerful adversary or rebuild the state. But this should not depress us; it should renew our confidence in ourselves and encourage us to aim at still greater achievements in the next decade or two. The philosophers of olden times maintained that 'the scholar may not be without breadth of mind and vigorous endurance; the burden is heavy and the way is long'. Pessimism and depression will never help us to shoulder this heavy burden over such a long road..."

But Dr. Hu Shih is not universally popular in China. Only the other day his arrest was demanded as a subversive agent. He is taking an encouraging view here, but his condemnation of existing systems at other times is too thorough-going for his countrymen.

The League of Nations' Educational Mission to China

Reference has already been made to the report of the experts sent to China by the League of Nations to examine and advise upon the working of the educational system, and it is now time to consider this report in greater detail.

At the May, 1931, session of the League, the Chinese Government asked the technical organizations of the League to send a mission to China to assist in the development of the Chinese educational system, and facilitate intercourse between the centres of intellectual activity in China and abroad. This course was approved. The experts chosen for the purpose were Professor Carl H. Becker, of the University of Berlin, former Prussian Minister of Public Education, Professor M. Falski, Director of Primary Education of the Polish Ministry of Public Education, Professor P. Langevin of the Collège de France, and Professor R. H. Tawney of the London School of Economics and Political Science.

The mission reached China on 30th September, 1931, and remained there about three months. They visited some of the principal centres of education in the central and northern provinces, and one of their number went to Canton. "At

Nanking," their report reads, "we began a systematic study of the documentation placed at our disposal by the Government, and we had several interviews and exhaustive discussions with the Minister."

In the introduction to their report the experts say that the ideas and judgments set forth in the report were not based exclusively on their own personal obervations, but, to a very great extent, on the views expressed by Chinese experts. The figures reproduced are based exclusively on official data.

It is clear then, quite apart from the shortness of their stay, that the League experts had very largely to rely on evidence which their experience of the Chinese did not place them in a good position to sift. It is therefore not strange that the facts they relied upon were not invariably above suspicion. For instance, the most important conclusion of the mission, and one in which they are supported by native educationalists, was that "there was great danger of creating a carefully educated social élite not closely connected with the general needs, which may become transformed into an unproductive clique enclosed within the narrow bonds of its own interests". This danger, indeed, is sufficiently apparent from the official statistics which show a great overloading in favour of higher education, but the persons who supplied the mission with facts were determined that this conclusion should be reinforced by the study of all the tendencies in modern Chinese education. Thus we find the statement concerning the early Christian missions that "they occupied themselves with establishing unrelated schools, designed not so much for the people as for privileged individuals. The missions," the report says further, " directed their chief attention towards the establishment of secondary and higher schools. Not many primary schools were established, and, moreover, as appears from the reports, it was the children belonging to the higher and middle classes who were instructed in them. The effect was rather to create a social élite, a governing intelligentsia class."[1]

Against this we have the statement of Dr. Kuo Ping-wên (see p. 50) that the schools of the early missions were " confined to the children of the humbler classes ". " The few who acquired a Western education therein," he says, " had little prospect of employment in the government." The thousands of children who in half a century attended the mission schools because their parents could not afford to send them to the ordinary schools, who were in many cases bribed by free food and clothing to attend, and whose chances of obtaining a government post were of the poorest, would have been startled to hear themselves described as " social élite " and " governing intelligentsia ". As regards the present day, missionary education is top-heavy, but not more so than the official education. The truth is that the missionaries are convenient scapegoats, but are in no sense the real culprits.

But the mission has to a great extent realized its limitations, and has confined its recommendations to matters which come within its competence. The result is that it has put forward a large number of valuable suggestions on administrative points, and the report can be recommended as the best existing description of the Chinese educational system, *qua pedagogic system*, at work. But it does not deal with what I conceive to be the root problems in anything but a general way, and to see the report in perspective it should be read in conjunction with Mr. Peake's *Nationalism and Education in Modern China* and the present work. The language problem, in particular, which is behind everything, is dismissed in two short pages, and even then the mission's remarks suggest that it does not clearly understand the nature of the problem.

[1] p. 20 of the mission's report.

THE PRESENT PERIOD

The mission is unanimous in its report. Recognizing the progress that has been made, it nevertheless observes the danger that the schools and institutions are developing rather as independent organisms modelled on the forms and ideology of private education instead of being included in an organized system of public education related to immediate social problems. The danger, it says, is related to the insufficient strength of public spirit in China in general and to factors concerning the organization of education as such.

> "Above all, Chinese educational tradition plays an important rôle, chiefly through schools established by separate families or groups of families for the needs of their own children, not passing, as regards organization and spirit, beyond the narrow bounds of interest and private financial considerations."

The mission finds the needs of the masses not sufficiently stressed. Many expensive universities have been founded, but no initiative has been taken with a view to the wholesale organizing of public education.

The conclusions of the mission in this respect are expressed with more force than in the report, by the British member in a book of his own [1] :—

> "Chinese education, with all its virtues, has some resemblance to a pyramid standing on its point. The schools and colleges giving practical education in agricultural or industrial technology, though some of them are important, are few relatively to the needs of the country. The number of primary schools is uncertain; but there were stated in 1931 to be under 9,000,000 in modern primary schools, out of a total population of something near 400,000,000.
>
> "The result is that the universities appear sometimes as to to be suspended in the air, that intelligence, which ought to be employed in the spreading of a way to a better existence among the mass of the population is wasted in a demoralizing scramble for openings into careers which are already overcrowded, and

[1] *Land and Labour in China*, by R. H. Tawney.

that practical life, which in China overwhelmingly means the life of the countryside, is deprived of the stimulus it might derive from the influence of education."

The second danger noted by the mission is that the foreign institutions introduced, especially American, are not subjected to the internal modifications necessary to permit of the realization of the potentialities of the great traditions which are specifically Chinese. There is too often purely formal imitation of foreign civilizations. European and American ideas spring from conditions that are peculiar to Europe and America. China should seek to modernize her own natural and historical individuality. In fact, the experts seem to think that she should use the recipe of the *intelligentsia* of the National University of Peking (see Chapter III).

The mission goes on to speak of the " alarming consequences of the excessive use of the American model in Chinese education ". The cultural conditions of Europe are more suitable for adaptation to Chinese requirements.

The use of manuals in foreign languages for instruction in secondary schools, the mission says, should be altogether proscribed. All science taught in a foreign language remains foreign to the mind of the child. Any ideas to be deeply assimilated by a child must be imparted in its own language, by means of symbols around which all his anterior knowledge has been organized. Manuals in Chinese must be got out at once, but first the new vocabulary " special to each discipline " must be determined.

This recommendation, as we have seen, begs the whole question.

In connection with the mass instruction of adult illiterates and the attempts that have been made to reform Chinese writing, the mission makes the following curious remark :—

" We noted that attempts are at present being made to reform writing, and what is worse, reformers spread their

THE PRESENT PERIOD

theory and practice independently in various centres and neighbourhoods, which is distinctly contrary both to the idea of linguistic unity and practical good sense."

The expression " what is worse " suggests that the mission regards writing reform as a bad thing, but from a study of other parts of the text it is clear that this cannot be what is meant.

A list of concrete proposals is appended to many of the chapters of the report. The powers of the Ministry of Education should be increased, the division of education budgets should be stricter, the payment of teachers should be more evenly proportioned, the division into higher and lower primary should be abolished, children should enter school at seven instead of at six. A large number of other administrative and pedagogic suggestions are set out which there is no space here to summarize.

The Need of a New Æsthetic

The shortcomings of education in modern China are most apparent in the art, needlework, and music classes. I have visited dozens of schools where in the entrance hall or other prominent place are displayed selected examples of the pupils' drawing and handiwork. One could see at a glance that Chinese boys and girls are unusually good at drawing and neat with their fingers, but one could see just as immediately that the models they used were corrupt. The traditional native designs have practically disappeared—the prunus blossom, the dragon, the variations on the character *shou* (壽) ; Western " realism ", or " direct from nature " methods have taken their place. And the result is deplorable. It is the same with the needlework. The girls still have the clever little fingers which produced the fine embroideries of a generation ago, and when they work character scrolls or old Chinese designs the results are pleasing, but here again realism in the Western sense has intruded and the girls seem to have lost all sense of colour values. Music, too, means for the most part Western music. How often have I lingered outside a classroom trying to identify the cacophony coming from inside and later discovered that it was " Broadway Melody " or the " theme song " from some film or other.

I should say that what China and Chinese education require above all is a new æsthetic. There is evidence that the Chinese themselves realize this in a subconscious way in their typography and shop signs. The authorized form of the written character was fixed many centuries ago in five different kinds of script. A candidate who formed a single character wrongly would fail to pass his examination. Nowadays the sign writers, and to a lesser extent the type cutters, take every known liberty with the script. Strokes are twisted, curtailed, or omitted just as suits the writer's idea of design. The influence of several kinds of Western script can be traced—the block letter, the romanized German, the trick effects of the poster artist and cover designer, besides the complications due to instruments like the spray-writer. In Japan the type cutters have impressed on the beautiful Chinese character an ugly squat utilitarianism. Most of the efforts of the Chinese sign writer are merely fanciful or grotesque, but there are some that have succeeded in giving a new artistic twist to the old characters. This I conceive to be the spirit of creation turning uneasily in its slumber. So far pictorial design has not been delivered from the crude imitation of the worst Western models, but there are signs that the Chinese art sense will make something new of them in the end.

Chinese women's clothes are the most promising evidence of success in combining Chinese and Western patterns. The exquisite cut of the coat, especially the sleeves, has been retained, and a modified Western skirt and silk

THE PRESENT PERIOD

stockings and high-heeled shoes have been adopted—though Chinese women look best in their native flowered slippers. The same good results have not so far been achieved with men's clothing. In particular the semi-military uniform with a peak cap, which is adopted in so many schools, copied from the Germans via Japan, is an eyesore. So long as Chinese parents send their children to school in this unseemly dress, there can be no serious improvement in Chinese education.

With the finding of a new æsthetic the Chinese will have gone far towards the solution of their problems.

Conclusion

The great majority of the foreign experts who have advised and are advising China have gained their experience in Europe and America, and have little knowledge of the cultural background of China. In education the only assistance they can offer is in selecting the technique for westernizing China according to what they consider to be the local requirements. Thus it is that the report of the League of Nations' experts is concerned exclusively with method; it leaves entirely untouched the question of how much, if any, of the traditional teaching is to be retained and how the classical system of thought is to be reconciled with the Aristotelian. The palæstra of discussion on the major issues has thus been relinquished to the Chinese intellectuals and the few foreigners with enough knowledge of China and the Chinese to enable them to form an opinion on these issues.

It is remarkable that the principal advocates of root and branch reform are Chinese, and the main supporters of conservatism are foreigners. There are, of course, many hundreds of native scholars who are attached to Confucianism, and many of these have expressed their opinions in books and journals, but the method of argument they use is for the most part on the traditional model, the "rhythm sequence". So when I say that the supporters of the traditional China and of Confucianism in particular are foreigners, I mean that it is the foreigners who are articulate in the medium understandable to those educated under Western conditions. The radical intellectuals of China, besides being the most in public prominence, are well able to clothe their ideas in the language of logical persuasion.

Let us imagine two friends of China, holding very different views, debating the question of what is China's best course to follow in education. I will call them Ion and Crito, but they are not to be identified with any real persons.[1]

Ion. The banishment of the Confucian ethic from the school curriculum was the greatest mistake that the reformers have made.

Crito. It had to go. It was obsolete and quite unsuited to the present age. Besides, it is long since it was a living force. China cannot hope to survive in the present contact and conflict of races without renewing herself. She must adopt the complete technique of Western thought if she is to become united and strong, to resist the Western economic machine, and to oppose conquest and aggression.

Ion. But China cannot remain a nation if she is to be deprived of her ethical system. She has created a religion which has held her together for thousands of years. The West has Christianity as the motive force of its civilization. What is the motive force of China if not Confucianism? What are you going to put in its place?

Crito. I very much doubt whether Christianity is any longer the motive force of the West. Faith has waned, and the current ethics of Europe and America are very different

---

[1] The summary of Confucianism in this dialogue is drawn and adapted from Sir Reginald Johnston's *Confucianism and Modern China*, London, 1934, but the arguments in its favour are purely the responsibility of Ion.

from those inculcated by the Scriptures. Moreover, the interpretations of the multitude of churches and sects are diverse and opposed on many fundamental points. There is, in my opinion, not enough in common amongst all of them to justify their classification as units of the same religion. I speak, of course, of the ethical teaching, not of the common recognition of the Godhead of Christ. To group Christians according to their essential ethical tenets you would have to do it by a cross section through churches and sects. There are, for instance, Catholic puritans and Protestant puritans agreeing very closely on the proper conduct of life, and, for that matter, there are Chinese puritans. No, the motive force of modern Western civilization does not derive from any unity of Christian conviction, but from the stream of the common cultural heritage, with its fount in Ancient Greece, enormously reinforced by the scientific spirit.

Ion. Science as a motive for life has failed. You will find that the great Western scientists are confessing that the mere search for knowledge is not enough; there must be faith and there must be dogma. But I am not speaking as a Christian. "The moral patrimony of every individual cannot be sought for elsewhere than in the native soil which has given birth to himself or to his ancestors." It is not Confucianism which has brought China to the state she is in to-day, but the neglect of Confucianism. Scientific ethics cannot produce anything more suitable for China than the high morality of the Four Books. And, contrary to what you say, ethical principles are not undergoing a kaleidoscopic change in the centuries. They are steadfast. The Decalogue is as true a guide for modern Europe as it was for the Israelites in the time of Moses. Think what Confucianism teaches. First: man is the noblest thing on earth. There you have the anthropocentric idea which is essential for man's progress; man's belief in himself.

Second: imitate the men of noble character, but when you meet the inferior look inward and examine yourself. Third: the gentleman is slow in speech, resolute in action. That is a radical guide for conduct which an Englishman, at least, must approve. Fourth: the Master gave his ambitions to be to give rest and peace to the aged, to be loyal and faithful to his friends, to give loving care to the young. In this Confucianism is at one with Christianity. Fifth: uprightness belongs to man by virtue of his birth; if he loses that he is in peril. How superior this is to the doctrine of original sin! A man is assured that he is good by nature; to depart from his true nature imposes all responsibility on himself. He cannot blame " circumstances ". Sixth: in his teaching the Master made four subjects his chief concern—scholarship, right conduct, loyalty to duty, and sincerity. Can you better this in any of your modern educational systems? Seventh: the wise are not shaken by doubt, nor the good by anxiety, nor the stout-hearted by fear. This is the sum total of all philosophy. Eighth: the rules for social conduct are in domestic relationships, a balance between familiarity and reserve; in affairs, courtesy; in general intercourse, loyalty and good faith. Even for uncivilized peoples one must have sympathy. Ninth: reciprocity. "What you do not wish others to do to you, do not do unto others." Tenth: human nature has its essential dignity; the humblest man need not surrender his soul. Eleventh: the gentleman is free from unreasonable likes and dislikes. He stands for what is right. Twelfth: have no fear of death; there is no Heaven or Hell; if a man has sought truth he may meet death without repining. Thirteenth: among the truly educated, there is no distinction of classes. The Chinese, of course, attained their ideal no more than the Christians attained theirs, but it was the striving to do so that created the civilization of China.

Crito. I have no doubt that many of the principles of

Confucianism are constant and would form part of any good ethical system. At the same time I say that the Confucian code as a whole no longer fits the facts. Since it suited another quite different state of society a long time has elapsed. Confucianism has been moribund for centuries and Chinese civilization moribund with it. Can any of these precepts enable the modern Chinese to decide whether they should make peace with the Japanese, engage in guerilla warfare with them, or concentrate their energies on strengthening their diplomatic position until such time as the League of Nations or an alliance of interested Powers shall intervene to save them from the enemy? Can the Confucian gentleman decide from his scriptures whether China should rely on centralization at Nanking or on a federation of the provinces? Can these ancient principles be reconciled with co-education, birth-control, or sexual equality under the civil law of the Republic of China? You may say that the first two questions have nothing to do with morals: I reply that morals and conduct in any particular cannot be separated. If you say that the answer to my third question is "No", I reply that in this case Confucianism is contrary to the biological development of mankind...

And so the debate continues. The positions of Ion and Crito are irreconcilable and it is unprofitable for us to follow the debate any further.

Now, to avoid ending this study of education in modern China on a negative note, I will imagine that I have been asked by the Chinese to advise them what they should do to bring into being a cohesive educational system. It is only a dream and I confess to some diffidence in entertaining it, but here is the advice I should give.

Cease to attempt to combine in one system the "rhythmic thinking" of Chinese civilization with the "chain thinking" of the West. Does this mean, then, that the traditional literature of China should be consigned to limbo once and for all, and that the country should deliver herself over to the Western system entirely ? No, what I suggest is this. For five hours out of the twenty-five and a half hours a week in the Upper Primary School (to choose a specific instance), the pupil shall learn purely traditional subjects : for the remaining twenty and a half hours he learn purely modern subjects. But, you will exclaim, this is nothing but a reversion to the 1903 syllabus ! No, the 1903 syllabus attempted to realize the saying, " Let Chinese learning be the essence, and Western learning provide material efficiency," by containing Chinese and Western subjects in one system. The twelve hours given to the classics did not, for one thing, leave time for the modern subjects. The pupil was the subject of a diarchy at the same time that he was supposed to be subject to an undivided rule. Both the Chinese classics and the Western teaching were offered as practical guides to knowledge and conduct. Since the two systems were of an entirely different nature and, literally interpreted, were frequently in conflict, the pupil was hopelessly confused. The result in the end was that the classical subjects were sacrificed to the Western ones and the present system came into being.

What I propose is quite a different thing. The instruction in traditional subjects is not to be considered as having a direct practical bearing on the pupil's life, but only a literary and æsthetic one. He will be in a sense the subject of a diarchy, but he must be conscious of this diarchy, and pass from one rule to the other with a clear sense of passing from one plane of reality to another. The five hours a week of traditional study is to consist of a certain amount of learning by rote, and a certain amount of excogitation. But the pupil shall no more seek directly to model his life on the *Chung Yung* than the pupil under a classical system in the West is expected to guide himself in daily conduct by his reading of Plato's *Republic*. He is to be taught that China has an unsurpassed literary and æsthetic tradition, but that the time when the Confucian teaching fulfilled its function as a complete guide to personal conduct, to government, and to actual life is now remote, and that an entirely changed set of circumstances has meant that China must develop an empirical system suited to her present needs. In the five hours available, the pupil will not be able to memorize the same great tracts of literature as his predecessor under the old scheme, and much of the lumber of the traditional syllabus must be cleared away. Much attention will be paid to calligraphy, and to the more spontaneous creations of Chinese literature such as the poems of the T'ang Dynasty. The whole idea will be to bring the attention of the young mind to the really enduring aspect of Chinese culture—its special sense of beauty. The history of native porcelain making, of lacquer, of the Sung painting, of Han and T'ang sculpture, of Ming engravings on wood, shall be explained by means of drawings and shall be made actual from the practice of the central art of calligraphy. The Confucian teaching, so far as there is time to bring it to the pupil's notice, shall not be treated as a dead thing, but as a thing still existing in a far-off China whose significance for the present day is the trailing glory of decorous behaviour, of serene ritual, and of living with music and rhythm. For the remaining twenty and a half hours a week the pupil will be educated under a modern, practical system. I would even recommend, were it practicable to arrange it, a change of costume in passing from the traditional to the modern side of the school.

I do not attempt to say what this modern system shall be. I can only say that it will have to be chosen piece by piece to suit actual needs. As the League experts, and all who have had any experience of the matter, say, it is useless to transplant a complete system from America or anywhere else and expect it to work.

My expectation is that the traditional study will be subjective, and the modern study objective. If the pupil's native instinct is inspired by his instruction in native literature and art it will well up in an enthusiasm which will spill over into the utilitarian modern side. In a century or so the two sides will coalesce.

But before this or any other system can be made effective it is necessary that the Chinese shall feel dismay at the non-realization of any programme they have undertaken, in fact that they shall practise the most valuable and perpetual of the Confucian virtues, *ch'êng* (誠), or sincerity.

APPENDIX

Analysis of Representative Chinese Textbooks

(*Prepared for The Royal Institute of International Affairs*)

" Sociology," " Foundation " Text Books, Vol. iii
Commercial Press, Shanghai, 1932.

Class.—Lower Elementary.

The whole book is about China except for references to Foreigners on pp. 18, 19, 21, and 22.

Treatment of War.

There is one picture of soldiers with fixed bayonets marching proudly with what appears to be the national banner in front on the celebration of the " Double Tenth ", the 10th October, 1911, when the Revolution started. Flags are flying from the windows of houses.

On p. 10 there is an illustration of prehistoric men driving away other prehistoric men with sticks, and the letterpress, " Prehistoric men, with regard to their own territory, would not allow men of foreign (i.e. different) tribes to encroach, and if they came on a hunting expedition the others drove them out with sticks." On the next page (p. 17) there is a move forward some thousands of years to the present day and the text, " In the last 100 years there have been several places in our country which have been annexed by foreigners and made into ' leased territory '. We must rise up, band together, and get back all our lost territory." On p. 18 there are questions for answer by the pupil. " Why and how should we get back these territories ? " There is an illustration (p. 18) of a European (English) policeman in Shanghai (?) beating a Chinese coolie's rickshaw (apparently " traffic control with violence "). The recovery of the Treaty Ports, Hong Kong, etc., it seems, justifies war if necessary.

Treatment of Nationalism.

The nationalistic references are :—

(1) Recovery of Treaty Ports by force if necessary (part of K.M.T. (Kuomintang) programme).

(2) "Sun Yat-sen was the founder of the Republic, we ought to revere and love him much" (p. 20).

(See note under "Treatment of War" as to foreign encroachment.)

(No references to 1848, 1870, or to Versailles or other treaties.)

Treatment of Religious Questions. Nil.

Treatment of Colonization.

China has suffered territorial loss at the hands of foreign powers. She must regain her territory.

Treatment of Race Questions. Nil.

Treatment of Economic Questions.

The steamship and railway train are favoured by implication (illustration, p. 22). Economic self-sufficiency is advocated (p. 21). "This is" (referring to illustration) "a market for national goods". Praise given to "national goods". Moral implied—we must buy Chinese goods to the exclusion of foreign goods when possible. No reference to class-consciousness.

Constitution and Political Organization.

Democracy favoured by implication. Also Socialism, which is part of Sun Yat-sen's "Three Principles". The rule of the K.M.T. is supported by implication.

Treatment of Industrial Co-operation. No reference.

Treatment of Biographical Incidents.

Sun Yat-sen established the Republic on 10th October, 1911, "we should revere and love him" (p. 20).

"SOCIOLOGY," "FOUNDATION" TEXT BOOKS, Vol. iv

Commercial Press, Shanghai, 1931.

Class.—Lower Elementary.

One section refers to the habits of savage tribes in the tropics and another to the Eskimos and their hunting.

Treatment of War.

p. 9 (illustrations of soldier, cannon, revolver, sword, knife, and spear), "The soldiers of our army are to protect our country.

APPENDIX

They use military weapons to a great extent. If our country is in danger they will protect us."

p. 10 (picture of Chinese boy scouts), " sometimes they practise military exercises."

Treatment of Nationalism.

p. 7, map of China.

p. 8, picture of national flag (includes K.M.T. flag in corner).

Treatment of Religious Questions. Nil.

Treatment of Colonization. Nil.

Treatment of Race Questions.

Friendly, but rather patronizing attitude towards inhabitants of tropics (Malays, etc.?). Term " savage " used for people who seem to be Malays.

Treatment of Economic Questions.

The economic basis of life is stressed—implements of primitive man, hunting of Eskimos. Gradually the implements improved. There is a description of the aeroplane, the train, etc., but no suggestion that they were invented outside China.

Constitution and Political Organization.

Picture of national flag (this flag has K.M.T. party flag in its corner).

Treatment of International Co-operation. No reference.

Treatment of Biographical Incidents. Nil.

" SOCIOLOGY," " FOUNDATION " TEXT BOOKS, Vol. V
Commercial Press, Shanghai, 1932.

Class.—Lower Elementary.

Treatment of War.

p. 13. Illustration of Chinese of the Han dynasty shooting down men of the Miao tribe of aborigines who are said to have attacked the Han (illustration of Han soldiers in coats of mail shooting arrows at the half-naked savages).

Treatment of Nationalism.

Map showing Mochang where the Revolution started in 1911, and letterpress explaining why it should be a place of national remembrance—pp. 9–10.

p. 11. Further history of the Revolution.

Treatment of Religious Questions. Nil.

Treatment of Colonization. Nil.

Treatment of Race Questions.

p. 13. The aboriginal *miao* are described as being defeated and absorbed into China (the miao, an aboriginal race, are still found in some provinces of China).

Treatment of Economic Questions.

Several pages on the economic devices of early man. pp. 24–5 describe metal and paper currency and their use (with illustrations).

Constitution and Political Organization. As in vol. iii.

Treatment of International Co-operation. No reference.

Treatment of Biographical Incidents.

p. 14. History of Sun Yat-sen and founding of Republic.

p. 15. Sun Yat-sen's sayings.

" SOCIOLOGY," " FOUNDATION " TEXT BOOKS, Vol. vi

Commercial Press, Shanghai, 1932.

Class.—Lower Elementary.

Treatment of War.

p. 9. " If we Chinese want to make our country strong, we must first make our people strong." " Everybody must cultivate the ancient fighting spirit." p. 10. Picture of boy scouts drilling, pp. 10–11, and letterpress.

Treatment of Nationalism.

p. 7. Commemoration of Sun Yat-sen's death and Revolution of 1911.

Treatment of Religious Questions. Nil.

Treatment of Colonization.

We must recover the " treaty ports " and conquered territory, p. 21 et seq.

Treatment of Race Questions.

pp. 21–2. Japan's aggression. Description of country's suffering at Japanese hands. " The 9th of May is a day of humiliation for the country."

pp. 24–5. The wrongs of the " unequal treaties ".

APPENDIX

Treatment of Economic Questions.

Descriptions of China's land and water-ways, railways, and roads. p. 32. " Sun Yat-sen said, ' If we improve our waterways and extend our wealth, our glory can exceed that of England and America.' "

Constitution and Political Organization.

As vol. iii. Democratic methods and speeches advocated on p. 15. Picture of Sun Yat-sen and the crossed flags of China and K.M.T.

Treatment of International Co-operation.

No reference. The first thing China has to do, it seems, is to recover her lost territory and make herself strong.

Treatment of Biographical Incidents.

pp. 7–8. The death of Sun Yat-sen at Peking in 1925. Celebration of memorial day in China.

" SOCIOLOGY," " FOUNDATION " TEXT BOOKS, Vol. vii

Commercial Press, Shanghai, 1932.

Class.—Lower Elementary.

The ten pages referring to the West refer also to China.

Treatment of War.

p. 27. " Opium and the country's shame." " Foreign relations after the Opium War." References to the first China War of 1839–1842. The lesson is that England forced war on China to force her to accept her opium. Discussion of the " unequal treaties ".

p. 31. Russia and the Chinese Eastern Railway. More imperialistic aggression. " We must never forget these incidents."

p. 30. " England massacred the students at Shanghai " (30th May, 1925). " Japan forced the twenty-one demands on us." France and the second China war. Aggression because of the death of a missionary.

Treatment of Nationalism.

p. 5 et seq. The national capital Nanking. Events leading to the Revolution.

p. 9. The Nationalist Party (K.M.T.). The creation of the Kuomintang by Sun Yat-sen. The institution of the " Three Principles ". The K.M.T. and Labour.

p. 11. Nationalism. "The sufferings of China from Imperialism." "The oppression and injustice China has suffered." (These expressions repeated over and over again.) "We must overthrow Imperialism."

Treatment of Religious Questions. Nil.

Treatment of Colonization.

Several pages on China's territorial losses.

Treatment of Race Questions.

The details under "Treatment of Nationalism" refer to the questions of race and Imperialism.

Treatment of Economic Questions.

p. 25. "Home-made China goods and patriotism."

p. 1. The Chinese must be patriotic and buy Chinese goods and not foreign goods.

p. 24. In ancient times there was no aristocracy; that was a later creation.

p. 23. Imports and exports.

p. 16. Our Country's trade.

p. 17. The invention of the steam-engine and the telephone.

Constitution and Political Organization.

The history of the Kuomintang is given. By implication, rule by K.M.T. and Principles of Sun Yat-sen are favoured.

Treatment of International Co-operation. No reference.

Treatment of Biographical Incidents.

p. 17. Watt's invention of steam engine.

p. 18. Franklin's observation of electricity. (Nationality of these persons not mentioned.)

"Sociology," "Foundation" Text Books, Vol. viii

Commercial Press, Shanghai, 1932.

Class.—Lower Elementary.

Treatment of War.

pp. 19–20. "Casting greedy eyes on China, the Western powers forced many 'unequal treaties' on China."

p. 23 et seq. The causes of the Great War are explained. The cause of the war is explained as a contest for power among the belligerent nations.

APPENDIX

Treatment of Nationalism.

Several pages incorporate Sun Yat-sen's nationalistic ideas from the " Three Principles ".

p. 22. Imperialism is shown as encroaching on China's rights.

p. 20. Chinese emigrants who are industrious have been exploited by the foreigners abroad. The National Government has protected them so that they shall not again be submitted to ill-treatment and insult.

Treatment of Religious Questions.

p. 18. One reference to the Portuguese coming to proselytize in China. Christianity not mentioned.

Treatment of Colonization.

Many pages devoted to the history of imperialistic aggression by foreign powers. Also statement that Chinese emigrants abroad need protection from insults and exploitation.

Treatment of Race Questions.

p. 4. " Now in the world the strength of the white races is greatest and they are always oppressing the red and black races " (" red " includes Malays, etc.).

Treatment of Economic Questions.

The economics of the " Three Principles " are inculcated, p. 12, etc. (The " Three Principles " has been translated into English. Published in 1927 by Commercial Press, Shanghai.)

Constitution and Political Organization.

Rule of K.M.T. and principles of " Three Principles of People " advocated.

Treatment of International Co-operation.

No direct reference, but implication is that China must make herself strong and get rid of foreign aggression before international co-operation can begin.

Treatment of Biographical Incidents.

Sun Yat-sen and his " Three Principles " mentioned.

" SOCIOLOGY," " FOUNDATION " TEXT BOOKS,
1st Vol. (of two)

Commercial Press, Shanghai, 1931.

Class.—Lower Middle (i.e. Secondary).

242   APPENDIX

Nearly all the book refers to foreign countries.

Treatment of War.

This is a straightforward outline of history. Military events like Alexander the Great's conquests are treated without comment, but there is a tone which seems to condemn conquest.

Treatment of Nationalism. Nil.

Treatment of Religious Questions.

Buddhism and Christianity are treated historically without bias.

Treatment of Colonization. Nil.

Treatment of Race Questions.

No specific reference. No particular racial bias.

Treatment of Economic Questions.

Favourable treatment of Society (including " Guild " economic organization) of Middle Ages in Europe.

Constitution and Political Organization.

No particular bias indicated except that democratic, as opposed to monarchical, rule favoured by implication.

Treatment of International Co-operation. No reference.

Treatment of Biographical Incidents.

Historical personages of East and West treated without bias.

" FOREIGN HISTORY FOR LOWER MIDDLE SCHOOLS,"
2nd Vol. (of two)

Class.—Lower Middle (i.e. Secondary).

Commercial Press, Shanghai, 1931.

Treatment of War.

Napoleon's history set out in a succession of facts with little comment. The fact that he brought war to Europe is not emphasized. His " code " and the things he did for internal government are dwelt on. No abhorrence of war is expressed. Section 31 deals with the growth of imperialism. The European nations were bent on territorial acquisition. China suffered loss of territory after the Opium War. The Great War is described in detail with the events leading up to it, " each country was out for its own profit " (p. 80). The point is that China (i.e. the K.M.T.) is only interested objectively in foreign countries. There is no pacifism taught, since nationalism and the strengthening of China may involve military action by the Chinese.

Treatment of Nationalism.

p. 120. Sun Yat-sen in a speech said, " The Three Principles of the People is the complete method of building the new State of China." Many pages in the book dealing with modern history emphasize " the dangers of Imperialism ".

Section 38 deals with the " world of to-morrow ". The great contest of the future will be between Socialism and Imperialism. " There are two great forces in the world—one is Imperialism and the other Socialism. Imperialistic Governments are represented by England, America, and Japan. Of Socialistic Governments the U.S.S.R. is the representative. The contest of to-morrow will be between these forces."

Treatment of Religious Questions. Nil.

Treatment of Colonization.

In the nineteenth century imperialism spread over the world. Imperialism is a danger to China which the " Three Principles " can counteract.

Treatment of Race Questions. Nil.

Treatment of Economic Questions.

The great contest of the future is to be between Imperialism and Socialism (Sec. 38). The People are under the heel of Capitalism, p. 117.

Constitution and Political Organization.

In the final section an account is given of Sun Yat-sen and his " Three Principles ". The latter are explained—nationalism, democracy, and economics are the three requisites. Self-determination is necessary for each country before it can be in harmony. The rule of the K.M.T. is to be supported. (Picture of Sun Yat-sen, p. 118.)

Treatment of International Co-operation.

Nil. (The pre-requisites of international co-operation is the self-determination of peoples, i.e. nationalism. Then the world will be in harmony.)

APPENDIX

Treatment of Biographical Incidents.

Pictures of Napoleon, Lenin, President Harding, Sun Yat-sen, Mustapha Kemal, Mussolini, Walter Scott, Tennyson, Wordsworth, and dozens of others are given. Persons are treated without animus, the facts of their lives being stated without comment.

NEW GENERATION CHINESE HISTORY TEXT BOOK, 2nd Vol. (of two)

Commercial Press, Shanghai, 1931.

Class.—Lower Middle (i.e. Secondary).

Treatment of War.

Section 7 describes the misfortunes suffered by China through the Opium War, the " unequal treaties ", etc.

Section 9, the Second China War. " Military and naval action—burning of the Summer Palace, etc.—the Boxer trouble."

Section 10. The War with France.

Section 11. Sino-Japanese War of 1894—" Russia and England's savage disposition." How Mongolia, etc., was lost from China at the time of the Republic.

Section 25. " China used to be a more powerful country." " We have become weak because we have lost our spirit of nationality, therefore we must recover the spirit of nationality." " To recover the spirit of nationality we must first of all understand the extreme danger we are in." " We have often suffered the oppression of foreigners." There is no glorification of war ; neither is there any condemnation of it. The evils of War-Lordism are dwelt upon. (Section 21.)

p. 118. " For ten or more years the arrogant soldiery rebelled and caused disorder, the violent generals fought among themselves, the Republic was lost sight of, foreign Imperialism encouraged 'war-lordism' and made a tool of it, and 'war-lordism' flourished with foreign help." (The reference is this—the powers for long only recognized the " illegal " northern government and smiled on the dictator-like activities of " war-lords " like Wu Pei-fu, but refused to recognize the Socialist government of Sun Yat-sen at Canton on the ground that it was unstable—as indeed it was. The country was, and still to some extent is, at the mercy of military commanders who in many instances are no more than bandit chiefs.)

APPENDIX

Treatment of Nationalism.

See note under " Treatment of War ".

p. 138. " China and the World." " China has a history of the length we have described, its position in world history is extremely important. Formerly China was very powerful, a very civilized country, the most powerful country in the world. Now the position of England, America, and France is higher. The principal reason for this is that we have lost our national spirit." (This lesson, like others, is straight from the " Three Principles ".)

Treatment of Religious Questions.

Section 2. Roman Catholicism in China. This section treats Christianity mainly from the point of view that its missionaries (Ricci, etc.) introduced Western science into China.

Section 13 says that the reason that the Roman Catholics were suppressed in the early eighteenth century was the fear of secret societies undermining the Government. Christianity, Mohammedanism, and Buddhism are viewed historically, not with bias towards any one of them.

Treatment of Colonization.

China is opposed to her territory being used for colonization by foreign powers. China must protect her own colonists (emigrants) who go and settle under a foreign flag.

Treatment of Race Questions. No special reference.

Treatment of Economic Questions.

No special treatment. Section 24 treats of the progress of science and its bearing on national education.

Constitution and Political Organization.

Section 22. Reform of the Kuomintang organization. The " Three Principles " are to be put into operation through the agency of the K.M.T. K.M.T. rule during the period of political tutelage.

Treatment of International Co-operation.

p. 138, Section 29. " China and the World." There is no advocacy of international co-operation ; the sole lesson is the weakness of China and how to make her strong by the revival of the national spirit and by the use of science. ("The Twenty-one Demands," "China and the Washington Conference," and other sections, stress China's rights, not her obligations.)

Treatment of Biographical Incidents.

Various historical persons mentioned, but no special point in biographical treatment.

NEW CHUNG HUA CHINESE HISTORY, 2nd Vol. (of two)

Chung Hua Publishing Co., Shanghai, 1931.

Class.—Lower Middle (i.e. Secondary).

Treatment of War.

The treatment of war is very similar in effect to that of the above volume, only the language is rather less restrained. There is, for instance, a "map of China's shame" (No. 36), showing China's territorial losses. The "oppression of Imperialism" before and after the establishment of the Republic is treated at length. The Powers did all they could to embarrass and oppress the new republic of China (Sec. 62).

"Imperialism and the oppression of China "—" In the Ch'ing Dynasty England and Russia both wanted to usurp Tibet," " Mongolia, Southern Manchuria, and Eastern Mongolia questions ... England, Russia, and Japan took advantage of China's distress to encroach upon China's territory." "Yüan Shih-k'ai in alliance with the Powers dissolved the K.M.T."

p. 68. " The banks of England, America, France, and Germany negotiated a loan of £15,000,000 (to Yüan Shih-k'ai) and later Japan and Russia entered the Banking Consortium, they wished to take control of China's finances (as security) ... the inner cabinet were opposed, America also did not consider this right and left the Consortium. Then Yüan Shih-k'ai, because he wished to crush the second Republican Army, entered into an agreement with the banks of the remaining five powers whereby the loan was secured on the Salt Gabelle, thus allowing the foreigners to counter China's former financial rule."

Treatment of Nationalism.

Nationalism and the treatment of war cannot well be separated. This volume faithfully renders Sun Yat-sen's views on nationalism and the oppression by foreign powers by war and economic forces.

APPENDIX

Treatment of Religious Questions.

Section 3. The coming of foreigners to trade and the arrival of foreign missionaries. The importance of the latter is considered to be that Western science first came with them. No anti-Christian bias observable.

Treatment of Colonization. As above.

Treatment of Economic Questions.

Section 6. China's Industrial Revolution. The coming of European and American educational methods. The adoption of modern industrial methods must continue. " Science " is the keynote of development.

Constitution and Political Organization. As above.

Treatment of International Co-operation.

As above. China is in danger of Imperialism. The great question of the time is the Pacific Ocean question and China is the focus of this question.

Treatment of Biographical Incidents.

Sun Yat-sen " featured " as in above volumes.

NEW GENERATION HISTORY (Approved by the Ministry of Education)

Commercial Press, Shanghai.

Class.—Higher Elementary.

Treatment of War.

This little book is only a bare outline of world history. There is little comment on war as such, but the bias against " Imperialism " and propaganda against the country responsible for the Opium War emerges fairly distinctly.

Treatment of Nationalism.

Nothing special. The various national movements are described without comment.

Treatment of Religious Questions. Bare references.

Treatment of Colonization.

No direct reference but inference as above.

Treatment of Race Questions. No specific reference.

Treatment of Economic Questions. No reference.

Constitution and Political Organization. No specific reference.

Treatment of International Co-operation. Nil.

Treatment of Biographical Incidents. Bare references.

NEW GENERATION HISTORY (Approved by the Ministry of Education), Vol. iii

Class.—Higher Elementary.

Treatment of War.

pp. 26–7. "China's oppression by foreign powers," territorial losses, losses of power over customs, over waterways, losses of mineral rights. No special treatment of war. The inferences to be drawn are the same as in the above volumes.

Treatment of Nationalism.

See under "Treatment of War". p. 29, "The History of the K.M.T." p. 27, "The Establishment of the Republic."

Treatment of Religious Questions.

Several sections give the history of religious movements—Nestorian, Christian, Buddhist, etc. The treatment is impartial.

Treatment of Colonization. As above.

Treatment of Race Questions. No specific reference.

Treatment of Economic Questions. No reference.

Constitution and Political Organization.

One section (No. 18) on the Government of China by K.M.T. describes the establishment of K.M.T. Government.

Treatment of International Co-operation. Nil.

Treatment of Biographical Incidents.

pp. 28–9. Sun Yat-sen and his foundation of K.M.T.

NEW GENERATION GEOGRAPHY (Approved by the Ministry of Education), Vol. ii

Class.—Higher Elementary.
Commercial Press, Shanghai.

Treatment of War. Nil.

APPENDIX

Treatment of Nationalism.

p. 1. Map of place where Revolution started 1911, " This is our country's place of national remembrance."

Treatment of Religious Questions. Nil.

Treatment of Colonization. Nil.

Treatment of Race Questions. Nil.

Treatment of Economic Questions.

China's natural resources described, also railways. Reference (p. 31) to Sun Yat-sen's economic programme in the " Three Principles ".

Constitution and Political Organization. Nil.

Treatment of International Co-operation. Nil.

Treatment of Biographical Incidents. p. 31. Reference to Sun Yat-sen.

INDEX

Abstract idea, 115
Academia Sinica, 209
Achievements of Chinese civilization, 217
Addis, C. S., 59
Aelfred, King, 131
Aesthetic, need of new, 225
Afforestation, 185
Agrarian population, 195
Agriculture, small-holding scale, 149
Aldersey, Miss, 52, 68
Alexander the Great, 242 (Appx.)
Alexander VII, bull of, 46
Allen, C. W., 46
America, 170, 175, 176, 181, 198, 203, 224
American Board, 52
American Methodists' Girls' School, 52
American Missionaries, 73
American Presbyterian Central Theological School, 53
America, students sent to, 58
American system of education, 71, 191
Amoy, 194
Amoy vernacular, 109
Analects of Confucius, 25, 38, 121
Ancient Greece, 229
Ancient morality, 200
Anglo-Saxon race, 203
Anglo-Saxons, 176
Anti-foreign feeling, 64, 72, 147, 164
Anti-foreignism, 196
Anti-foreign movement, 74
Anti-foreign propaganda, 201
Anti-foreign reaction, 51
Anti-foreign Teachings in New Textbooks of China, 165
Antithetical sentences, 21, 22, 23
Apes, 203
Archery, 3, 4, 63
Arch of Constantine, 41
Aristotle, 89, 134
Arsenals set up, 56
Associative classifications, 117

Astronomy, 127
Ātmân, 132
Authoritarian, Chinese society, 133
Autocratic government, 178
Avarice in Chinese character, 197
Axiom, 153
Ayscough, Florence, 91

Backhouse, Sir E., 22, 22 n.
Bacon, Francis, 80, 126, 127
Baltimore clippers, 47 n.
Banking system, 201
Banks, 246 (Appx.)
Banks, foreign, 196
Banks, native, 196
Banners (Manchu), 49
Barbour, 129, 131
Basic English, 160
Bachelor's degree, 29
Beautiful, 155
Becker, Carl H., 220
Bentham, Jeremy, 88 n., 89, 89 n., 99, 130, 153
Bergson, Henri, 77
Berr, Henri, 88 n.
Bessemer, Sir Henry, 82
Bible of New China, 163
Bible of Revolutionary China, 172
Bible, teaching of, 54
Bill of Rights, 129
Binary compounds, 21
Biot, 40
Birth control, 231
Bismarck, 174
" Black Haired Race," 138
Bland, J. O. P., 167 n.
Blood group, 195
Blundervil, 116
Board of Rites, 65, 69
Bolsheviks, 193
Bonnet, 128
Book of Changes, *see* Changes, Book of
Book of Rites, *see* Rites, Book of
Borodin, 189
Bourne, F. S. A., 31, 35
Boxer Indemnity, 197, 217

Boxer rising, 64, 170, 181, 244 (Appx.)
Boxer Year, 23
Boys and girls, model careers of, 4
Boys, education of, 4, 15
Bradshaw's *St. Werburge*, 140
Brailsford, H. N., 137
British Museum, Aurel Stein MS., 7
British Navy, 57
British police, 164
" Broadway Melody," 226
Browne, Sir Thomas, 127
Buddhism, 13, 15, 37, 46, 117, 127, 143, 242 (Appx.), 245 (Appx.), 248 (Appx.)
Buddhist culture, 83
Buddhist literature, 121
Buddhist priests, 103
Bulgaria, 211
Bullock, T. L., 97, 122 n.
Bureau, Educational Affairs, 65
Bureau of Publications, 208
Burma, 191

Callery, 5 n.
Calligraphy, 233
Canons of Filial Piety, 21
Cantlie, Sir James, 170, 202
Canton, 72, 81, 142, 159, 162, 171, 172, 188, 189, 198, 200, 220
Cantonese, 101, 105, 158
Cantonese coolies, 81
Cantonese Dictionary, Eitel's, 156
Canton " incident " (" Shakee " incident), 72, 173
Canton Medical School, 169
Capitalism, 149, 150, 152
Capitalists, 182, 183, 187, 189, 192
Cap of manhood, 27
Carnap, Rudolf, 126
Carter, T. F., 127
Catholic Church, 138, 167
Catholic point of view, 166
Catholic puritans, 229
Catholics, 52, 53
Catholic schools, 74
Causation, sense of, 101
Censorship power, 181
Central Advisory Committee of Kuomintang, 136
Central Executive Committee of Kuomintang, 136
Central Government, 162
Central Headquarters of Kuomintang, 161

Central Headquarters of National Government, 161
Central Political Council, 208
Ceremonial Rites of Chow, 6, 62
Ceremonies and Public Instruction, Minister of, 3
Ceremony, *see li*
Charioteering, 4
Chan Kuo period, 139 n.
Chang Chen-yu, 31
Chang Chih-tung, 58, 61, 62, 64, 66, 77
Chang Po-ling, 54
Chang Tso-lin, 172
Chang Ying-hua, 54
Changes, Book of, 3, 31
Chaucer, 120
Chê (in connection with *Chih*), 96
Cheating at examinations, 37
Chekiang, 104, 138, 208
Chên, 31
Ch'ên Chiung-ming, 162, 172
Chen, Gideon, 48 n.
Ch'êng-tse (tzŭ), 127
Ch'ên Tu-hsien, 105
Ch'ên Yüan-lung, 127
Chiang Kai-shek, 73, 173, 201
Chih, a genitive, 96, 97, 98
Chiang Mêng-lin (Monlin Chiang), 71, 127 n.
Ch'ien Tzŭ Wên, *see* Millenary Classic
China, population of, 216
China Review, 40, 136
China Year Book, 22 n., 70, 163 n., 204, 210
Chinese civilization, 89, 204
Chinese composition, 22
Chinese–English Dictionary, Morrison's, 50
Chinese girls' school, 68, 68 n.
" Chinese have no national spirit," 174
Chinese Imperial Naval College, 57
Chinese ineffectiveness, 211
Chinese language, 87 et seq.
Chinese Legation in London, 198
Chinese literature, 14
Chinese method of thought, 99
Chinese Press, comments in, 214–220
Chinese puritans, 229
Chinese race, 162, 174, 178, 203, 204
Chinese Recorder, 163 n.
Chinese Revolution, 166, 180

INDEX

Chinese science, 127, 127 n.
Chinese students abroad, 65 n.
Chinese thought, 90
Ch'ing Dynasty, 2, 37, 40, 68, 209, 246 (Appx.)
Ch'ing Penal Code, 199
Chin Lan-pin, 58
Chinoiserie, 41
Chin-shih, degree, 36
Chiukiang, 194
Choa Mei-pa, 101 n.
Chore, Mr., 25 n.
Chou Dynasty, 3, 4, 11 n., 42
Chou Hsing-ssŭ, 20
Chou Kung, 116
Chou Tzŭ, 120
Christ, 229
Christian education, purpose of, 53
Christian faith, 167 n.
Christianity, 37, 228, 230, 245 (Appx.), 248 (Appx.)
Christian knowledge, 50
Christian missions, 221
Christian nations, 141
Christian schools, 74
Christians in China, 46
Christian Socialists, 146
Christian Trinity, 49
Citizenship, 186
Civilization of China, 37 n.
Civil Service, 26
Ch'üan (rights), 129
Chihli, 138
Chu Hsi, 16, 17, 103, 123, 123 n., 127
Chü-jên 25 n., 31, 37
Chung, 55 n.
Chung Hua Publishing Company, 246 (Appx.)
Chung Yang Yen Chiu Yüan, 209
Chung Yung, 21, 34, 35, 90, 232
Church Missionary Society, 52
Chu-tse (tzŭ), 127
Chu Yin Tzŭ Mu (*Fu Hao*), 108 n., 109
Clan loyalties, 177
Clan system, 148
Classics, 21, 26 n., 42, 43, 53, 103
Class struggle, 189
Clavius, Father, 45 n.
Clement XI, bull of, 46
Co-education, 231
Cogito : ergo sum, 101
Cole, G. D. H., 146
Collège de France, 220
Colleges, modern, 58

Colleges, provincial, 24
Colenso, Bishop, 168
Colorado, 170 n.
Colour values, 226
Commerce and industry, first favourable mention, 64
Commercial Press, 30 n., 54, 114, 164, and Appendix
Commercial Press Chinese–English Dictionary, 109, 112
Commissioners of Education, 161
Common blood of Chinese, 174
Committee on Textbooks, 208
Communism, 72, 143, 168, 181, 188, 189, 201
Comte, Auguste, 126
Confucius and Confucianism, 1, 3, 15, 17, 19, 32, 34, 35, 37, 39, 40, 46, 62, 67, 70, 79, 154 n., 195, 219, 228, 228 n., 229, 231, 233, 234
Control Yüan, 136
Cosmopolitanism, 175, 190
Cost of education in China, 24 n., 216
Cotton, 186
Counter Reformation, 44
Couvreur, S., 52, 115, 140
Crook, A. H., 170 n.
Culture, Chinese lack of personal, 177
Culture group, 195
Curriculum committee, 163
Cursor Mundi, 129
Customs autonomy, 193
Customs, control of, 193, 196, 198
Customs receipts, 199
Cynewulf, 129
Czechoslovakia, 211

Dancing, part of liberal education, 4
Das Kapital, 166
David, Armand, 51
Debabelization, 6, 158 n.
Decalogue, 229
Decorum Ritual, 6
Deforestation, 195
D'Elia, Pascal M., 124, 163 n., 166, 167, 167 n., 170 n., 171, 171 n., 188 n., 203
Democracy, 134, 135, 137, 139, 161, 177–181, 192, 193, 203, 243
" Demism," 167
De Morant, Soulié, 170 n.
De Ruffe, M. A., 109 n.

Descartes, 101
Designs, traditional, 225
Des Rotours, R., 43 n.
Dewey, John, 71 n.
Diagrams, 116
Dickens, Charles, 106
Die-hard, foreign, opinion, 201
"Divine Right," 180
Doctrine of the Mean (*Chung Yung*), 35, 62
Dominicans, 46
Doolittle, 24
Douglas, 36
Dragon Throne, 147
Drawing, 225
Dubs, Homer H., 111
Dutch, 46, 47
Duyvendak, J. J. L., 89, 97 n., 100 n., 103 n., 105 n., 110, 122, 130 n., 139 n., 153 n., 157
Dyer Ball, 36 n.
Dynastic Histories, 77

Eclipse of 1636, 45 n.
Economic domination, 196
Economic oppression, 198
Education Committee, 210
Educational system threatened with collapse, 207
Education, Minister of, 81, 218
Education, Ministry of, 69 n., 225
Education, higher, amount spent on, 217
Education, primary, amount spent on, 217
"Eight-legs" essay, 23, 31, 39, 43, 63, 65, 66, 123, 155, 156
Eitel, 156
Elyot, 134, 143
Embroideries, 225
Empress Dowager, 49, 105, *see also* Tz'ŭ-hsi
Engelbrecht, H. C., 57 n.
Engels, 146
Engineering, mechanical, teaching of, 56
Engineers, Chinese, sent to England, etc., 58
England, 175, 176, 211, 239 (Appx.), 246 (Appx.)
English, the, 46
English language, 53, 54, 160, 213
English Presbyterians, 52
Europeans, contact with, 46
Equality, 179, 180

"Erasmus of the Reform Movement," 170
Euclid's *Elements of Geometry*, 56
Eunuchs, 15
Europe, 80, 229
European civilization, 176, 204
"Ever-Victorious Army," 49 n.
Evolution, 127, 128
Examination power, 181
Examinations, 26–37, 57, 65, 66
Examinations, military, 65
Examination *Yüan*, 136
Executive power, 181
Exhortation to Learning, 61 n.
Extra-territorial system, 193, 194

Fabians, 146
Fa Hsien, 46
Faithfulness, 177, 199
Falski, M., 220
Family-ism, 148
Family loyalties, 177
Famine, 195
Faraday, 47, 82
Fictions, theory of, 95, 95 n.
Filial devotion, 177
Filial piety, 143 n., 198
Finck, F. N., 94, 98
First China War, 42, 47
First National Education Conference, 161, 163
Fitzwilliam Museum, 41
Five Arts, 3
Five Canons, 28, 47, 61, 77, 206
Five-Power Group, 171
Five Virtues, 37 n.
Foochow (Fuchau), 56, 107
Food problem, 185
Food shortage, 193
Ford, Henry, 183
Foreign goods, 150, 186
Foreign capital required, 184
Foreign domination, 175, 185
Foreigners, 178, 199
Foreign loans, 190
Foreign Office, Chinese, 55
Foreign oppression, 196
Foreign policy, 162
Foreign trade, 150, 151
"Forest of Pencils," *see* Hanlin Academy
Forke, A., 111
"Form Arts," 164
Formalism, 50
Formosa, 144

INDEX

"Forty Symbol System," 105
"Foundation" Textbooks, 239 (Appx.)
Four Books, 21, 27, 28, 29, 37 n., 47, 61, 65, 77, 95, 206, 229
Fourth Gospel, 205
Flood, 219
Franklin, 240 (Appx.)
France, 57, 185
Fraser's Magazine, 139
Fraternity, 179
Freedom, 131, 133
French Concession at Shanghai, 171
French Revolution, 179
Fukien, 107
Fukienese, 105
Fu Tsêng-hsiang, 105

Garrison Commander at Nanking, 210
Gautier, Théophile, 13, 14
Gentry, local, 214
Geography, 61, 127, 164
Geometry, 56
German adviser to Chiang Kai-shek, 173
German letters, 226
German officers, 57, 60
German system, 71
Germany, 176, 198
"Gestures," 155
Gettysburg Oration, 170
Gibbon, 37, 41
Giles, H. A., 19 n., 37, 40, 46, 92, 93, 97, 97 n., 110, 114, 115, 146
Giles, Lionel, 8 n.
Girls, education of, 4, 5
"God," 46
Goddess of Mercy, 117
Godhead of Christ, 229
Goethe, 77
Goffe, Sir Herbert, 214 n., 217
Gordon, 49 n.
Gower, 119
Graduates, T'ang and Sung, 26
Grammar for Chinese, 92
Granet, M., 88, 88 n., 110, 143 n.
Graphs of pupils' activities, 213
Greased cartridge mutiny, 47
"Great Learning," see *Ta Hsüeh*
Great War, 176, 242 (Appx.)
Greece, ancient, 229
Greek, teaching of, 54
Greene, 116
Gregorian Calendar, 45 n.

Grimm, Jacob, 94
Guerrilla armies, 201
Guild Socialism, 242 (Appx.)
Guild society, 149

Hackmann, H., 110, 111, 156
Hai Kuo T'u Chih, 48 n.
Hailam children, 159
Hail, W. J., 49 n.
Hainan, 107
Hakka children, 158, 159
Haldane, J. B. S., 18 n.
Hallam, 134
Hamlet, 42
Hampole, 125
Han Dynasty, 2, 15, 26, 26 n., 31, 42, 138, 237 (Appx.)
Hanighen, F. C., 57 n.
Hankow, 194
Hanlin and Hanlin Academy, 36, 41, 42, 58, 70, 209
Han race, 174
Harding, President, 244 (Appx.)
Harmony, 177
Hart, Sir Robert, 55
"Heart" radical, 102
Herbart, 119
Heungshan, 169
High sea, 141
Hillier, 109
History, 61, 62, 164
History, teaching of, 56, 57
History textbooks, 244 (Appx.)
Hobbes, 120
Hokkien, 158
Holcombe, A. N., 166, 167
Homonyns, 12
Homophones, 108
Hong Kong, 158, 198
Hong Kong Medical College, 170
Honolulu, 169
Hopei, 216
Hopkins, L. C., 7 n., 8 n.
"House-that-Jack-built" construction, 122
Hsiao Ching, 21
Hsiao Hsüeh, 16, 61, 103
Hsiang dance, 5
Hsien, 208
Hsien Fêng, Emperor, 51
Hsin Ch'ing Nien, 105
Hsing T'o, 19
Hsin Wên Pao, 215
Hsüan T'ung, Emperor, 171
Hsüeh Pu, 69

Hsü Hsin, 39
Hsü Kuang-ch'i, 45
Hsün Tzǔ, 39, 119
Huang Yi-chou, 25
Huc, N., 25 n.
Humanistic teaching, 54
Hung Lou Mêng, 104
Hung Siu-tsuan, 49
Hu Shih, 2, 3, 45 n., 71, 78, 83, 105, 105 n., 106, 217, 220
" Huxley's Cockpit," 192
Hygiene, 164

Idea, 115
Ideology of Private Education, 223
Ille, 98
Imperial College, 3
Imperial Library, 126
Imperialism, 154 n., 175, 191, 203, and Appendix
Imponderabilia of translation, 98
Inconsistencies and errors in *San Min Chu I*, 202
Independent Labour Party, 146
India and Non-co-operation, 171
Indo-European tongues, 88
Industrial Arts, 164
Industrial Revolution, 47
Initiative, Right of, 181
Innocent X, bull of, 46
Inspection of fiefs, 30
Intelligence and ability of Chinese, 178
Intelligentsia, 222, 224
Intendant of Circuit, 214
International, 152, 153
Internationalism, 175
International co-operation, 237 et seq. (Appx.)
Interests of capitalists and workers reconciled, 182
Interpreters, training of, 55
Inventions, Chinese, 126
Irony, 153
I Shih Pao, 215

Jacobinism, 146
Japan and Japanese, 60, 60 n., 65, 82, 82 n., 83, 83 n., 84, 114, 147, 170, 171, 218, 226, 227, 231, 246 (Appx.)
Japanese academies, Chinese in, 65
Japanese crisis 1932, 136
Japanese system, 71
Japanese-German system, 71

Japanese " Twenty-one Demands," 71
Jesuits, 44, 45 n., 46, 51, 52
Joffe, 188, 189
Johnston, Sir Reginald, 22 n., 171 n. 228 n.
Journal Asiatique, 27 n.
Journal of the Ministry of Education, 106
Judicial power, 181
Judicial *Yüan*, 136
Julien, Stanislas, 20
Jus gentium, 1
Justice, 177, 199
Jupiter, 90

K'ang Hsi's dictionary, 11 n., 105
K'ang Yu-wei, 58, 60, 77, 78, 170
Kao, Duke of, 5
Kant, 119
Karlgren, B., 7 n., 8 n., 9 n., 10, 11, 12 n., 26 n., 31 n., 94, 94 n., 96, 97, 98, 100 n., 112 n., 114, 160,
Kemel Mustapha, 244 (Appx.)
Kerensky, 169
Khuan Chung, 39
Kiangsi, 208
Kien Long (Ch'ien Lung), Emperor, 27, 175
King-chau Mui, 84
King George III, 47
Ko dance, 5
Kropatchek guns, 57 n.
Kuang Sü, Emperor, 28, 60, 63
Kung, Prince, 1, 2
Kuominchun, 173
Kuomintang, 73, 136, 137, 149, 163, 167, 171, 172, 173, 174, 180, 183, 189, 201, 205, 207, and Appendix
Kuo Ping-wên (P. W. Kuo), 3, 5 n., 6, 15 n., 50, 54, 55 n., 58 n., 60 n., 71, 222
Kuo Yü, 102, 106, 107, 108, 110, 112, 156, 159
Ku Yen-wu, 2
Kwangsi, 172
Kwangtung, 169

Lamb, Charles, 127
Langevin, P., 120
Langland, 120
Lang Son, Battle of, 57 n.
Language and Language Problem, 8 et seq., and Chapter IV
Lao Nai-hsüan, 105, 106

INDEX

Lao Tzŭ, 39
Latourette, K. S., 45 n., 51 n., 73 n.
Lavoisier, 47
League of Nations' Mission, 85, 211, 220, 221, 223
Legendre, A. E., 204
Legge, James, 2 n., 4 n.
Legislation, Principles of, 153
Legislative power, 181
Lenin, 112, 169, and Appendix
Leong, Y. K., 148 n.
Leroux, 144
Letters, God of, 18
Li, 3
Li Chieh-san, 104
Liang Ch'i-chao, 60, 77, 78, 106
Libel Eng. Policy, 140
Liberty, 131, 132, 179, 200
Li Chih-tsao, 45
Li Chi, see Rites, Book of
Li Hung-chang, 56, 57 n.
Likin, 186, 186 n.
Lin Chin-nan, 106
Lin, Commissioner, 48 n.
Li Po, 77
Literacy, 25
Li Tuan-fên, 61
Livelihood, Principle, 162, 181–7
Li Ying-lun, 189 n.
Logic, 121, 124
London School of Economics, 220
Loyalty, 142, 143, 147, 192, 199
Lu Ch'uang-chang, 104
Lu Hsi-shan, 127
Lu, Kingdom of, 62
Lun, 23
Lun Yü (Analects), 21, 35, 95 n.
Lydgate, 118

Macao, 45, 170
MacNair, H. F., 49 n., 169, 169 n., 170 n., 171 n.
Manchu Dynasty, 49, 126 (*see also* Ch'ing Dynasty)
Manchu Emperor, 49, 171
Manchu schools, 24
Manchus, 135, 147, 186, 198
Mandarin dialect, 107
Marco Polo, 4
Maritime Customs, 55, 136, 186, 203
Martin, W. A. P., 3 n., 17 n., 18 n., 21, 21 n., 22 n., 25 n., 38 n., 40 n., 55, 55 n., 59
Marx and Marxism, 146, 166, 169, 182, 183, 184, 188, 193, 196

Maspero, Henri, 1 n.
Mass education, 86
Mateer, C. W., 53, 93 n., 102, 107
Mateer, Mrs., 114, 152
Mathematics, 1, 4, 54
Mazzini, 153
Mencius, 21, 97, 116, 154, 154 n.
Mesopotamia, 204
Miao tribe, 44, 238 (Appx.)
Middle Kingdom, 55 n.
Military colleges, 69, 70
Military officers, improved status of, 60
Millenary Classic, 19 n., 20
Ming History (*Ming Shih*), 45 n.
Mirror of History, 61
Missions, Missionaries, and Mission Schools, 51, 52, 53, 54, 58, 73, 74, 207
Moerbeke, William of, 134
Mohammedanism, 143, 245 (Appx.)
Molière, 77
Mongol Dynasty, 104
Monlin Chiang, see Chiang Mêng-lin
Morgan, Evan, 113
Morgan, L. G., 156, 157, 170 n.
Morrison, Robert, 50
Morrison Education Society, 52
Morse, H. B., 47 n., 49 n., 169, 169 n., 170 n., 171 n., 194
Mo Ti, 39 (*see also* Mo Tzŭ)
Mo Tzŭ, 1, 77
Moule, A. C., 45 n., 92 n.

Nanching Shu-yüan, 25
Nankeens, 150
Nanking, 136, 161, 170, 174, 203, 221, 239 (Appx.)
Nanking Government, 167
Nanking, Treaty of, 50, 54, 59
Nanyang College, 60
Nation, 195
National Assembly, 170
National Government, 136, 162, 206, 210, 241 (Appx.)
Nationalism, 73, 81, 139, 161, 162, 174–7, 187, 190, 195, 196, 200, 201, and Appendix
Nationalism and Education in Modern China, 164, 222
National Peoples' Assembly, 137
National Phonetic Alphabet, 108 n.
National Reconstruction, 162
National University of Peking, 105, 224

s

Naval schools, 56
Navy, Chinese, 82
Neo-Confucianism, 13
Neologisms, 111
Nestorian Christianity, 248 (Appx.)
New China Review, 45 n.
New Culture Movement, 86
Neitzsche, 119
Nile, 204
Non-Mandarin speaking provinces, 159
North China Daily News, 109 n.
Northern Government Telegraph College, 56
Noumenon, 116
Numerical categories, Chinese fondness for, 19

Odes, 13, 19
Odoric, Friar, 44
Official Gazette of the Ministry of Education, 210
Ogden, C. K., 88 n., 95, 99, 158 n.
" Opium War," 47, 194 n., and Appendix
Organic Law of the Constitution, 137
Organic Law of the National Government, 207
Owen, Robert, 144, 146
Oxford Dictionary, 114

Pacific Ocean Question, 247 (Appx.)
Pai Chia Hsing (" Century of Surnames "), 20, 20 n.
Pai hua, 105–110, 157, 219
Pailey's *World History*, 218
" Pamela," 112
Pandean pipes, 4
Pantoja, Diego, 45
" Paper " schemes, 213
Paris, 136
Parker, E. H., 24, 36 n.
" Parliamentarians," 171
Parsons, Charles, 82
Pa-tao, 195
Peake, Cyrus, 1 n., 70 n., 71 n., 164, 165, 222
Peffer, Nathaniel, 172, 187, 188, 189, 189 n.
Peiping, *see* Peking
P'ei Shou, 45
Peking, 173, 208
Pekingese, 12, 107
Peking University, 78

Phenomenon, 116
Philosophy and Philosophers, 118, 119, 166, 230, 254
" Phonetic Symbols," 105 n.
Physical education, 164
Pi, 19
Pictographs, 8, 9, 10, 95
Ping (" soldier "), 113
Plans for National Reconstruction, 162
Plato, 119
Platonic philosophy, 116
Plato's *Republic*, 232
Poe, Edgar Allan, 50
" Poetic Revolution," 60
Poland, 211
Polytechnic Institution, 57
Population of China, 203, 216
Portuguese, 44, 241 (Appx.)
Pottinger, Sir H., 203
Presbyterian schools, 52
Price, F. W., 81 n., 129, 169, 170
Priestley, 47
Primary education, 25 n., 162, 163, 210, 212
Protestants, 50, 52, 53, 54, 73
Protestant Episcopalians, 52
Provincial Colleges, 24
Prussia, 211
Psyche, 154 n.
Psychological Reconstruction, 162
Ptolemy, 44
" Public," 140, 141, 142
Purcell, Victor, 91 n., 108 n.
Purcell, V. A., 83 n.
Puritans, Catholic, 229
Puritans, Chinese, 229

Queen's College, Hong Kong, 170
Quintuple-Power Constitution, 162
Quoc Gnu, 109 n.

Race and race questions, 195 and Appendix
Realism, Western, in art, 225, 226
Recall, Right of, 181
Referendum, Right of, 181
Refinement, absence of Chinese personal, 200
Reform movement, 63, 64
Reign of Terror, 180
Reinsch, Paul, 84
Religious instruction, 79
Religious questions, Appendix
Reybaud, 144

INDEX

Remington Small Arms Company, agent of, 57 n.
Remington-Lee rifles, 57 n.
Renaissance, 44
Renan, Ernest, 111 n.
Reorganization of Education in China, The, 211
Republicanism, 58
Republic, Chinese, 217, 218, 231, 246 (Appx.), 248 (Appx.)
Republic, constitution of, 73 n.
"Returned Student," first, 52
Revenue, Board of, 135
Revolution, Chinese, 105, 133, 148, 170, and Appendix
Rho, Giacomo, 45
Rhyming Dictionaries, 30 n.
Rhymes, 30
Rhythm and "rhythmical thinking," 101, 228, 231
Ricci, Matteo, 45 n., 51, 56, 245 (Appx.)
Richards, I. A., 154
Richardson, 112
Richard, Timothy, 53
Rights, 129, 130, 135
Rights of Man, 129
Rites, Book of (*Li Chi*), 2, 3, 3 n., 4, 6, 16, 62
Ritual, 38
Romaunt de la Rose, 142
Roman Catholics, *see* Catholic Church, etc.
Romanticists, 153
Rome, 191
Ross, E. A., 80
Rousseau, 1, 179, 204
Royal Institute of International Affairs, 164, 165, 214 n.
Ruggieri, Michele, 45
"Running dogs" of the Imperialists, 74
Russell, Bertrand, 38 n.
Russia, 172, 175, 211, 244 (Appx.), 246 (Appx.)
Russia and Chinese Eastern Railway, 239 (Appx.)
Russian Five-Year Plan, 213, 215
Russian influence on Sun Yat-sen, 172
Russian Revolution, 176
Russo-Japanese War, 65, 66
Rutherford, Lord, 82

Sacrifices of Heaven and Earth, 29

Saigon, 109 n.
Saikwan, 142
Saint-Simon, 146
Salisbury, Lord, 170
Salt Gabelle, 136
San-ho Hui, 148
San Kuo Chih Yen I, 104
San Min Chu I, 6 n., 38 n., 73, 73 n., 81 n., 115, 117, 124, 129, 135, 139, 145, 147, Chapter V
San Tien, 148
San Tzŭ Ching, see Trimetrical Classic
Schaal, Adam, von Bell, 45
Schneider, 197 n.
School hours, 18
Schools, 6, 24, 51, 53, 66, 67, 69, 75, 156, 217, 221, 223, 224, 231
Schools, Catholic, 74
Schools, Christian, 74, 75
Schools, girls', 68
School of Law, 130 n.
Schopenhauer, 77
Science, 46, 62, 78, 79, 126, 127, 155, 157, 162, 203, 247 (Appx.)
Scientific department of the T'ung Wên Kuan, 55
Scientific Socialism, 182
Science, teaching of, 54
Scientific terms, 209
Scott, Walter, 106, 244 (Appx.)
Secondary Schools, 208, 221
Second China War, 54, 244 (Appx.)
Secret Societies in Straits Settlements, 148
Sericulture, 186
Sex equality, 231
"Shakee Incident," *see* Canton "incident"
Shakespeare, 77
Shanghai, 57, 60, 172, 198, 203
Shanghai "massacre", 72, 164, 173
Shensi, 208
Shang Yang, 39
Shao dance, 5
Shastras, 121
Shaw, G. B., 79, 144
Sheridan, R. B., 214
Shou, 225
Shih-lien Hsü, 39 n.
Shou T'i, 27
Shou T'ou Tzŭ, 108 n.
Shun, Emperor, 32, 32 n., 33, 34, 35, 119
Shuo Wên, 2 n., 7 n.

Shu-yüan (Provincial Colleges), 24, 25, 65, 66
Sino-Japanese War, 56, 59, 170, 244 (Appx.)
Six Arts, 4, 26
Six Praiseworthy Actions, 4
Six Scripts, 11 n.
Six Virtues, 4
Slaves, the Chinese are, 177
Smith, A. H., 23, 142
Social Democrats, 146
Socialism, 144, 145, 146, 147, 149, 150, 168, 181, 182, 183, 193, 243 (Appx.)
Socialism and Capitalism, Intelligent Woman's Guide to, 79 n.
Social Contract (Contrat Social), 204
Society for the Unification of the National Language, 108 n.
Society for the Unification of Pronunciation, 108 n.
Society in China, 37 n.
Socius, 147, 148
Sokikusha (Press Association), 165
Soothill, 166, 190 n., 191, 204
Sophists, Chinese, 123 n.
Sovereignty, meaning of, 177
Spencer, Herbert, 126
Spenser, Edmund, 131
Spinoza, 120
Ssŭ-ma Kuang, 77
Starkey, 144
State, Country, 137, 153
Stein, Sir Aurel, 7
Stevenson, R. L., 144
Students, 69, 179, 207
Students, returned, 71, 77
St. John's College, Shanghai, 218
Summer Palace, 41, 244
Sung Dynasty, 24, 41, 42, 123, 127, 233
Sung Emperors, 39
Sung History, 148 n.
Sun Yat-sen, 6, 38 n., 54, 63, 72, 73, 81, 115, 124, 130, 136, 139, 145, 147, 148, 149, 153, 161 et seq., 187, 188, 189 n., 190, 191, 192, 193, 194, 195, 196, 197, 198, 199, 200, and Appendix ; death of, 172
Su Tung-p'o, 77
Switzerland, constitution of, 180
Synoptical Gospels, 205

Ta hsiâ, dance, 5

Ta Hsüeh (Great Learning), 21, 43 n., 122, 124
Ta Hsüeh Yüan, 161, 161 n., 207, 208
T'ai P'ing Rebellion, 49, 49 n., 54, 56, 203
Takemaye, R., 83 n.
Ta Kung Pao, 214, 217
Taku Ultimatum, 173
T'ang and Sung graduates, 26
T'ang Dynasty, 13, 25 n., 39, 41, 42, 43 n., 233
T'ang Leang-li, 25, 26 n., 78, 85
Tang Principles, 208
T'ang Shao-yi, 153 n.
T'ang Yu-lin, 81
Tao, 5 n.
Taoists and Taoism, 15, 37
Tao, L. K., 148 n.
Tao Tê Ching, 14 n.
Tartars, 46
Tawney, R. H., 220, 223 n.
Teaching of Science to the Chinese, 156
Technical terms, 209
Terminus, Roman God, 144
Textbooks, 159, 164
Thackeray, 150
Theocratic government, 178
Theory of Fictions, 88
Thibetan Buddhism, 143
Thibet, 191, 246 (Appx.)
Thinking, Chinese method of, 89, 231
30th May Incident, *see* Shanghai " massacre "
Thomas, 45 n.
Thomson, Sir J. J., 82
" Three Principles of the People," *see San Min Chu I*
Ti, 98
Tientsin, 57, 105, 106, 173
Tientsin, Treaty of, 54, 55
Tientsin, University of, 60
Ting, V. K., 78
Tiuchiu, children, 159
Tobar, J., 61 n.
Tokyo, 165, 170
Toyoda loom, 82 n.
Translations, 58, 154
Treaty ports, 149, 151, 152, 238 (Appx.)
Triad societies, 148
Trimetrical Classic, *see San Tzŭ Ching*

INDEX

"Triple Demism," 163 n.
Ts'ai Yüan-p'ei, 48, 70, 71, 133, 207, 209, 210
Tsêng Kuo-fen, 49 n., 56
Tsingtao, 197
Tsungli Yamen, 55
Twenty-four Filials, 21
Twenty-one Demands, 106, 246, (Appx.)
Tuan Ch'i-jui, 172
T'ung Chien Kang Mu, 61
Tung Chung-shu, 39
Tung Kung Pao, 215
T'ung Meng Hui, 149
T'ung Wên Kuan, 55, 58
T'u Shu Chi Chêng, 20
Tz'ŭ-hsi, Empress Dowager, 63, 64, see also Empress Dowager
Tzŭ-Kung, 32, 33
Tz'ŭ Yüan, 30 n., 101, 114

"Ultimatum," 113
"Unequal Treaties," 186, and Appendix
United States, see America
Universal Education, 60, 211, 216
Ursa Major, 135
Ursis, Sabbatini de, 45
Usk, T., 118
Utopian Socialists, 182

Vale, 116
Variétés Sinologiques, 27 n., 31, 52
Verbiest, Ferdinand, 45
Vissière, 27, 27 n.
Von Bell, Adam Schaal, see Schaal, Adam

Wade's *Dispatches*, 199 n.
Waley, Arthur, 14 n.
Wang, 21
Wang An-shih, 15 n., 39
Wang, C. C., 54
Wang Chao, 105, 106
Wang, C. T., 54
Wang Ch'ung-hui, 54
Wang Shih-chieh, 218
Ward, 49 n.
Watt, inventor of steam engine, 125

Watts, 125
Weiheiwei, 194, 197
Wênli, 60 n., 93, 102, 105, 107, 108, 110, 112
West, the, and Western civilization, 44, 46, 48 n., 50, 53, 60, 61, 62, 65, 78, 79, 82, 85, 86, 136, 147, 160, 196, 225, 228
White races, 175, 191
William, Maurice, 187, 188
Williams, 48 n.
Williams, C. A. S., 12 n.
Williams, S. W., 16 n., 108
Williams, Whiting, 188
Wilson, President, 176
Women, education of, 67 n.
Wong Fun, 52
Woodbridge, S. 61 n., 63 n.
Wo Tao-tzŭ, 155
Wuchang, 58
Wu, Duke of, 5
Wyclif, 131
Wylie, A., 39 n., 40 n., 48 n.

-y, 99, 100
Yale University, 58
Yang Chu, 77, 119
Yang Kuei-fei, 155
Yao, 32, 33, 34, 35
Yen Ching University, 54, 117, 217
Yen, W. W., 54, 158
Yin and *Yang*, 87
Y.M.C.A., 218
Young, A., 150
"Young China Party," 170
Yuan Shih-k'ai, 69, 70, 72, 171
Yüeh, Kingdom of, 62
Yuen Po, 62
Yuen Ren Chao, 107 n., 108 n.
Yu Hsüeh Shih-t'ieh, 20
Yunnan, 107, 138, 172
Yung, 19
Yung, 31
Yung Chêng, 28
Yung Wing, 52, 56, 58

Zen Buddhism, 13
Zi, Etienne, 27 n.
Zikawei, 51

Printed in Great Britain by Stephen Austin and Sons, Ltd., Hertford.